#HOCKEYSTRONG

A Novel

E. Robuck

Elysian Fields Press
2017

Published by Elysian Fields Press
Elysian Fields Press (USA), Maryland, 21032, U. S. A

All rights reserved under International and Pan_American Copyright
Conventions. Published in the United States by Elysian Fields Press,
Maryland, U. S. A.

Robuck, Erika
#Hockeystrong/Erika Robuck
ISBN 978-0-9822298-1-1

PUBLISHER'S NOTE
This is a work of fiction. Names, characters, places, and incidents are
either the products of the author's imagination or are used fictitiously.

For my spouse.

And my hockey player.

And his siblings.

Author's Note:

From youth scrimmages to professional sporting events, the author of this novel has spent thousands of hours on the sidelines of thousands of practices and games. However, #HOCKEYSTRONG is a work of fiction. Names and characters are a product of the author's imagination. Though sports families will see many types and scenarios similar to situations they have no doubt encountered in the world of youth sports, any resemblance to actual events or persons, living or dead, is coincidental.

"While the law of competition may be sometimes hard for the individual, it is best for the race, because it ensures the survival of the fittest in every department."

Andrew Carnegie

#HOCKEYSTRONG

Your average northeastern U. S. suburb
2015

Chapter One
8 Months to District Playoffs

 Kate Miller's Status Update: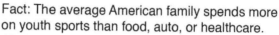

Fact: The average American family spends more on youth sports than food, auto, or healthcare.

Cars line up at the rink like a series of oversized dogsleds: Tahoe, Suburban, Lexus, Escalade, Hummer, a scattering of minivans. All of them are white—white as snow, white as nine-tenths of the players, white as the muffs around the tops of the armies of Ugg boots slapping the pavement in the pre-dawn on a summer day.

Charlie Miller parks his gray sedan next to an SUV with a stick figure family plastered to its rear view mirror. Most of the cars at the rink have them. The families vary from tidy, symmetrical lines of Mom, kid, kid, kid, dog, Dad, to creative takes. Potato Heads. Minions. Dinosaurs eating stick people.

"Ah, the little figure families are growing," says Charlie to his wife Kate. "Do you think the Churches added so many pets because they feel inadequate for having only one child? Should we get a hermit crab?"

"I have no judgment of stick figure families at this time," says Kate.

She reaches in her gym bag and pulls out a set of flip-flop stickies: one large and masculine, one medium-sized and feminine, one small and kiddish.

"No," says Charlie.

"I did."

"Why?"

"A glass of wine. Online shopping. A moment of weakness. A deep-seated wish to blend better with the hockey families this year."

"Kate."

"We're too standoffish. Maybe we'll have a better season if we make a real effort."

Charlie places his hand on Kate's forehead.

"Oh no," he says. "The fever. Starting already."

Kate swats him away and grins. She drops the flip-flop family back in the bag.

"I don't know what came over me," she says.

"No, take it out. Put it on the car. As a reminder."

"Of what?"

"The insidious nature of the onset of sports-parent madness."

They sit in the sedan sipping coffee, watching other cars arrive, working themselves up to wake their eleven-year-old son Brett in the back seat to begin the season that will last as long as a pregnancy, and cost as much as a small island in the Caribbean—especially now that the Polar Bears have qualified for an *extra* tournament league that could get them nationally ranked at district playoffs. When they had asked Coach Butch last year what was so special about these districts everyone had been buzzing about, he had replied that they were the Stanley Cup of youth hockey. That answer had somehow made sense during the endless winter months spent in pack-like travel with hockey families, but less now, in the warmth of off-season, when the summer had thawed the brain.

"It's the hockey stickers I love most," says Charlie.

Kate surveys the parking lot.

DRIVER CARRIES NO CASH.
OUR KIDS PLAY HOCKEY.

PENALTY BOX MOM.

MY HOCKEY MOM CAN BEAT UP
YOUR SOCCER MOM.

"That's my favorite," Kate says, pointing at Coach Butch's pickup truck.

HOCKEY ISN'T FOR PUSSIES.

"It's good we have a guy like that in our son's life," says Charlie.

"Yes, you're way too soft."

Sal and Louise Gardenia arrive in their Cadillac. Sal has all the associated health problems of Type 2 diabetes, and doesn't have to work anymore due to the successful settlement of a personal injury claim against the auto shop franchise where he used to change oil; some kind of machine failed and took his right pinky and ring finger. The Cadillac —paid for in the settlement—has no hockey slogans, only stickers that reveal Sal's passion: politics.

SPAY AND NEUTER LIBERALS

EXTREMIST ONBOARD

DRIVING A SEDAN MEANS I HAVE MORE MONEY FOR AMMO

"Do you think Sal was locked in a basement closet as a child?" asks Charlie.

Kate laughs. She reaches back, squeezing Brett's knee. "Wake up, bud. Time for hockey."

Even with his eyes closed, Brett smiles.

"Hockey," he says with a happy sigh.

"How is he our offspring?" says Kate.

"I think it comes from your side," says Charlie. "Ultra-competitive sportsy people."

"Ah, let's not forget your father. Lieutenant Colonel?" she says. "He'd make Coach Butch cry."

"Butch doesn't have feelings."

As they climb out of the car, the little hockey players greet and tumble over one another like a litter of puppies. Coach Butch stands unsmiling in the doorway of the rink, blocking entrance to the parents while instructing the kids to walk in under his arm. In the distance a dog barks, a sprinkler ticks, a teenaged girl wearing a lifeguard tank top and towel draped over her shoulders pedals past them on her bike.

"This time of year most people can barely remember a sport like ice hockey," says Charlie.

"That's why *those* people's children aren't on *this* team," says Kate, in her best Coach Butch voice.

By the time the Millers reach Coach Butch, Charlie can see that Kip—father of defenseman, Kyle—is perturbed. Kip's a firefighter of muscular build who likes to talk about his hockey days (though he made it through only two seasons at the division-three collegiate level), and carries a binder for his son that says *Kyle's Path to Hockey Greatness.*

"I need to get first day pictures," says Kip.

Piper Caldwell sniggers. Her husband Justin nudges her with his elbow. Piper is platinum blond and six feet in stilettos, which is all she wears. Their son, Aiden, a forward with perfect hair and nice, white tennis shoes, has a hockey bag that never smells and skates that are always sharpened. His sisters—two girls, ages five and three—are hypnotized by their iPads. Like most hockey siblings, they will spend the greater part of the next year staring at screens in dirty rink corners, not an adult in sight, likely texting with child predators disguised as little girls on the Webkinz site.

"Piper's spiced tea perfume is clashing with the pumpkin spice of her latte," whispers Kate.

"Are they serving those already?"

Coach Butch raises his arms. Charlie notes the ruddy hair and beard Butch usually grows out to lion's mane size throughout the season have been recently shorn, probably the result of lice from his hunting stand.

"Read this before entering," Butch says.

His wife Helen—an odd, shifty-eyed woman—passes out the two-paged, single-spaced document.

"I'll summarize," Butch says. "This year parents are not allowed in locker rooms. You will not be on the bench. I do not recommend lingering during practices, or the hour before games. If your son--"

"Or daughter!" yells a voice in the crowd. Zoe's mom.

That a girl got on a team coached by a misogynist is of no concern, but there is a rumor going around that she's related to the program director.

"—gets injured, do not come running to the bench unless I summon you. If your child misses one practice, he gets a warning and cannot play a period in the next game. If he misses two—he sits a game."

"What if he's sick?" asks Mee Maw, Henry's grandmother. Her gray-brown hair is teased and smoothed into a perfect, chin-length mushroom, sprayed with enough Aquanet to make it hard as a hockey helmet.

"The same rules apply. I don't care about illness, visiting family, or studying for a test. If your kid made this team, hockey is number one. I can call up seven kids on a waiting list any day of the week to take your kid's spot. Don't forget it."

"When will we see the tournament and game schedule?" asks Piper. "We have a ski trip in February, but we might be able to change the dates if necessary. I just need to know in advance."

"It's July. How do you expect me to know that far in advance? As I said, hockey comes first. There are times I will call practices with an hour's notice. Be ready."

"When will you name team captains and assistant captains?" asks Tina Church, the team mom.

"Ooh, good question," says her husband, Bob.

"Once they've proven themselves."

"Who will supervise the kids in the locker room?" asks Mee Maw.

"The kids will be alone until ten minutes before game time, during which time I will enter with my assistant coach. Which brings me to post-game. The players are not to begin taking off their uniforms until I have debriefed them on how they played. They are not to leave until I give them permission."

"Did I black out during try-outs?" whispers Kate. "Why did we sign up for Butch's team again?"

"You agreed because of the extra tournament league," Charlie reminds her in a hush.

"I did *not*. You were all about that."

"No, it was because Brett loves his line mates. He wanted to stay."

"He could have loved new line mates."

"Butch pulled me aside and specifically asked me if we'd keep Brett in the program. He's proven himself. Maybe Butch will be different with him."

Butch clears his throat.

"If I think they are not paying attention to me," he says, glaring at the Millers, "they will sit a period of the next game. And for those of you who are new to me, I yell. Kids are hardheaded and can't hear me on the ice. If you don't like your little sissy getting yelled at, get out of here. Everything I do—even if you don't understand—is meant to prepare these players for the ultimate goal: getting to district playoffs. That is why your kid is a Polar Bear. All of their training will lead to victory, but not if you stand in our way. A great man once said, 'Uncoachable kids become adult losers; let your kids get used to discipline, or get out.'"

Butch turns and enters the rink, letting the door slam behind him.

"I don't think that's the quote," says Piper.

"This was a mistake," says Kate. "It's not going to be different this year."

"What, Butch seems more thoughtful," says Charlie. "He took the time to write a whole manifesto."

The parents stand in huddles, eyes darting over the words in the document.

"Who is this assistant coach he mentioned?" asks Tina.

"It's Butch's oldest son," says Sal. "Great kid."

Nothing Sal says can be trusted. He's Butch's toadie.

"The stoner?" whispers Kate.

"At least there will be one mellow person on the bench," says Charlie.

Charlie flips the paper over and continues to read. He feels a sudden cramping in his stomach and wonders if he ate something bad.

"Did Butch ever get the lesson in school about *to, too,* and *two*?" says Kate. "And I don't think 'supposably' is a word. Isn't it 'supposedly'?"

"Phrase of the Day," says Piper. "Copy Editor: One who proofreads and fact checks material before publication."

Several of the parents laugh.

"What does she mean," says Charlie. "What's 'Phrase of the Day?'"

"Butch has started posting them on Facebook," says Tina. "He likes to put up words and phrases of the day. He must think it's inspirational."

"No, they can generally be read as passive-aggressive jabs at parents," says Kate.

Tina shrugs.

"I'm glad I'm not on Facebook," says Charlie.

"You should be," says Tina. "We have an awesome team page."

"You'll need it by middle school, at least for Brett," says Kip. "College recruiters need a place to find stats and highlights."

"They're U12, Kip," says Kate.

"You're already late getting started," says Piper.

No way, thinks Charlie.

9

The barking dog again calls Charlie's attention from the hockey parking lot. A terrier digs in the dirt next to a father and daughter fishing at the pond across the road. Memories of the charter his family took off Islamorada come back. Was it only two weeks ago that they were watching sunset over the Florida Keys? They had started talking seriously about moving to Florida last February—when they were all in the throes of seasonal affective disorder, aggravated by the insanity of hockey with Coach Butch—but the summer made them forget. How could they forget?

Kate opens the door to the rink, icy air hitting Charlie's face.

"I changed my mind," he says. "I'm not ready."

"Come on," says Kate. "Hockey's not for pussies."

Chapter Two

Justin awakens to the clicking sound of his wife's phone. He turns over to see Piper's face glowing cadaver-blue in the light of the screen. The clock over her shoulder reads 4:16. He slides his hand under the sheets and tries to snuggle. Piper shifts so her back is to him, and continues to type. A moment later she launches from the bed, throwing back the sheets.

"Come back," he says.

"You know Aiden has to be at camp."

She crosses the wood floor to the bathroom.

"Hours from now."

"I'm not going to that rink looking like Kate Miller, with her mousy brown hair in a ball cap and wearing godawful sweatpants."

"Aren't they called yoga pants?"

Justin thinks Brett's mom is hot. She has big brown, heavily-lashed eyes that focus on you when you talk to her, and she's fit and petit. He once almost suggested Piper get a pair of those yoga pants with the hot-pink lines down the sides that Kate wears; Piper would look great in them. But Piper likes to keep the illusion going that her beauty is natural. She wouldn't be caught dead wearing athletic clothes in public.

Piper groans as she starts the shower.

"What?" he says.

"Tina posted her camp photos from yesterday before me, and she already has sixty likes. Now she's going to think I copied her."

Another round of clicking is followed by the clack of a phone hitting the tile tub edge and the slam of the shower door. Justin drifts off again, only to awaken with a start. He remembers it's Piper's birthday. He reaches for his own phone, opens his music, and cues the song. Once the shower shuts off, he gets out of bed and turns up the volume.

50 Cent. *In Da Club*. She tries not to smile while he dances around her.

"The timing of the birthday trip you planned for me is less than ideal," she says.

"We get to take Aiden to camp today. Your mom can manage the rest of the week."

"Yes, but she doesn't stay at the rink. She just drops off."

"That's all my parents did when I was his age."

"Well, you probably didn't have a crazy-ass coach like Butch."

"At least we wouldn't have to deal with other hockey parents."

Justin looks in the mirror as he throws his boxer briefs in the hamper and turns to flex.

"Look at my perfect dad-bod, Pipe. Big biceps, soft stomach, muscular legs. Impeccably groomed hipster beard kept just short of Duck Dynasty, trimmed enough not to look like a terrorist."

"Noooooo," she says, leaning her face an inch from the steamed mirror. "I have a gray hair in my eyebrow."

"Well, you are thirty-nine today. It's about time."

"Stop reminding me."

She leans closer to the mirror until her sharp angular nose rests on it.

"Wait!" she says. "Emergency cancelled. It's blonde."

Piper's phone buzzes, wiggles, and dings from where it now rests by the sink. Her life is a seamlessly fluid conveyer belt, where she switches between physical tasks like putting on make up, assembling meals, and driving to swimming pools, schools, tumble gyms, ballet studios, salons, and hockey rinks, to the virtual tasks of keeping up with endless texts, emails, and social media notifications. Justin is glad he works in the city—twenty miles away from this suburban queen-dom—where he and Piper met at the commercial real estate firm, when they didn't have social media or three children involved in three activities a piece.

"Since you told me I can't commit to one more thing," she says, "I've decided to let Tina take team mom duty this year."

"Obedience; this is new. I have other suggestions. Open your notes app."

"Tina really does deserve it. I mean, I'm simply not willing to wear Polar Bear hockey clothes, bring blue balloons to playoff games, bring blue doughnuts and coffee for early morning games..."

13

"I remember someone in this bathroom painting her nails Polar Bear blue last year."

"That was just for playoffs! Tina paints hers blue all season long."

"Yeah, and her husband has major team spirit. Bob's entire casual wardrobe is hockey apparel with his son's name and number all over it."

"The real reason I don't want to be team mom is that I can't deal with Coach Butch any more than absolutely necessary. He's an animal."

"Cosign."

"Did you see he has started posting a 'Word or Phrase of the Day' on Facebook?"

"We talked about that yesterday."

"He's a semi-illiterate troll who practically lives in his filthy little cubby of an office in the rink. On top of that, Tina says she heard he steals from the vending machines. This is a major adult role model we have in our son's life."

"Ah, I remember telling you we should go to the Ice Dogs this year, but no, you said the Polar Bears are doing the extra tournament league so we have to suffer through Butch another year. The Ice Dogs are in the same league now, by the way."

"That wasn't a guarantee during try-outs," says Piper. "And I don't regret it. This will be good for Aiden's development as a player. He's dying to win the district playoffs, and the time he has invested with this team will pay off. I know it."

"You know he's eleven years old, right?"

"Once he has a districts win on his hockey resume, we can move on. We just have to reinforce that Coach Butch's behavior is not how adults should act."

"Just the berating of kids part? Or the stealing? Or letting his obnoxious son play every other shift? Or screaming at refs? I feel like we should focus on one really bad behavior, or Aiden will just tune us out."

"Ugh. Guess what his latest 'Phrase of the Day' is? *'Helicopter Parents: Parents who take an overprotective or excessive interest in the life of their children.'*"

"He has a point."

"My Phrase of the Day: I wouldn't have to helicopter my kid if the coach wasn't such an asshole."

"That's more of a sentence of the day. It lacks the punch of the phrase."

Piper groans, turning out the light on her way out of the bathroom, leaving Justin in the dark.

"Happy Birthday," he calls.

Chapter Three

  Kate Miller's Status Update: ⚙

Article Link: Little Quitters
70% of kids quit sports by age 13.
#1 Reason: It's no longer fun.

Charlie thinks practice wouldn't be so bad if there were only the sounds of blades scraping over fresh ice, whistles, children's voices. But Butch never fails to plug his iPhone into the sound system, blast music that sounds like it would feel to have someone punch you repeatedly in the ear, and scream commands over it with his grating growl. Sal Gardenia pounds the air over his head, hits the glass, and reaches around Justin to bang Charlie on the shoulder, leaving a sting.

"Pumps 'em up! Eh, buddy?" says Sal.

"AC/DC," is all Charlie can think to say.

Charlie stands with Justin and Sal, in that order, their heads forming a mountain peak, with Justin's at the summit. Respectively, they are brunette and bespectacled, black-haired and bearded, and bald and mustached, and clad in cargo shorts, skinny jeans, and athletic shorts. Sal will wear his shorts all through the winter, paired with tank tops or tee shirts that reveal every aspect of his three-hundred pound, heavily tattooed form. Sal is never cold and never without a pocket full of candy bars, a fistful of soda.

"It does feel like the *Highway to Hell* being here this early in the summer," says Charlie. "I'd give anything to be back in Florida."

Justin and Sal look at Charlie as if has spoken a language they do not understand. Should he repeat the words louder, slower? Sal steps almost imperceptibly away from the group, as if putting distance between himself and Charlie in case what Charlie has is contagious.

"I have to admit; I didn't think so at first, but I'm pumped," says Justin. "There's nothing like hockey."

Nothing? thinks Charlie. *How about fishing, boating, drinking pina coladas with rum floaters, swimming in blue-green water with manatees?*

"We've been counting down the days!" says Sal. "Hockey can't start early enough for us. We've had Mario training since try-outs ended. He's been on the ice four days a week."

"Aiden's only been on two a week," says Justin. "Piper signed him up for tennis camp at the club and forgot to get on the list for power-skating camp. At least he's kept up with his trainer."

An unpleasant sensation roils in Charlie's gut. Brett hasn't set foot in a rink in months. Besides their week in the Keys, Brett has spent every nice day at the community pool, and every rainy day hunting snails and worms at the pond. He and his pool friends even formed a band, with Brett using a set of buckets as drums. They made up songs about catching fireflies, and squishing caterpillars, and eating bacon—all the things boys love.

"Trainer?" asks Charlie.

Justin looks at him, his face a mixture of pity and perplexity.

"Aiden's lifting with a trainer," says Justin. "Twice a week, hour and a half. The guy's really reasonable. Let me know if you need his number."

"Sure," says Charlie.

My teacher's salary should cover that, he thinks.

They stand at the end of the ice where the back-up goalie, David, makes his usual miserable misses. He fails to block most shots, and when the puck gets past him he bangs his helmet on the goal post. His fourteen-year-old sister, Amy, paces behind him. She has autism, tourettes, ADHD, and anger management issues, and tends to erupt during tense situations or when she thinks David is upset, often verbally and physically abusing the nearest male in reach. Sal groans when the hundredth puck shoots past David in the net. He leans in to whisper to Charlie and Justin.

"I heard Tom paid a little 'extra' to get David in the net."

"To who?" says Charlie.

Sal looks at Butch, and shrugs.

"Why would his dad pay extra for him to never play?" says Justin.

"To say his son is on a Triple A team."

David surrenders another goal.

Charlie screws up his face in disbelief. A parent wouldn't really do that at the Pee Wee level, would he?

Slap! Amy strikes the back of Charlie's head, knocking him into the glass. She runs away crying.

"What was that for?" says Charlie, rubbing his forehead and righting his eyeglasses.

"Better you than me," says Justin.

Charlie glances around, seeking Kate. Five minutes in the rink, and he's already injured and feeling guilty, inadequate, and mildly nauseated. He finds her talking to Piper and Tina—her eyes on him. She mouths, "Oh my God," and nods up toward the warming room.

#####

The warming room overlooks the rink and is coated in a fine layer of dust. Younger siblings of hockey players have graffitied the dust on the long center table with stick figures not unlike those on their families' cars, names with I's dotted with hearts, and a rogue "FUK You!" The vulgarity and misspelling would suggest Sal's youngest son, Dante, has been here.

Kate sits heavily at the seats along the glass and groans.

"You're rethinking this team, aren't you?" says Charlie. "You wish we had signed Brett up with the Ice Dogs."

"If I could rate my panic on a scale of one to ten it would be a definite eight."

"Not ten, though, so that's good. What set you off?"

"What set *you* off?" she says. "Your face matched mine."

Kate has noticed they do this. They punt questions to each other like politicians, gauging how they should feel by measuring their emotions off the only other sane adult they know of in the rink. They talk each other into and out of a million feelings a season, convince each other of their intellectual superiority to the other parents, their pure motives. Neither of them played hockey or came from hockey families. Kate ran track and Charlie played club soccer through college. He refs for the intramural soccer league at the middle school where he teaches art. Brett was the one who found hockey after Charlie's father took him to a Florida Panthers game. The next week, Brett had taught himself to skate in the driveway with a rusty pair of roller blades. He used a golf club and wiffle ball as a stick and puck, and begged Kate and Charlie to sign him up for hockey until they relented. Kate remembers the text message Charlie sent his father and its response like it was yesterday, and not four years ago.

--THANK'S A LOT. AFTER THAT HOCKEY GAME, BRETT WANTS TO PLAY THE SECOND MOST DANGEROUS AND FIRST MOST EXPENSIVE SPORT IN THE COUNTRY.

--ATTA BOY!

The exchange was extraordinary for two reasons: one, Charlie's father never replied to text messages; and two, the old man was excited about something—something of Charlie's. Well, something of Brett's, but Charlie was as pleased as if his father were excited about something he did. Brett had played rec hockey for five months before the coach told the Millers that Brett was a natural and needed to play travel. The rest was history.

"Justin wants to give me the name of a personal trainer for Brett," says Charlie.

"Stop."

"Mario's been on the ice four days a week all summer."

"Wow."

"Yeah, and I don't know if we're hurting Brett or helping him by not subscribing to the madness."

"Helping, of course," says Kate. "Kids lifting weights at a young age stunts their growth and leaves them susceptible to injury."

"I would think it stimulates growth. And maybe he'd eat more."

Kate rolls her eyes.

"You see him out there," she says. "He skates just as well or better than all the others, without special trainers."

"You're right," says Charlie. "So what got you?"

"Tina's trying to get me to host a #HockeyStrong party."

"What on earth is that?"

"She's a 'Style Captain' for a new line of sports parent clothing. You know the stuff Bob always wears with Bobby's numbers on it. There's a company. It's growing faster than the founder can keep up with it. Tina wants me to start selling it."

"You did say we should make more of an effort with team families."

Kate slaps Charlie's shoulder, which still stings from Sal's thump. It's only seven in the morning, and he has been assaulted by three people.

A new song begins. *Welcome to the Jungle*, by Guns and Roses.

"Ah, yes, the live version," says Charlie. "There are several F-Bombs throughout."

"Glad to see Butch is sticking with tradition and using last year's playlist," says Kate. "The kids really connect to hard rock from the seventies and eighties."

"Sal digs it."

They look down and see Sal bobbing his head to the music. Dante runs up to him and shouts something at his father. They argue for a moment. Sal clearly denies some request. Dante is in full tantrum mode now, one so epic his mother—who can rarely be seen away from Butch's wife Helen's side—wanders over with disgust on her face, and

21

chews out Sal. Sal reaches in his pocket to dig out change. Dante skips to the soda machine.

"So, do you want to seriously try to switch to the Ice Dogs?" asks Charlie.

"It's too late. They filled their roster at try-outs."

"Things can be done. I know one of the assistant coaches. I taught his son last year."

Kate looks out on the ice. Brett skates with Justin's Aiden and Tina's Bobby. They weave in and out of one another with the speed and grace of the Blue Angels—it's as if they know the other's moves before they make them. Brett digs out the puck and sends it to Aiden, who scores against Viktor—the good goalie. The boys skate to each other and hug, knocking one another over in a tumult of laughter.

"No," says Kate. "He's happy here."

The new dad, Jack, enters the warming room and nods before setting up his laptop in the corner. Jack's son Dominik plays offense. He doesn't speak to the other parents and no one knows where they live. All through try-outs and now, at pre-season camp, Jack just sits, typing incessantly on his computer.

Kate and Charlie watch the rest of practice from the warming room, where they can observe everything but don't have to interact with anyone. Helen once made a comment that real hockey parents never watch from the comfort of the warming room, as if she thinks her presence on the boards somehow helps her son. They watch Sal make the rounds, dipping in and out of conversations, gathering information he'll report to Butch. Piper alternates between staring at her phone, yelling at Aiden's little sisters, and sipping her latte. Kip snaps photos and dodges punches from Amy.

Even through the glass, they can hear Butch's screaming. He berates the kids, stopping often to make them do push-ups on the ice or skate suicides. Practice ends with laps to *God and Guns*, by Lynyrd Skynyrd, and *Another One Bites the Dust*, by Queen. Sal bangs the glass to show his approval. Butch nods and salutes. Zoe pukes over the side of the boards and Butch yells in her ear, probably reminding her of the waiting list of players who won't puke when pushed to the limit.

Chapter Four
Seven Months to District Playoffs

 Piper Caldwell's Status Update:

Pre-season party at the club! Blue streamers hung, sports music station streaming, ice cream sundae bar open for business. Love these kids.

#MemoriesofaLifetime #HockeyStrong

Justin is pissed. It's the team mom's responsibility to organize the pre-season pool party, but Piper took it over, even after saying she'd stop signing up to run every committee.

"We have the club pool," she says.

"Tina could have figured something out."

"She was considering Kate's suggestion to have it at some nasty pond, with bugs and fishing and picnic tables."

"The kids would have loved that."

"Please."

Piper had custom invites made with the silhouette of a scantily clad blonde woman in large sunglasses, margarita glass in hand, poolside. She indicated the time, directions, and dress rules, including the bit about men having to wear collared shirts on their way through the clubhouse to the pool. This rule has spurred their first controversy, and since the tropical flower arrangements are just being delivered (late!), Piper told Justin to deal with it. It seems Sal is causing trouble with the greeter.

"I'm sorry sir, but a collared shirt is required," says the greeter. She is about seventeen years old, and unaccustomed to dealing with men who wear tank tops and Confederate Flag bathing suits.

"I'm only walking to the pool," says Sal.

Louise stands behind him, attempting to pry Mario off Dante, where they brawl in the slate walkway.

"I do realize that," says the girl. "But I could get fired if I don't enforce the rules."

"So you're going to deny my kid a party with his teammates because I can't walk forty friggin' feet without a collar?"

The manager glides over, holding a white golf shirt. He's tall, has hair greying at the temples and perfectly manicured fingernails.

"Sir, our club was chartered in 1926, and we take pride in the order established here for the pleasant atmosphere of our paying members. You either wear the collared shirt I am happy to provide for you to walk to the pool, or your son doesn't come in. Simple."

The man looks with distaste at the wrestling boys. Dirt spills onto the walkway where they have unearthed a bed of Black-Eyed Susans.

"Just put on the damned shirt," says Louise.

Justin hates to be associated with the Gardenias, but since he wouldn't put it past Sal to punch the manager, he has no choice but to intervene.

"Louise," Justin says. "Wonderful to see you. Please take the boys to the pool."

She disentangles them and pulls them down the hallway, muttering curse words.

"Sal," says Justin. "Desserts are out and the beer's cold. Just throw it on, man, and we can talk hockey."

Sal gives the manager a threatening look before grabbing the golf shirt and squeezing it on, giving him the appearance of an oversized marshmallow. Justin slaps Sal on the back and guides him down the hallway. When they get to the pool, they see that Mario and Dante have removed their shirts and flip-flops, left them in a pile in the middle of the walkway, and cannonballed into the pool without realizing it's adult swim. The lifeguard blows the whistle and yells at them.

"Gimme a break!" says Louise, red faced. She bends over to pick up the boys' castoffs.

Sal pulls the collar of the golf shirt, tearing it off and dropping it on the path.

"Never again," says Sal.

Sal catches Mario and Dante being reprimanded by the lifeguard, and storms over to the teenaged boy, leveling him with a shocking series of expletives.

Piper joins Justin. He grabs the margarita from her hand and downs it. As Piper begins to complain, they are hit with a cloud of spray sunscreen, and turn to see Tina holding her son Bobby by the arm and attempting to douse him with sunblock.

"I swear she just did that like five minutes ago," whispers Piper.

Bobby is able to extricate himself from his mother's grip and runs off to join his linemates, Aiden and Brett, on the volleyball court. Kate wanders over, followed by Kip and his wife Lucy.

"No Charlie today?" says Justin.

"No, he's reffing summer soccer," says Kate.

"Soccer's become an all-year-rounder," says Kip.

"All sports are," says Kate. "Remember when we could just play outside in the summer?"

"We've already started Kyle's little bro with hockey," says Lucy. "He's only three."

"Been on skates since he could walk," says Kip.

"He couldn't even poopy on the potty when he started ice skating," says Lucy.

"You ever read that book about the ten thousand hours?" says Kip. "The one that says the best hockey players are born early in the year?"

"We had in vitro to make sure both boys would be born in January."

Justin hears a noise come from Kate that sounds like a laugh, but isn't a laugh. It's more of a choke. Or a gag. She looks at Justin with wide eyes, as if to confirm he's on her side, and Kyle's parents are insane. The in vitro thing is definitely crazy, but getting a kid on skates early? You can't get them on too young.

The whistle blows, ending "adult swim" and the boys run to the pool, shouting like warriors on the battlefield. They jump in and begin dunking one another, starting games of sharks and minnows and Marco Polo. Kip shakes his head.

"Now that the season has started, they shouldn't be swimming," he says.

"Why?" asks Kate.

"Pools are a major factor in bringing down hockey players. They dehydrate, the chlorine tires them out, the lack of gravity messes with their legs so they can't skate well."

"Who told you this?" she says. "Is there science behind it?"

"When I played hockey in college, my coach forbid us swimming during tournaments, and if he forbid it, there's science."

"Maybe he just didn't want you getting hurt or staying up too late."

"No, there's a definite thing it does to the legs."

Justin has noticed that Kip finds a way to work his crushed hockey dreams into most conversations. He has told them all about the shoulder injury that side-lined him, made him take too much time off, and resulted in the end of his hockey career. He wants his boys to carry the torch. Justin gets it. Whether people want to admit it or not, the success of their kids matters. It's a reflection on the parents.

"This needs to be the last time they swim until next summer," says Kip. "We invest too much in our sons and hockey to compromise their performance for silly parties."

"Invest," says Kate. "That's a strong word."

Justin thinks it's cute seeing Kate flustered and combative. She is a full head shorter than Kip, but she's got her hands on her hips, legs in a wide stance, and she's looking up at him as if she'd like to punch him.

"It's the right word. The time, the money, the emotional support—if my parents had invested better in me, there's no telling where I'd be. If they'd started me earlier, if they'd hired trainers, I wouldn't have gotten injured, I would have made it to the NHL."

Piper threads her arm through Justin's, leading him away from Kate and the Howards. Her margarita glass is full (again) and she has a terrible case of the hiccups.

"What's so interesting?"

"Kate and Kip are debating about whether or not the boys should be allowed to swim once hockey season starts."

"Let me guess; Kate thinks kids should just be allowed to be kids, and who cares how swimming affects ice skating?"

Suddenly, Bob Church hurls himself full speed down the diving board—wearing a bathing suit with his son's jersey number on his rear end—and does a cannonball that causes an uproar. Piper jumps back just in time to avoid the worst of the splash, and nearly falls into the ornamental grasses. The hockey players wrestle and jump all over one another in the water. Members are starting to gather their children and swimming accessories into their oversized monogrammed bags. Many aren't hiding their displeasure with the Caldwells for bringing this element into their club.

"We're going to have to move," Piper says. She hiccups and covers her mouth.

"Probably," says Justin.

"Excuse me."

It's Henry's grandmother. Justin can never remember Henry's grandparents' names, though they are the ones who attend all hockey events. They refer to themselves as Mee Maw and Poo Poo, but he refuses to address grown adults in such a way.

"Henry has a nut allergy," says Mee Maw. "You have bowls of macadamias all over the tables."

"I'm sorry," says Piper. "I told the club caterer to avoid anything that causes allergies. She was trying to go with a tropical theme. I'll have them removed right away."

Hiccup.

"He's also allergic to gluten, dairy, and mango."

A quick survey of the food table reveals that Henry will be able to eat exactly nothing. One would think the grandparents would have brought the boy some food, since he is so limited in what he can ingest.

"When our kids were growing up, no one had food allergies," says Mee Maw in her most sanctimonious tone.

"Yeah," says Piper, "but you probably smoked with the windows up and didn't have car seats, so we're even."

Did she just say that out loud? Justin thinks. Piper might have had more to drink before this party than she confessed.

Mee Maw gives Piper's nearly empty margarita a look of distaste before looking to Poo Poo for reinforcement, but Poo Poo only has eyes for Henry. He stands next to the pool, waving at the boy every time he surfaces for air.

"Why don't I introduce you to the caterer," says Justin. "You can see if they have anything in the kitchen that might do for Henry."

"Great idea!" says Piper.

Their youngest daughter runs up to Piper and begins pulling on her mesh cover up.

"Pee pee," she says.

Normally the girls annoy Piper whenever their basic needs call, but Piper abandons Justin in a hurry to escape this conversation.

"Henry wants to show us his cannonball, and he's getting in line now," says Mee Maw. "I don't want to miss it. Couldn't you just talk to them?"

"Fine," he says.

As he walks away, he hears Mee Maw address Poo Poo.

"We'll host at our house next year so Henry doesn't have to feel different from everyone else. *And* there's no alcohol."

Chapter Five

The last weekend in August is a wash. Torrential rains have cancelled both soccer games Charlie was supposed to referee, as well as Butch's off-ice training session at an outdoor track. Charlie is delighted; not only will they not have to see Butch, but Kate and Brett can help him move the rest of his art supplies and teaching materials to his new classroom. They have been carrying and unpacking boxes for hours through the non-air-conditioned school, and in spite of the gusty wind, the building remains musty and hot. They finished the pizza they ordered, and are now eating the Italian ice Charlie surprised them with from a mini fridge he has stored in the cloakroom.

"Why did they move you?" asks Brett, scraping at his lemon ice. "Your other room was bigger. And not on the second floor."

"This room gets better light. And they wanted all the science classrooms together. They're turning my old art room into a shared science lab."

Charlie drops his last box of art books and opens the window, letting in a blast of wind, sending posters flying all over the room. Kate scrambles to pick them up, placing a bust of Van Gogh—sans lower ear—on the pile. As thunder rumbles, Charlie wipes the fog from his glasses and turns to his family.

"Isn't this great?" he says.

Brett and Kate give each other strange looks.

"Sure, Dad," says Brett.

"Come on. Are you telling me you would rather be running endless laps—with Coach Butch screaming at you —than helping your dad set up his classroom?"

"Nah, I guess I'd rather do this. Besides, I lifted boxes today. Those are like weights. I can tell my lineys I've been working out."

"Your who?" asks Kate.

"My lineys. Linemates. Aiden and Bobby. Aiden has been lifting weights with a trainer. I wish I could do that."

"That's not good for you at this age, bud," says Kate.

"You don't know that," says Charlie.

"I do know that. In fact, Brett's pediatrician said no weights except his own body weight until puberty."

Brett sniggers.

"I was actually doing a little reading on the subject," says Charlie. "They say if you use low weights with more reps that's better for kids than heavy weights with less reps. There's even a group who thinks it builds bone density."

"So can I?" asks Brett. "Can I get the weight trainer?"

"No," says Kate. "Even if it were good for you, it costs too much. We already pay a ridiculous amount for hockey."

"I thought you made good money."

"Brett," says Charlie. "First of all, our finances are none of your business. Second, your mom does do well as a recruiter, but the job market is slow right now."

"Besides," says Kate, "it's not just about the cost; it's about the principle."

"I think Bobby's going to sign up, too. His mom and dad were talking to Aiden's parents about it."

"The Churches are very competitive with the Caldwells," says Kate. "And everyone, for that matter."

"We don't have to compete, because you're the best on the team," says Charlie.

"Charlie!" says Kate.

He shrugs.

Brett smiles and digs back into his Italian ice. After a few moments, he asks, "What's a skullet?"

Charlie snorts.

"Where did you hear that?" says Kate.

"Coach Butch. He said Bobby's dad has one, and Mr. Gardenia laughed."

"Lovely," says Kate.

"Do you know what a mullet is?" says Charlie.

"Yeah, like when your hair is shorter up top and longer in the back?"

"Yep. Well, a skullet means you're bald up top, with long hair in the back."

Brett giggles.

"That's not very nice," says Kate, trying to suppress a smile.

"Coach Butch is not very nice," says Brett.

"Do you want to move teams?" asks Kate.

"No," says Brett. "I love my lineys."

"At least there's that," says Kate.

"And at least we get a break from Butch this weekend," says Charlie.

"Amen," says Kate.

As they finish their Italian ice, Charlie's cell phone starts buzzing. They search the piles, but can't find it in all the mess. By the time they locate the phone at the bottom of a mountain of smocks, it has stopped ringing. Charlie sees that it's Coach Butch who called.

Thunder rumbles.

He listens to the voicemail, his spirits sinking lower with every word.

"What is it?" asks Kate.

Charlie puts the phone on speaker and holds it up so Kate and Brett can hear Coach Butch's message.

"Polar Bears. I got Mike's school to open their gym for me. You need to be there for off-ice training at sixteen hundred hours—that's in sixty minutes, for you civilians out there. If you don't show, consider yourself benched for the first period of the Labor Day Tournament.

Chapter Six
Six Months to District Playoffs

Piper Caldwell's Status Update: ⚙

Some people are so rude. You try to do something nice, and they don't appreciate it. New phrase: Helicopter Grandparents. Yeah, it's a thing.

💚 💬

Piper and Tina scroll through social media apps while waiting for the Labor Day tournament to begin.

"Nice Vague-Booking," says Tina, reading Piper's status update. "Aren't you worried Henry's grandmother will see?"

"I'm not friends with Mee Maw on Facebook," says Piper.

"I'm friends with Henry's mother, are you?"

"I wouldn't even know what she looks like if I passed her in a rink. What's the deal? Why are the grandparents always here?"

"No idea."

Piper spots the new defensemen's parents. Butch cut Zoe for puking at pre-season practice, and he replaced her with twin thugs, Franklin and Gordie, whom he poached from the Ice Dogs. He promised the boys' father Hank that the twins could be the starting line of defense, and Hank could work the penalty box any game he wants, which was apparently important to him because of how much time his sons spend there. Hank has greasy hair and a red, runny nose he wipes with a wilted hankie. The mother, Dawn, has a shock of dyed red hair and a bedazzled t-shirt screaming over her massive boobs.

"Former stripper?" says Piper.

"In the eighties," says Tina.

"Those leggings reveal an unfortunate lot."

"She should have given them to Goodwill thirty pounds ago."

"Do you think she has that make up tattooed on her face?"

"I can't get past the spikey pink nails," says Tina. "Those should be illegal. Along with the out of date breast implants."

"Time for a redo, honey."

Piper feels herself literally recoil as Coach Butch saunters into the lobby. He looks Dawn over from head to toe, and adjusts himself in his favorite sweatpants—the ones with the hole in the crotch.

"The season starts in ten minutes," he says. "Once that buzzer goes off, those boys are mine. Don't interfere. Don't even feel like you have to stay. They need to focus on me if we are going to get to districts this year."

Amy stands behind Butch and yells, "Piss off, you filthy lot of you!"

Mee Maw raises her hand. "We should emphasize that the children—eleven and twelve-year-olds—are here, first, to have fun."

Butch looks at her as if she has just walked out of lobotomy surgery wearing a hospital gown opened in the front. He doesn't dignify the statement with a verbal response.

"Oh, one quick announcement," says Tina. "Be sure to let me know the name—full name, nickname, whatever—your son wants on his end-of-season trophy. I have to get those orders in before October first to get the discount."

Butch's face turns redder than Tom's Washington Capitals jersey.

"Trophies?" says Butch. "There will be no trophies unless we have winners."

"Hockey's not for pussies!" yells Amy.

"These are Pee Wee hockey players," says Mee Maw. "Every Pee Wee gets a trophy."

Mee Maw never knows when to shut up, thinks Piper.

"David's counting on it," says Linda, the back-up goalie's mother.

Piper snorts.

"You want a trophy," says Butch, "have them play rec for the rink down the road. Maybe you'll even get participation ribbons."

"And orange slices!" says Sal, with a snort.

Amy slaps Sal on the head.

"Youth hockey has become ridiculous," says Butch. "Back when I played, there were no face cages, no mouth guards, no water breaks. You could body check the minute you got on skates."

"Yeah, Buddy," says Sal, patting Butch on the back. He glances around to make sure he's safe from Amy, but she's hiding under the bleachers.

"There were no team pool parties or trophies unless you won the whole damned league," says Butch. "There will be no trophies here unless we win districts."

Butch enters the rink, slamming the door behind him, and for once, Piper finds herself in agreement with him.

#####

Usually Piper prefers to stand along on the boards on whichever end Aiden is shooting, taking video footage of his shifts with her phone so she can post to social media when he scores, but not today. She has two issues: one, her new stilettos are killing her feet, and two, Justin has been snippy with her since the team pool party. She tried to argue with him that she wasn't taking over team mom duties again, and really, the party wasn't that bad. But she'd argued that position after consuming an obscene amount of margaritas. Also after a mishap with her heel getting stuck in the grout around the pool coping that had sent her plunging into the swimmers' lane, and resurfacing with a wardrobe malfunction that Sal, Butch, and Kip had apparently seen and enjoyed.

She walks swiftly past the goalie parents—Nikolai the Russian is unintelligible, and Tom and Linda are total bores with coffee breath. She finds a space on the bleachers a little away from the other parents.

She soon overhears Kip's conversation with Kate. He stands in front of Kate with his foot up on the riser, muscles bulging through his too tight tee shirt and jeans, regaling Kate with tales from his hockey days. A quick scan of the rink reveals that Lucy is not in attendance. Kip likes to put the moves on other hockey moms when he's not under Lucy's watchful eye.

"It was tied up, and there were ten seconds on the clock," he says. "My shoulder felt like it was being prodded with a hot poker, but I saw the opening, took the shot, and scored. Won the championship game."

"Impressive," said Kate, staring ahead at the Zamboni making its final swipes.

"I had to have surgery after that. Killed my career. Got me addicted to opioids for a while. But at least I went out on a high note. Made my momma proud."

"I'm sure your mom felt your pain."

"How's that?"

"I read an article about mom's having their kids cells actually in their brains. We can literally feel the pain of our children."

Piper rolls her eyes.

Kip pulls his leg down from the riser. His eyes glaze over and his smile falls. Kate has killed his hard on.

"I get why moms become so obsessed with their kids, but what about dads?" she continues. "They get every bit as obsessed. It's like we all live through them now. Our parents didn't behave this way."

He makes a polite *yeah* sound, and looks at the clock as if willing warm ups to begin.

"We feed off the kids and their accomplishments or failures. Inside all of us—sports parents in particular—are these dormant volcanoes, just waiting for the right conditions to erupt."

Shut up, thinks Piper. Kate is always spewing nonsense about parenting articles, sports articles, science findings. Piper cannot for the life of her figure out what Justin finds attractive about Kate. He's always trying to get Piper to buy yoga pants to wear in public. She wouldn't be caught dead in the hockey-mom uniform.

The music begins pounding through the rink sound system. Kip can't get away fast enough. Kate catches Piper watching, and rolls her eyes as if to say, "What a creep." Piper gives Kate a tight smile before turning her attention to the team.

The boys wait outside the doors to the ice like bulls at a rodeo, their breath fogging in the cold air. They stomp from skate to skate, chew their mouth guards, bang their helmets together, and slam their sticks on the ground. Assistant Coach Andy opens the door. Its thick metal scrapes like the bars of a prison cell. The boys begin their battle cry and rush to the ice, skating laps to get warmed up. The energy gives Piper a thrill; it's electric. Each year it never fails: the boys get exponentially faster and taller and more skilled, upping the intensity from season to season like the knob on an amplifier. Piper feels as nervous as if she were a player, and hopes Aiden has calmed down. He puked as soon as they got to the rink, but he does that often before games; he's a head case.

The warm-up clock counts down until the final buzz, and before Piper knows it, the game has started. She is pleased to see that Aiden's line is out first. He and Bobby and Brett are the best line; they get it done. She just wishes Aiden were center. Brett has that honor, and while he is good, he doesn't seem that much better than Aiden— especially now that Aiden is lifting.

Wait! Goal, Brett.

The crowd goes wild.

She looks at the bench, but Butch doesn't react. He expects them to win. They won't get any praise from him.

Fine. Kids get enough back slaps these days.

With one minute left in the first, the other team screens their goalie and sends a perfect shot into the top right corner. Nikolai slams his stick on the ground. Brett skates over and head butts Nikolai, patting him on the shoulder and encouraging him not to get down on himself. Tina cues Taylor Swift's *Shake it Off*. The other forward line is out and loses the faceoff, but Piper can't see what happens next because her five-year-old is in her face.

"I'm hungry."

"Not now. There's only one minute left in the first period."

"We never ate lunch!"

"Yes we..." Piper stops herself, notes her growling stomach, and looks at the clock. One forty-five. *Oops.*

"How are we supposed to squeeze lunch in when we had to drive an hour to this rink—an hour early. I'll get you something later. It wouldn't kill you skip a meal anyway."

Piper notices Kate giving her a horrified look. She's so judgmental. Kate reaches in her purse and pulls out a package of pretzels.

"Is she allowed to have these?" says Kate.

Sure, just give my chubby kid a bag of carbs when I deny her.

"She's fine. But thanks."

"Mommy!"

"Ugh, whatever, just don't stand in front of me during the game."

Kate passes the pretzels to Piper's daughter, who climbs down the bleachers and tears open the bag like she hasn't eaten in days. She shares them with her little sister, and they get back to whatever it is they do on their iPads all season.

Just before the second period begins, Charlie Miller rushes in, skin clammy, out of breath, glasses askew. Kate kisses him and gives him an update on the game, and when Brett sees his dad from across the ice, he does a little hop and waves. Coach Butch taps Brett on the helmet and points at the ice as if to say, "Pay attention."

"Sorry I'm late," says Charlie.

"It's okay. They're tied. Brett had the first goal!" says Kate.

"Awesome!"

Charlie sits heavily and runs his hands over his eyes.

"What's wrong?" says Kate.

He lifts his sweatshirt sleeve to reveal red, claw-like marks on his arm. His warm-up pants have grass stains on the knees.

Good Lord, was Charlie Miller, of all people, in a fight? thinks Piper.

"I had to break up a brawl."

"Where?"

"At the soccer field. Between two mothers. Of eleven-year-old soccer players."

"Please tell me you're joking," says Kate.

"I wish."

"Why were they fighting?"

"One of them forgot the players' snacks for the end of the game. When a mom got on her about it, the forgetful one told her that maybe if her kid ate fewer snacks he'd have more speed on the field."

Piper snorts.

"It got ugly fast," says Charlie.

Their conversation stops as soon as the next period begins. Dominik, the new kid, scores, but his goal is quickly

42

answered by the opposing team. Piper cannot believe Nikolai has let in two goals. He has had the most shutouts of any Pee Wee goalie in the tri-state area. His father is losing his mind, screaming in Russian at his son.

In the third period, the opposing goalie trips Mario Gardenia, who gets up and pushes back. When the ref blows the whistle, it's Mario who gets the penalty. He throws his arms in the air at the referee in protest. Sal bangs the glass. Louise spews profanity. Her tantrum is so intense, the referee skates to where she stands and puts up his hand to warn her. This infuriates Louise even more, and finally, two rink employees move toward her and escort her from the rink.

Piper's girls look up briefly from their electronic devices. Something nags at Piper when she realizes they display no visible reaction to a grown woman being thrown from a youth sporting event for having a temper tantrum, but she doesn't dwell on it. The game is on again. The Millers can't move on, however.

"Louise is as much of a lunatic as Sal," says Charlie.

"The goalie did trip Mario," says Kate. "He was just getting back at him. Too bad he got caught."

Piper's eyes widen. That is not a typical Kate statement. Is she becoming a real hockey mom?

"Kidding," says Kate, giving a half-hearted laugh.

When Butch puts Brett in for the penalty kill, he looks up at his parents with a smile. At the end of the shift, Charlie gives Brett a thumbs up for a great job, but Brett is passed over for his next shift. Then the next.

"Maybe he's letting him sit since he was out for the whole penalty kill," says Kate.

"No, something's up," says Charlie.

Brett is passed over two more times. Piper sees that Charlie's face has turned red. She would be upset, too. They pay too much for their kids to get benched for bogus offenses, but it works out for Aiden's playing time, so she keeps her mouth shut. Bob Church scoots over to where they all sit and leans in to Charlie.

"Why doesn't Butch have him out there?" he says.

"No idea," says Charlie.

"We need a goal, big time."

"The man makes no sense," says Kate.

With two minutes left, Butch finally puts Brett back in the game. Brett chases a loose puck and takes it all the way to the goal, but before he can shoot, a defenseman on the other team nails him. Brett lies on the ice for a few seconds before standing, shaking his head, and skating to the bench. The other player is sent to the penalty box.

An ungodly, guttural, growling noise directed at the offending player comes from the stands. It takes Piper a moment to realize that sound came from Kate's throat. The dormant volcano has apparently erupted.

Brett is put back in with thirty seconds on the clock. He wins the face off, scoots the puck to Aiden, who feeds it back to him to score the winning goal. The Polar Bear spectators erupt with a series of whoops and hollers. Brett looks to his parents, and Charlie gives him a thumbs up. It might be Piper's imagination, but Butch appears to be glaring across the ice at Charlie.

No matter. Piper launches herself down the bleachers to take pictures of the kids with the winning scoreboard above them. She is thrilled to see she is the first to post the win on social media.

Chapter Seven

  Kate Miller's Status Update:

Article Link: Ultra-Competitive Parents:
Warning Signs & Red Flags

Kate ducks behind Charlie.

"Hide me," she says.

"Why?"

"Tina's here. She's all over me about hosting that #HockeyStrong party."

"Don't worry; she's talking to Hank's wife."

"She is?"

"Is that strange?"

"She and Piper talk about Dawn like she's a dog."

"I know why they're friends now," says Charlie. "Look."

Dawn wears a #HockeyStrong jacket with both of her boys' numbers on the back.

"That didn't take long," says Kate.

Tina calls the parents to order.

"Our first family fundraiser is coming up, and I expect to see each player represented at Caliente Tex Mex," says Tina. "I've made a banner you can all easily share on social media through the team page. Make sure all of your friends and family know so they can come to Caliente on Monday with big orders to support the Polar Bears."

"I heard that the Ice Dogs raised a thousand dollars through their Caliente night," says Piper.

"I expect at least two thousand from our families," says Tina. "And we'll need it, with all of these tournament fees."

"Every time I eat at Caliente, I have stomach issues for days," whispers Charlie.

"It's for the team," says Kate in her best Tina voice.

"Next order of business," says Tina. "I need copies of your son's birth certificates. I'm still waiting on a few of you to turn those in. The league requires it, and the boys technically should not be on the ice until they have it, but they'll give a grace period of a couple of weeks if you can't find the birth certificate."

There is a murmuring in the crowd, jokes about the tall boys lying about their ages.

"Mario only just turned nine," says Sal, puffing up his chest. "Thank God the kids can play up. He was skating circles around those benders at the Squirt level."

"He's only nine?" says Mee Maw. "Is that even safe?"

"Of course it is," says Sal. "He's a beast."

"It wouldn't be safe for kids his age to have Mario the Beast playing with them," says Louise.

"Did she just make a hashtag motion with her fingers when she said 'Mario the Beast?'" whispers Kate.

"She did," says Charlie.

The kids emerge from the locker room and head toward the ice for the game. The parents become alert, as if the Adderall that half the boys take oozes from their pores, perking up the spectators via osmosis. They file in behind the kids.

"Wait!" calls Tina. "I'm hosting a #HockeyStrong painting party next Thursday. Moms, raise your hands if you're coming! Bring a friend!"

Charlie forces Kate's arm in the air while she struggles to keep it down.

Slap!

Amy smacks Charlie in the back of the head.

#####

Thinking Tina will be running the score clock, Kate leads Charlie to the offensive zone. She soon realizes it's Helen's turn at the clock, however, and tries to sneak to the stands. Tina stops her.

"Is Brett ready for this?" asks Tina, lifting her eyebrows and nodding to the ice like it's the Stanley Cup Playoffs.

"If eating Fruit Loops and playing Minecraft gets a kid ready, he's in top form!"

Kate enjoys Tina's horrified look. Charlie gives Kate a squeeze in the side. He's more diplomatic with sports parents.

"Where's Bob?" he asks.

"He has the flu," Tina says with disgust. "If we get sick because of him and can't play, I'm going to be pretty P-O'd."

We, Kate mouths to Charlie. She thinks it's ridiculous when parents use the "we" pronoun when referring to their kids' sports. *We won in overtime. We beat the best team in the league.*

They are the players. Not the parents.

Kate turns her attention to the game, and soon wonders if Bobby might be sick. He's not skating well, his face is white, he's favoring one side like he's sore on the other. Kate can sense Tina's tension. Tina keeps muttering, "Come on! Man up!"

A nervous energy buzzes in the rink. The Polar Bear defense has been particularly aggressive, making foolish penalties over and over, leaving only three or four Polar Bear players on the ice while the offenders serve time in the box. And whatever Bobby's issue is seems to be intensifying.

"What's wrong with him?" asks Tina. "Do you see how he's limping? It's like he's only putting weight on one foot."

Tina taps the glass and makes a motion with her hand like *speed up*! After the next whistle, the limping worsens. Bobby can't get any momentum, and the bits of his face that can be seen through his helmet cage are now blood red.

"Oh no," says Tina.

"What?" says Kate.

"He's hurt. I thought I caught Bob wrapping his foot the other day. Oh my God."

"It might just be twisted," says Kate.

"Yeah, but if it he can't skate through the pain and needs to take time off, he might get cut!"

"No way; you're the team mom," says Charlie.

"But Butch always talks about that waiting list he can call at any moment to take one of our kids' spots. God, and I was really starting to feel a connection with Coach."

While Kate looks at Charlie with raised eyebrows, Piper and Justin join the group.

"What's with Bobby?" says Piper, barely suppressing her thrill over Bobby's drama. Kate has seen Piper in action last season. Injury gets her off, especially if it makes her son look better on the ice.

"Nothing," says Tina. "I'm sure he's fine. Just an ankle twist. Why is Aiden coughing so much?"

Piper's face turns red.

"He was up all night," says Justin.

"Not all night," says Piper, slapping Justin's arm and giving him a *Don't air our dirty laundry* look. "We gave him a double dose of cough medicine and slathered him with Vicks. He'll be fine."

Louise and Sal join the crowd. Tina looks as if she's going to get sick.

"What's with this line?" asks Louise with disgust. "Aiden is coughing like a TB patient, and Bobby looks like a cripple."

"Bobby's fine," says Tina through gritted teeth. "Just a little ankle twist, I'm sure."

"I hope that's all," says Louise.

"Don't worry; he'll be fine against the Ice Dogs tomorrow."

"My cousin has a friend whose son plays for them," says Louise. "She said their coach has been telling them to stick it to our boys when the refs aren't looking."

"Butch has been prepping our guys at practice all week," says Sal. "He gave them the player numbers of their best guys; we'll get our goons on them. And Mario knows how to hit the boards and fall like he's real hurt when he's not."

"We can beat them clean," says Kate. "No need for tricks."

"They've got it coming," says Louise. "Their starting center boarded Mario at summer camp, and that kid is going to get it."

The whistle blows. Bobby is down, rolling around and clutching his foot. Butch sends Assistant Coach Andy over to investigate, and Andy has to practically peel Bobby off the ice and carry him to the bench. Tina starts toward him but Louise holds her back.

"Butch isn't going to want you over there," she says.

"If he's hurt, I might have to take him to urgent care."

"Just wait until the end of the game."

"Half the time they just perform for their mommy's sympathy," says Sal.

"Mario knows better," says Louise. "He won't get any of that shit from me."

Louise and Sal leave and resume their post across the boards, where they can gossip and critique other people's children in privacy. Tina frantically punches at her phone, likely questioning sick Bob about Bobby's injury. The Polar Bears end up winning one to nothing, but only because Viktor brought his A game. Bobby doesn't return to the ice, and when it's over, Andy attempts to lift Bobby.

Charlie hurries over, and assists Andy in delivering Bobby to Tina.

"I'm sorry, Mom," Bobby says.

Bobby struggles not to cry. Kate feels awful for the kid; she can only imagine the pressure Tina puts on him.

"What do you think it is?" Tina asks Andy.

"What?" says Andy.

"His foot. Does it look swollen?"

Andy shrugs, and his phone dings. He pulls it out of his pocket and picks at a pimple on his cheek while he reads a text.

"Did Butch say anything?" says Tina.

Andy looks up at her as if she's a buzzer that won't stop going off.

"About?"

"What will happen if Bobby can't play tomorrow?"

"Whoa, I don't think Coach considers that an option."

Bobby whimpers.

Tina runs her hands through her hair and groans.

"Let's go," she says to Bobby.

"I need my bag!"

"Coach Andy will get it."

Andy looks annoyed, but obeys. Bobby stands and tries to take a step, but cries out the moment his left skate touches the ground. He slams back down on the bleachers, and puts his face in his hands.

"Oh my God, Bobby, really?" says Tina. "Do you want Coach Butch to see you like this? You don't want him thinking you're weak."

Kate feels sick.

Dawn emerges from the crowd. She gets on her knees in front of Bobby—ample cleavage exposed in her plunging neckline—and uses her pink claws to untie his skate.

"Okay, Baby, let me see," says Dawn.

Suddenly there is a crowd, mostly male. As Piper comes closer, eyeing the foot, Kate can almost hear Piper silently hoping for injured reserve so Aiden will have more playing time. It will only be a matter of minutes before the gathering parents start making their sideline diagnoses and prognoses. Kate has seen it before.

"Please, this isn't necessary," says Tina.

"It's no trouble," says Dawn. "I'm a nurse."

Dawn slides off the skate and Bobby's sock. The foot almost visibly expands in the cold air. It's black and blue, swollen, and clearly in need of medical attention. There is a collective intake of breath. Piper stares down at the foot with a mixture of horror and fascination. Helen saunters forward and raises one eyebrow. She gives Louise a knowing look.

"Broken," says Helen. "Four weeks."

"Six," says Louise.

"Get him to the car," Kate says to Charlie. She doesn't want this poor child subjected to the creepy injury wishes of psycho sports parents.

As Kate hurries to hold open the door for Charlie, Piper's voice rises above the crowd. It sounds malicious, triumphant.

"Eight."

#####

An hour after they turned out the light for bed, Charlie continues to toss and turn. Kate rolls over and faces him.

"What's wrong?" she says. "Still thinking about Bobby?"

Charlie sits up, puts on his glasses, and reaches for his phone.

"Partly," he says. "The pressure Tina puts on that kid is frightening. And the parents are sick."

"I know."

The light from the iPhone screen reflects in his glasses.

"What are you looking at?" she says.

"I feel silly."

"Tell me."

"Okay, so I know this is crazy, but I started keeping track of Brett's ice time. He was only out there for an average of twenty-two seconds per shift."

"You were timing line changes?"

Charlie runs a hand through his hair. "Um, yeah."

Her initial thought is *Nuts*. But then she realizes she has been keeping track in her head, and she has noticed Brett seems to get short-shifted.

"Not a bad idea," she says.

"I'm glad you don't think I'm crazy."

"I'm right there with you."

"Butch has his kid covering two positions," says Charlie. "Mike goes from his usual offense to defense for the penalty kills, so he gets double the playing time."

"Nepotism."

"Which I get. If I coached I'd probably let Brett play more than the other kids."

"No you wouldn't. You'd even give David equal time in goal."

"I would not."

"Yes, you would."

"I told you there are rumors his dad paid to get him on the team, right?"

"You said Sal told you," says Kate. "He's like a grocery store tabloid—only fifty percent accurate."

"Eighty."

"I'd personally like to start a collection to pay David to leave the team."

"Kate!"

She loves to play up her crazy for Charlie. It scratches an itch, and also lets him release some of his private insanity. It's not healthy to keep these feelings suppressed, but they have to be careful not to do it around other hockey parents.

"When he's in goal, it's open season," she says.

"I'm shocked."

"Just kidding. Ish."

Charlie again scrolls through the list of shift times.

"I just want to figure out why Butch is punishing Brett," he continues. "If Brett was messing around in practice or not running the plays, I'd understand, but as far as I've observed he listens to every stinkin' direction Butch gives."

"I don't know how any of them can understand a word of Butch's instruction. He's always screaming in that hoarse voice. I keep praying his vocal chords will collapse. They have to be getting close to death."

Charlie is quiet for a moment.

"Do you think Butch is mad at *me*?" he says.

"For what?"

"I have no idea, but he keeps glaring."

"God only knows what sets him off," says Kate. "But I wouldn't lose sleep over it."

Chapter Eight
Five Months to District Playoffs

 Piper Caldwell's Status Update:

You know how gyms have childcare rooms? I'm going to start a nationwide movement for ice rink childcare rooms. Sibling Sitters.
Oh, and aerosol sanitizer to disinfect the air. I'll make a fortune.

#SiblingSitters #HockeyStrong

Piper surveys the rink and sees several kids sneezing, including her own son, and Bob Church, spreading his germs along the bleachers. He's talking to the other team's parents, and likely going on about how great his son is, while pointing to the kid's name and number on his shirt, his hat, and the sides of his sweatpants. He lands a wet sneeze in his arm, but keeps talking like he didn't just get snot all over his jacket.

"This place is disgusting," says Piper. "We're all going to catch it."

"Did you give Aiden cough medicine?" says Justin.

"No. He looked sluggish yesterday. I think it affected his performance."

"Bad decision. If he gets on a coughing jag, he might start wheezing. I think he's working up to asthma."

"Don't even say that out loud."

Slap!

Amy strikes Justin's face. Piper sees that Justin looks like he wants to hit back.

"I hope he chokes to death," says Amy. She tackles Justin with a bear hug. "I'm sorry. I'm sorry!"

While Justin struggles to extract himself from Amy's grip, which has wandered south to his backside, Butch walks over wearing head-to-toe camo. His hair and beard are reaching lion's mane status, and his fingernails are crusted with dark red, probably from an animal he shot and gutted earlier that morning.

"Hank's sick," he says. "I need someone in the penalty box."

Justin volunteers, and succeeds in removing Amy from his body. Once he's gone, Kip slides next to Piper and nudges her shoulder with his.

"As much time as we spend together, you could be my hockey wife," he says.

It must be her turn for his attention. *Whatever*, she thinks, *at least he's pleasant.*

"I've been meaning to tell you," says Kip. "You're in great shape. I can't believe you have all those kids. How do you do it?"

"Starvation. Surgery. Whatever it takes."

"LOL," he says. "Keep doin' what you're doin'."

He gives her a fist bump.

The ref blows the whistle and drops the puck to start the game. The Ice Dogs have come out to slaughter. They are skating twice as fast, hitting twice as hard, and shooting twice as much as the Polar Bears. Butch's screaming can barely be heard over the rising crowd noise—especially Nikolai's Russian tirade.

Now that the game is on, Kip tracks Kyle's every movement, hunter-style, with his sports and video cameras. When he catches a good play, a penalty, or a goal, he waits until after the camera is turned off to cheer. He notes Kyle's stats in the binder after each whistle. But even Kip is beginning to get distracted by the level of game intensity.

An Ice Dog center charges the goal, knocking the net off its posts and flattening Viktor. Nikolai screams and slams the glass. Franklin and Gordie grab the kid off Viktor and begin punching him, and the other players pile on. The refs pull the kids apart and blow their whistles. Dawn has a teenage boy with her, presumably an older son, who screams at the Ice Dog who punched one of the twins. He runs down the stands, climbs on the boards, and shouts: "You little dickhead! I'll smear your ass all over the parking lot!"

How embarrassing, thinks Piper.

She takes a long drink from her portable coffee mug, savoring the flavor of the Bailey's she added at the last minute. So what if it's early. The booze will keep her warm and chill. Her youngest walks over, eyes on the psychotic teenager, and taps Piper's leg.

"What?"

"Pee pee."

"Seriously? Not now. You always wait until the game has started. You'll just have to hold it until this period is over."

Henry's grandfather Poo Poo manages to coax the screaming teenager to the bleachers, but Coach Butch and the Ice Dog coach are now in a shouting match. Luckily, they can't duke it out since they are separated by the scorekeeper and penalty boxes.

"I gotta go bad," says the girl, jumping from foot to foot.

Coach Butch starts to climb over to the other team's bench, but Justin stops him.

"Mommy!"

"Not now!"

Two players from each team are ushered into their respective penalty boxes. Butch stops cursing and shakes off Justin's hold. He high fives his players who have entered the penalty box before returning to the bench.

Her daughter begins to sob.

"What?" says Piper.

Her pink leggings are soaked.

#####

Piper ends up having to buy toddler figure skating pants for a small fortune in the pro shop, and by the time she returns to the game, the third period is underway. A huge, husky woman wearing overalls has taken her place along the boards, so Piper stands on the other side of the woman just as the Ice Dogs score on a power play, tying the score 2-2. The woman hoots and bangs the glass.

The Polar Bears are angry enough to come back hard. They are in the offensive zone, firing puck after puck at the Ice Dog goalie. After he almost lets one in, the woman in overalls bangs the glass and growls at the kid, who Piper assumes is her son.

"Get pissed!" the woman says. "You gotta get pissed to stop these guys!"

58

On the next play, Kip's son Kyle makes a breakaway, and when he gets within a stride of the goalie, the kid uses his skate to knock the goal off its posts. Kyle shoots and the puck goes in the goal, but the refs wave it off and reset the net.

"Come on!" yells Kip. "The goalie cheated! That's the third time he's done that!"

"Shut up, asshole!" yells the goalie's mother. "Get your eyes checked."

Kip appears so shocked the woman has spoken to him this way that he's momentarily silenced. Boos come from the stands.

In the last minute of the game, Aiden's line heads full speed down the ice. The Ice Dog defense and forwards pull tight around the goal. Brett feeds the puck to Kyle at the point, and he makes a slap shot from the blue line. The puck speeds through the air and finds an opening in the top corner of the goal. The Polar Bear fans cheer, but the refs blow the whistles and again wave off the goal. The net is off.

"That little cheater did it again!" yells Kip. "How can you not see this for what it is!"

"Shut up, dick!" yells the goalie's mom. "There's obviously a problem with the settings."

"The problem is your son!"

They continue to argue while the Polar Bear spectators heckle the referee. The game ends with a tie, and Piper follows a mass of grumbling, unsatisfied parents into the lobby. Even the Millers appear to be bickering.

"Why do we we pay this much for travel hockey," says Charlie, "for our kid—who scores and assists ninety percent of the goals—to get short-shifted for Butch's made up misdemeanors, while Butch high-fives kids who start brawls?"

"I told you last year we should have switched."

"That's baloney, Kate. You agreed."

"I'm not arguing about the past anymore. What's done is done."

Piper takes a swig from her mug. This is better than *The Real Housewives of Beverly Hills*! She catches another parent argument—this time between Ice Dog dads.

"I can live with a tie," says one of them.

"You would say that, loser," says the other guy.

"Why don't you kiss my ass?"

"Why don't you start thinking like a hockey parent? A tie. Idiot!"

Kip slams the doors on the way out, and is followed by the goalie mom.

"You just keep running your mouth and see what I do," she says.

Justin walks over to Piper. "WTF? Is this kids' hockey or a war room?"

"The chick in the overalls is the cheating-goalie's mom," says Piper. "She and Kip are going at it."

Kip flips the woman off.

The woman makes a move toward Kip, but a parent from her team takes her shoulders and guides her out toward the parking lot.

"And you just missed two Ice Dog dads yelling at each other because one said he could live with a tie," says Piper.

"Nuts."

"But that's not the craziest thing! The Millers were arguing!"

"Charlie and Kate?"

"Yes, Charlie and Saint Kate."

"About what?"

"Charlie's upset because Butch keeps short-shifting Brett."

"He should be pissed. Brett's the best forward out there."

"Excuse me, have you forgotten your son?"

"No, but statistically, Brett has the most points."

"Traitor."

"Don't be ridiculous."

"Whatever, Justin. Yes, Kate's son is the best. How could he be anything but the best with a mom like that?"

"Piper!"

Piper is getting so tired of his ridiculous crush on Kate. She finishes her coffee and shrugs off his hand, leaving him standing in the lobby.

Chapter Nine

 Kate Miller's Status Update: ⚙

Photos: Brett as a baby, Brett in his hockey uniform

Happy Birthday to our favorite fish-catching, air-drumming, worm collecting, high-diving, hockey-playing kid! We love you Brett!
♥ 💬

Charlie removes the towel of ice from the back of his head.

"Has the bleeding stopped?" he asks.

Kate shakes her head in the negative.

"Great. Great end to a great day."

"Amy feels bad. Look, she's cowering in the corner. I think she was trying to hug you."

"No, there was murder in her eyes."

"She can't help it."

"I know she can't, but where are her parents? Hi Linda and Tom. Sorry to interrupt your burrito feast, but your daughter physically assaulted me."

Every booth at Caliente is stuffed full of blue-and-white clad adults, while the private room in the back where the kids remain unsupervised whizzes with spit balls, hot sauce packets, and refried beans. At least, that's what Charlie hopes he sees running down the wall. One can never be sure when

62

Dante Gardenia is involved. Charlie is starving, but his stomach is already rumbling at the thought of Caliente and its inevitable aftermath.

"How was work?" Kate asks.

"Well, while I was explaining Frida Kahlo's fruit-and-bride still-life as a model for one the kids had to paint, one of my more precocious eighth graders told me that she loves Frida because of the sexual freedoms depicted, even in her fruit representations."

"Clever."

"Yes, but she said this while the principal walked in for a surprise observation."

"Oh."

"And when the lesson was over, the principal asked me how I planned to handle the angry parent emails that would result from my teaching about sex through art in middle school."

"But you weren't teaching that."

"I know you understand, but I don't know that my boss does."

"Eek. Sorry."

"And just as I finished hanging and displaying all of the student art showcased at the public library, I realized I was missing one kid's piece, which he left in the kiln after I reminded him about fifty-seven times to put it with the showcase pieces."

"Then he doesn't get his piece shown."

"It's not that simple. His mother is a lunatic. She has been asking about the viewing times for weeks, and told me she invited the boy's grandparents, aunts and uncles to see his work."

"That's nice."

"No, it's not. The whole reason we applied for this showcase was because her sister's son's class got to do it, and all the grandparents went, and her nephew's art made it in the paper."

"Oh, Lord."

"Yeah. Which is why I had to fight rush hour traffic to go back to school to pick up his sculpture, to take back to the library, so it's ready to be viewed tonight by his family."

"Which is why you're late."

"Yes. And I didn't tell you the bad part."

"Oh, God; what?"

"His cat sculpture lost its tail in the kiln. I had to superglue it. Pray that it stays."

"I will."

"How was your day?" he says.

"Fine."

"Good. Let's serve the cupcakes and get the hell out of here."

"Look, I know you're grouchy from work."

"And being attacked. And having to come to this circle of hell for a fundraiser for a team led by a coach who is Satan's son."

"Yes, all that. But it's Brett's birthday."

Mee Maw taps Kate on the shoulder, staring at Brett's birthday cupcakes as if they are covered in anthrax.

"Excuse me," says Mee Maw. "Tina told me you plan to serve cupcakes. I need to see the nutritional information because of Henry's allergies."

To Mee Maw's absolute delight, Kate reaches into her workbag and produces a single cupcake in a box with a PEANUT/TREE NUT/DAIRY/GLUTEN FREE label slapped on its cover.

Kate rounds up the players for a noisy round of "Happy Birthday," which Dante feels the need to accompany with armpit fart sounds and conclude with a loud burp. Sal and Butch snort, but when Butch sees Charlie he stops grinning and glares at him. Then he leans over and whispers something in Sal's ear that makes Sal look at Charlie and laugh.

This is the cherry on today's shit sundae, and he's in no mood. Charlie throws the towel on the table and crosses the restaurant, planning a speech on the way. His courage depletes with each stride, and by the time he stands over the table, Butch's withering stare makes him want to curl in a ball. He can't imagine what a kid must feel like to be on the receiving end of it. While he reminds himself that Butch is an ice rink manager who steals from vending machines, Nikolai scoots over and invites Charlie to sit.

"Come, come!" he says. "You eat us."

Charlie would look rude to refuse, so he smooshes next to Nikolai. The odor of cigarette smoke on the Russian is enough to make him want to puke.

"Good Brett goal, hey?" says Nikolai. "Game winner."

Charlie looks at Butch, who pretends to be interested in watching children eat cupcakes. Charlie uses the opportunity to praise his son. It was a good goal, and Butch needs to be reminded of it.

"Yeah, we were really excited," Charlie says.

"He practice much?"

"In the driveway, in the dark, the rain, the snow. He's always practicing."

"Viktor, too. I shoot him."

"I wish I could help Brett. I played soccer."

"I did, too," says Sal.

Charlie is surprised. Sal's physique would not suggest exercise had ever been a part of his life.

"Really. Where?"

"Just through high school. Didn't go to college. I didn't need any liberal douchebags filling my head with their bleeding-heart nonsense."

Butch high-fives Sal.

"I was pretty jacked until I hurt my knee. Even dabbled in body building," says Sal. "Then I lost my fingers, so that was that."

He holds up his stumpy hand. Charlie tries not to cringe.

"No more working out for me!" Sal laughs, finishing his soda with a slurping noise.

"How did Mario get into hockey?" asks Charlie.

"Cause this fool's my neighbor," says Sal, slapping Butch's shoulder. "He started dragging us to the rink since the boys were two. Passes down all of Andy's old stuff to Mario. We're all in now."

"Nice," says Charlie. He looks at Butch, trying to make a human connection with the man. If Butch invited a kid to play hockey, he must be somewhat decent. Maybe there's hope. "Hey, we have some old pads Mario or Dante could have. We don't have any other kids to pass them on to, and Mario's a little smaller than Brett."

"Sure, Buddy, thanks," says Sal.

Suddenly the day is better. Charlie chastises himself for being so negative. Maybe he's paranoid. There is so much tension in hockey, it can seep into your brain and make you think the worst. Charlie excuses himself to order a burrito and rejoins the man-table during a hearty conversation about Dawn's assets, which are on display in full body spandex. He's not attracted to her, but goes along with his new buds with the hopes of making a stronger connection with them.

As he stuffs the last bite of burrito in his mouth, he does a quick scan for Kate and sees that Tina has cornered her—no doubt trying to get her to host a #HockeyStrong party. But Kate isn't looking at Tina; she's glaring at Charlie.

#####

Following Caliente night, Charlie was home for two days with a wrecked stomach and a chilly wife. Kate wasn't normally the jealous type, but something about him discussing Dawn's assets with the cavemen rubbed her the wrong way. He thought he could joke with her about it, but she wasn't taking the bait. Charlie wasn't able to pay her too much attention since he spent the greater part of each day in the bathroom, but when he could finally emerge for more than a few hours, she mostly avoided him. In spite of the stomach issues and trouble with Kate, however, he considered Caliente night a net positive: he had been texting with Sal all week, and that felt like an in.

It was Thursday, and they had the night off hockey because of the curling competition at the rink. Tina's #HockeyStrong painting party was at seven o'clock, but Kate had already declared she'd rather hunt with Butch than attend.

"It might be fun," says Charlie.

"Oh, please. If you go into each of their homes a week from now, you'll find the same picture hanging on their walls as a sort of obscene testament to what happens when women get bored and are forced to participate in fundraisers. What's next: adult coloring books?"

Charlie's phone bings. Sal sent him a link to Groupon for the trainer.

"Sal," he says, holding up his phone. "He's like my *paisano* now."

"Lucky you."

Kate gets up and starts clearing dinner. Brett puts his plate in the sink and races toward the door to go out and hit pucks in the driveway.

"Did you finish your homework?" Kate calls.

"Yes!"

"Did you study for Science?"

"Yes!"

Once Brett is outside, Kate slams doors and dishes. Clearly she is not going to move on without a discussion.

"Are you still upset about Caliente?" says Charlie.

"How observant of you."

"Come on. It was harmless banter."

"I didn't know you that night."

"What are you talking about?"

"The nasty mood. Fraternizing with Neanderthals. Ogling Dawn."

"Sometimes you have to meet people where they are."

"By being a fraud?"

"I'm trying to form bonds with these men. At the beginning of the season, you said we should try to blend better. You bought a flip-flop family, for God's sake."

"I didn't mean by talking about women like they're meat."

"Come on, Kate. You know I'm not attracted to a woman like that."

"Of course I know; that's not the point."

"Then what is?"

"For all of her make-up and big boobs, Dawn is actually intelligent."

"Kate, men don't talk about women's brains when they are together. I'm sorry. It's just not what we do. Besides—if Butch and his toadie, Sal, befriend me, Brett might not get benched as much."

"Butch is just as evil to Sal's kid as he is to every other player."

"Not as bad," says Charlie. "How about a little credit for trying to make relationships with these people, instead of judging them all the time?"

"Don't act like I'm the only judgy one."

"You're not, but the way we've handled the season so far isn't working out, is it? Let's try a new tack."

"So under your line of reasoning, maybe I should start flirting with Butch. I mean, if that gets Brett more playing time, why not. Hey, maybe I could sleep with him."

"That's ridiculous, and you know it."

"You don't see my point at all?" she says.

"No," he says, grabbing a towel and wiping down the counter.

"You don't think I have any right to be aggravated?"

"No. You should be grateful. I hate those guys as much as you do, and I resent being lumped in with them."

Kate's mouth hangs open. She stares at him a moment, then her gaze hits the fridge. She pulls off the **Painting and Pino** flier, grabs her purse, and walks out the door.

Chapter Ten

 Piper Caldwell's Status Update:

Painting and Pino: Perfect Pairing!

#MomsNightOut #GoPolarBears
#HockeyStrong

The shade of blue on the studio walls reminds Piper of toilet disinfectant. The instructor is a tall, thin man with an auburn pompadour. And the wine—she can't even: bargain bottles of the tackiest crap you'll find at school fundraisers and family holiday parties in suburbs across the U.S. All evidence that allowing Tina to be team mom was a mistake.

"Isn't this fab?" says Tina.

"The fabbest."

"And I'm pleased to see Helen here. It's good to bond with the coach's wife. Maybe it will give our lineys a little extra time on the ice."

Tina is such a brown-noser. She has been trying to build a relationship with Helen for years in the hopes that it will lead to improved playing time for Bobby, or maybe even the honor of assistant captain. Everyone knows the coach's son will be captain, but the two assistant spots are up for grabs. Piper takes a long gulp of merlot, working hard not to shudder once it's down the hatch. She'll have to double down so she gets drunker faster.

"OMG," says Tina. "Kate Miller just pulled into the parking lot."

"Stop," says Piper. "Is she wearing her work clothes or her yoga pants?"

"She's actually wearing leggings with brown boots, a long denim top, and a scarf."

"I guess it would have been too much to hope she'd have plucked her eyebrows."

"Or put on a drop of make up."

"Kate! What a surprise," says Piper.

"Thanks," she says, uncharacteristically flustered. "I heard something about wine?"

"Pick your poison," says Dawn. Tonight's bejeweled shirt says *Hot Mess Express*.

"Sauvingnon Blanc."

"Hmmm. Don't see that."

"Your choices are the bargain Chardonnay or the bargain Merlot," says Piper.

"Any white will do," says Kate.

Tina glares at Piper and walks over to the instructor. Dawn has only just poured Kate's drink when the man begins barking orders. He's like a well-groomed version of Coach Butch. This party was supposed to be for ladies only. Not to mention that wine and painting parties are supposed to be soothing, not stressful. Another strike against Tina.

The hockey moms settle in chairs like geese flying south, facing a picture wall of a beach with a palm tree. Each has a glass of wine on a table next to a palette full of paint. They all work on the same picture, step by step, under the command of Slender Man. Aside from Mee Maw and Lucy, the rest of the moms have made it. Tina is the only one not painting; she's here to sell apparel.

Helen and Louise are engrossed in gossip, so Tina starts collecting orders on the opposite side of the room. When she reaches Kate, Piper sees that Kate hasn't kept up with the painting steps. She stares into the distance with a blank expression.

"Kate, hello!" says Tina. She waves a #HockeyStrong catalogue in front of her.

"Sorry," says Kate, shaking her head. She takes the catalogue and begins leafing through it.

"Make sure you put in your order before the end of the painting party," says Tina. "#HockeyStrong donates ten percent of all sales to your team, so don't be stingy."

Tina slips a pen in Kate's free hand.

"Sweatpants with your kid's name and number, $120," says Kate. "Sweatshirts, $110. Hand-stitched Jerseys, $320. Long-Sleeved Tee Shirts, $80. Short-sleeved Tees, $60. #HockeyStrong Bejeweled Tee Shirts, $160. Seriously?"

"These prices are actually pretty good," says Tina. "Bob and I have had clothes made on other sites with Bobby's name and number before #HockeyStrong was around, and that cost a fortune. This saves us a ton."

"Yeah, but headbands for $36? Socks for $28?"

"Don't forget the team gets a percentage of the proceeds," says Helen.

Tina beams, obviously thrilled that Helen has backed her up.

"Maybe I should just make a donation," says Kate. She flips back and forth a few times before filling out the form for one pair of socks.

"You know shipping's a flat $20?" says Tina.

"So $48 for a pair of socks?"

"If you spend over a hundred, shipping's free."

Kate groans and takes back the catalogue. Piper refills her glass and returns, ignoring the instructor's ho-humming about people not focusing on the task at hand.

"I ordered the blanket," says Piper. "I wouldn't be caught dead in these clothes, no offense, Tina."

Tina gives Piper a tight smile and looks at Piper's wine glass.

"Not to change the subject, but how are you getting home? I don't want any DUIs after my painting party."

"For your information, I can Uber it, but it would take at least two Costco-sized bottles of this grape juice to have any effect."

"Ooh, I found a good deal!" says Louise from across the room.

"Did I miss the deal page?" says Kate.

"These fatheads are a steal! Life-sized, of your kid, $430, with free slogan fatheads! Hashtag Mario the Beast!"

Louise makes a hashtag mark with her fingers.

"Doesn't Sal complain about being broke all the time?" Piper whispers.

"He does, but the Gardenias know how to prioritize," says Tina, giving Kate a pointed look.

"With hockey fatheads?" says Kate.

"It's about more than fatheads," says Tina. "It's team spirit."

Kate stares at Tina a moment before scribbling a check for the $125 blanket, and handing Tina the order form. Piper watches Tina tally up the totals, and a smile of pleasure spreads over the team mom's face.

"Good night?" asks Piper.

"Banner!" says Tina. "This might give me the points I need to become a Head Style Captain. And Butch will be pleased to learn how much the Polar Bears will get toward a future tournament bus."

"You're not giving the money directly to him, are you?"

"Gosh, no," says Tina. She leans in and lowers her voice. "I'm sure he's doing well enough skimming off the vending machines."

When Louise gets up to go to the bathroom, Tina hustles over to Helen.

"Helen, I just noticed that with my totals tonight, I'll get a free accessory," says Tina. "Why don't you pick out something for yourself."

"You sure?" says Helen.

"Absolutely."

Helen snatches the catalogue and selects a scarf. Tina doesn't point out that scarves are not included since they're over fifty dollars, but she's stuck. She'll look like a jerk if she brings that up. Piper finishes another glass and returns to the wine table.

"So, I've been talking with Bobby's orthopedist," Piper overhears Tina say. "He's thinking Bobby won't be out as long as we originally thought."

"Mmmm," says Helen, gulping her wine.

"I know Butch will be glad to have the lines straight again."

Helen doesn't respond.

"It's a pity Bobby doesn't get to play with Mike, more," says Tina. "I've seen them working together at practice a few times, and they have a particular chemistry."

Piper stiffens. That little bitch is angling for time for Bobby on Mike's line.

"What's that?" asks Louise, back from the bathroom.

"Tina thinks Bobby has good chemistry with Mike."

Piper hears Louise snort, and her shoulders relax. Good. They've boxed Tina out. But seeing where Tina's true colors lie has given Piper an idea.

#####

Justin sees the reflection of headlights coming up the driveway, and goes to the window. Piper's white SUV weaves closer to the house at an alarming speed, and he sucks in his breath. She hits the breaks just before slamming into the garage door.

Drunk.

Justin wishes he could invent an app that would pause Piper two drinks in, when she's loose and flirty. Three or more and she's slurry, weepy, and a danger to society.

He's been stewing all evening about Kip, and how Piper encourages his attention. At practice, she leaned into Kip to watch his game footage, close enough so her hair rested on his shoulder. Justin was hoping to have it out with her tonight, but judging how she pulled in, she'll need to go right to bed.

He hears her come in through the side door—bracelets clanging, muttering to herself, hiccupping—and wishes he'd just gone to bed before she got home. She throws her hundred-pound black leather purse on the white counter and kicks her stilettos at the wall, leaving a mark.

He leans on the doorframe.

"You're still up," she says.

"I like to be ready in case I need to pick you up at the police station."

"Scuse me?"

"Uber. It's an app. Use it."

"Whatever," she says. "Tina had the cheap shit. It tasted like juice and snuck up on me about two minutes ago."

He notes the red wine stains dribbled down her expensive silk white blouse, and starts to comment, but sees by her swaying that he should just get her to bed.

"Your mother called," he says. "She can watch the girls for the Thanksgiving tournament."

"Good. Then I won't have to spend all the games in public bathrooms and in front of vending machines. The girls are such pains in the ass."

"I thought you said you weren't going to the Mom well as much because she gets too involved."

"I have no choice. I have literally never seen two more high-maintenance girls."

Apple doesn't fall far, thinks Justin.

"It will be good, too, if we want to grab a drink late-night with other parents. Aiden can stay alone. Kip says there's a great wine bar within walking distance of the hotel."

Justin suddenly feels hot. All of his rational thought—the futility of arguing with his drunk wife—is cancelled out at the utterance of the name Kip.

"Maybe I'll stay home with the girls," he says. "Then you and Kip can have Q-T at the wine bar."

"What?"

"You seem to really enjoy Kip's attention."

Her face flushes, from anger or guilt, he cannot tell.

"Are you kidding me?" she says. "He flirts with all the moms."

"But they all don't flirt back. Have you seen how Kate treats him?"

"Oh, God. Not Saint Kate!"

"This is tiresome."

"I can't for the life of me figure out why you think that plain-Jane is hot."

"Don't change the subject. I'm just saying she puts Kip off. You encourage him."

"For Chrissake, Justin. I'm not remotely attracted to Kip."

"Then act like more of a bitch. You don't usually have a problem with that."

"Maybe I do like the attention," she says, starting to cry. Mascara oozes down her face in grotesque streaks. "It would be nice if you made me feel hot every once in awhile."

"Please, Piper! Every time I make a move for you, you swat me away. *It's too early, Justin. I just put on my night moisturizing mask, Justin. We have hockey camp, Justin. Don't mess up my lipstick, Justin.* What do you want me to do? Plug it in your iCalendar so you can plan for it?"

She turns her back to him and almost falls, but catches herself on a column. She leans over on the kitchen island and begins to sob with her head down on the counter.

"It's just all this pressure!" she cries. "Hockey, dance for the girls, the club, my mother, my looks."

It's pointless to argue further.

He guides her up the stairs and toward their bedroom— trying to keep her quiet so she doesn't wake the kids—which is no small task. When he puts her in bed, she's so gone she doesn't even remember to wash off her make up.

Chapter Eleven
Four Months to District Playoffs

 Charlie Miller's Status Update: ⚙

Hockey's not for pussies.

#GoPolarBears #HockeyStrong

A little nagging voice has started in Charlie's head. It says things like, "Do you really pay an athletic trainer $90 a session to work with your twelve-year-old, two days a week, before school?" He imagines a tiny Amy swatting away the disembodied voice in his brain, and the thought makes him chuckle. He turns to share his thought with Kate, but remembers she is not with him. She said she'd be home, in bed, drinking coffee, perusing the internet for good therapists for him.

"See what I mean," says Justin, joining Charlie and Sal on the bench. "Top notch."

The trainer is an intense, Napoleonesque guy with a voice the wrong side of loud for this early in the morning. He is fit but pocket-sized, probably from lifting weights from too young an age. Charlie watches Brett struggle under a bench press bar, and stands to intervene, when Sal puts his stumpy hand on Charlie's arm.

"It's cool. He knows what he's doing."

"He's been training kids for years," says Justin.

"Remember that Olympic guy, the one who made all the shootout goals?" says Sal.

"T. J. Oshie!" says Charlie.

"No, not him," says Sal. "Some other guy, like from 2000. Anyway, he trained him."

"How did you hear about him?" says Charlie.

"Kip's recommendation."

"I'm surprised Kyle isn't here," says Charlie.

"Oh, Kip won't do group sessions; only one-on-one for Kyle," says Sal.

"It's all being documented for *Kyle's Binder of Hockey Greatness*," says Justin.

"Kip wouldn't want anyone else in the backgrounds of the photos," says Sal.

"Kip takes photos of the training sessions?" asks Charlie.

"And records the hours in the binder," says Justin.

"Haven't you ever seen the photos on Facebook?" says Sal. "He has this edit app that makes Kyle look like a pro."

"I'm not on Facebook," says Charlie.

After Charlie's brief enthusiastic high at the thought of his son training with a guy who trained some Olympic player, he is now lower than when he started. He thinks of Kate. She wasn't even mad at him for setting this up without asking; she just looked at him, shaking her head. It was the look one would give to a grandfather with dementia, or a schizophrenic who didn't understand the voices were imagined. He is starting to think he might be crazy, or at the very least, obsessed. He has dreamt about Butch three times now. In the dreams, Charlie is always a player on the team, usually ignored, occasionally berated, but in the one last night, Butch gave him a pat on the helmet. Charlie woke up feeling as good as if his father had reached out to him after all these years. Waking and processing the dream was disorienting, then distressing, though the memory of the imagined helmet pat continues to give Charlie false and erratic moments of pleasure.

"Good thing we got a Groupon," says Sal.

"What does this usually cost?" says Charlie.

"Like $50 more. A session," says Justin.

"Wow. How many sessions did we get?"

"Six," says Sal.

"That should be enough," says Charlie.

Sal and Justin give him the strange look again, the look like he's a lunatic. Charlie's right eye twitches.

Brett cries out and drops the bar into its holders. He lies on the bench for a minute before Napoleon tells him to get up and start jumping rope.

"You have to stay consistent," says Justin. "Otherwise, all the progress will disappear."

"Yeah, and then Brett will be back down there with the benders," says Sal.

"All right, what is a bender?" says Charlie. "It seems to be the big hockey insult."

"It's a kid who skates so bad his ankles bend in, making him look cow-toed."

"Yeah, like the little mites when they start," says Justin.

"Ah," says Charlie.

His mind returns to Sal's comment about Brett going "back down" with the benders. Is Sal trying to insinuate his son isn't very skilled? Charlie removes his glasses and pinches his forehead. He has not yet had coffee, and this all too much to process so early in the morning after such a poor night of sleep, dreaming of Butch's approval.

As if conjured, Butch walks in. Charlie stands on reflex. Butch watches the boys for a minute in silence, then looks at the dads. He nods, salutes, and leaves the workout room.

Charlie feels as if he has been patted on the helmet.

#####

Kate is certain that Brett's fatigue is from that ridiculous trainer. Throughout the first period of the game, Brett's legs might as well be made of lead. He's skating slow, coming off the ice bent over, coasting instead of going after the puck. She is worried something is really wrong. Finally, Brett scores a goal on a power play, but when he skates to the bench, it appears Butch is scolding him. Brett looks to Kate and Charlie when Butch is done with him, and Charlie gives him a half-hearted thumbs up.

"What's Brett's deal?" Charlie says, his voice agitated.

"I hope the trainer didn't do irreparable damage."

Charlie gives Kate an *Oh, please* look, and turns his attention back to the bench. Butch continues to yell at Brett.

"How can a kid can get yelled at for scoring a goal?" says Charlie. "Especially since I'm breaking ground with Butch."

"How so?" says Kate.

"Butch was pleased with the trainer, for one. Then before today's game, we talked hunting."

"You don't know how to hunt, Charlie. Blood makes you woozy."

"No it doesn't! Butch even offered to take me some time."

The buzzer sounds to end the first period, and Charlie pulls out his phone.

"Look," he says to Kate, holding it up on a Facebook page. "Did you see Butch's "Word of the Day? *Indolence*. Avoidance of activity. Laziness."

She's confused, and doesn't know how he wants her to respond, especially because he's smiling.

"He's not talking about us," he says. "*We* are the dedicated ones. *We* got in on the trainer."

"Wait, since when are you on Facebook?"

"I just got on so I could follow hockey stuff."

She stares at him a moment, and then pulls out her own phone. She clicks around, squinting her eyes at the screen in disbelief.

"You're friends with Butch, Sal, and Kip, and you didn't friend me?" she says.

"I just got on, like, yesterday."

"And you didn't start by friending your wife? What, you're only Facebook friends with psychos?"

"They asked me as soon as I liked the Polar Bears page! I didn't ask any of them to be friends. Well, I asked Butch. But not Sal and Kip."

"You asked for Butch's friendship before asking for mine?"

"Kate, get ahold of yourself. Look, I'll send you a friend request right now."

"Forget it," she says. "I don't want to be friends."

Charlie laughs. She knows this conversation is absurd, but she's still pissed. He reaches for her arm, but she pulls away.

Brett skates over and bangs on the door of the spectator side to get off the ice. Kate and Charlie hurry down the bleachers, and when they reach Brett, Kate takes off his helmet and feels his forehead.

"What are you doing?" says Charlie, glancing nervously from Brett to Butch.

"He's sick, Charlie," says Kate.

"With what?"

"I'm sure it's the flu. Half the team's had it."

"He seemed fine this morning," says Charlie.

Brett's face is so red it's almost purple.

"You lasted the whole first period," Charlie says. "It's only two more, bud. They need you!"

"Feel his head!"

"How can you tell if it's a fever or exertion?"

She gives him a murderous look. Charlie reaches for Brett's forehead, and when he rests his palm on his son, he flinches. Brett emits a horrible wet cough.

"Did you tell Coach Butch you were sick?" Charlie asks.

Brett nods.

"What did he say?"

"Nothing."

"Why did he yell at you after your goal?"

"I don't know," says Brett.

"How can you not know? It just happened?"

Brett coughs again.

"Enough," says Kate. "Get him some Gatorade."

Charlie obeys, and as he returns, the spectators erupt. The opposing team has just scored a goal. Butch throws his clipboard, hitting Assistant Andy on the back of the head.

"Charlie!" Kate calls.

He pulls his attention away and walks over to them, handing Brett the drink.

"We should go," says Kate.

"No," says Brett. "I want to watch."

"You need to rest. Your eyes are glassy."

"If he wants to watch, let him," says Charlie. "He can just as easily sit here as he can on the couch at home."

"Sitting on cold metal in an ice rink is not the same as lying on the couch at home."

"I want to stay," says Brett.

Kate glares at Charlie. She knows he's staying just to kiss up to Butch, but it's two against one.

By the end of the game, Kate wishes she had insisted they leave. Viktor is given a penalty for tripping a player, and has to leave the goal, putting in David. The opposing team scores on him immediately and wins the game. Butch storms off the ice without shaking the other coach's hand, and now can be heard screaming at the kids from outside the locker room.

Kate leads Brett to the parking lot, with Charlie in the rear, carrying the hockey bag. An enormous black SUV with a sticker of a hockey puck that looks as if it has smashed the glass has pulled in so close to them, Kate has to squeeze Brett in the passenger side. While Charlie loads the equipment, a kid from the other team passes them, smirking. Kate and Brett climb in the car, but just as she's about to close the door, she hears the kid say, "Bender."

Charlie slams the trunk.

"What's your problem, kid?" Charlie says.

"Cherry-picker," he says, with a laugh.

She's about to close the door, but hears Charlie say, "Shut your filthy mouth."

The boy's mother ushers him toward the car.

"Did you hear what he said?" Charlie yells at the woman.

"Let's go," the hockey mom says to her boy.

That horrid kid continues to laugh.

"You brat," shouts Charlie. "My son was sick. How dare you criticize him? He didn't make it to the second period, but he got a goal—with the flu—which is more than you can say, I'm sure."

The boy is a jerk, but Charlie needs to calm down. Kate calls to him. "Get in."

"But that kid…"

"Get in!"

Other families are leaving the building and staring at Charlie—a grown man, a teacher!—screaming at a child. He gets in his side, and at least has the decency to look ashamed. Kate slams her door.

"You're going to end up in jail!" she says.

"I know," he says, contrite. "I'm losing it."

"Clearly!"

"But that kid called Brett a bender. And a cherry-picker."

"What's a cherry-picker?"

"Someone who waits for others to feed him the puck so he can score."

Kate is silent for a moment. "Brett is not a cherry-picker."

"I know. That's why I lost it."

She looks out the passenger window and sees the kid staring at them, still laughing. She clutches the door handle, willing herself to calm down, but feels electrocuted. Kate squeezes out of the car and rushes over to the boy.

"Oh my God," says Brett from the back seat.

Kate begins a tirade. She knows she doesn't make sense, but she doesn't care.

The boy's mom rolls down the window and screams at him to get in the SUV. He finally obeys, looking as if he's going to cry. Once he's in, the mom begins to pull forward, but Kate jumps in front of the vehicle. While Kate crosses around and bangs on the driver's side window, Charlie hurries to collect his wife. The other mom has her hands up, as if in surrender. The kid puts his head down in the back seat. Charlie approaches Kate the way one would a bear in the wild, gently places his hands on her shoulders, and guides her back to the car. The woman peels wheels as she speeds out of the parking lot.

Except for Kate's heavy breathing, it is silent in the Millers' sedan. Their earlier conversation comes back to her. She pulls out her phone, opens Facebook, and accepts Charlie's friend request.

#####

Charlie paces in the garage, watching the clock on his phone. Butch texted him that they needed to talk at 9:00 PM. He didn't even ask—just gave the order like a damned lieutenant colonel. Charlie needs privacy when he speaks with Butch because he'll probably end up raising his voice, and doesn't want to wake Brett, who's in bed, sleeping off the flu.

8:58.

Time could not move any slower.

Charlie has been fantasizing about this conversation all afternoon, and he is prepared to tell Butch to stop criticizing his son. Brett is the leading scorer on the team. The other parents constantly tell Charlie and Kate how awesome Brett is. Brett doesn't give Butch any trouble, and he has never missed a practice or game until today, when he had to leave because he was sick.

8:59.

Bullies only back down when they're challenged, and Charlie is angry enough to do so. He has had it with the turmoil Butch has brought to their household, and he's not going to take any more.

9:00.

Charlie presses call. The phone rings four times, but Butch doesn't pick up. He's probably doing this as a power thing. Charlie paces around the garage until 9:06 when his phone rings. He forces himself to wait until the third ring to accept the call.

"We need to get some things straight," says Butch.

"What's up?" *Steady, now.*

"Do you know how to play hockey? Do you even know how to ice skate?"

"No."

"That's right. But I do. I'm the coach. I've been coaching for two decades. I've been on the ice since I could walk. I probably know a thing or two about the sport, right?"

"Yes, but…"

"No but," says Butch. "I told you parents at the beginning of the season that the boys need to look to *only* me for coaching. So when I see you over there, giving Brett a thumbs up every time he comes off the ice—whether or not he's had a good shift—it bothers me."

"Are you telling me that I can't give my son positive feedback?"

"Question: Do human beings want pats on the back or discipline?"

Charlie recalls the dream he had where Butch pat his helmet.

"Pats, of course, but…"

"And if there's a guy across the stands giving you thumbs up—even if you got beat in a face off, or didn't back check, or missed a shot—and a guy behind you (not exactly Mr. Sunshine, but there to make you a better player) who are you going to pay attention to?"

"I'm not a 'guy,' Butch. I'm his father. And you never give him praise."

"Do you want Brett to be a winner?"

"Of course…"

"Do you think Wayne Gretzky is a legend because he got a thumbs up every time he left the ice?"

"No, but…"

"I am here to make these kids into hockey players. If you want trophies, and first place medals, and thumbs ups, send him to a crafting club."

"But if you could just balance your yelling with some positive feedback."

"I give them positive feedback when they deserve it. Doesn't Brett ever tell you things I say about his scoring record in the locker room?"

"Well, no, but…"

"I just gave him the game puck last week for scoring on the penalty kill. Did he tell you that?"

"No."

Charlie begins to forget why he was so angry. Brett can't remember what Butch said to him five minutes after he got yelled at, so it makes sense that he wouldn't share the good things. Charlie is embarrassed by how much he's worked himself up for this conversation. Maybe Butch wasn't screaming at Brett at all in the game. Maybe he was yelling "Good job!" Charlie picks at the flip-flop family on the back of the car.

"Of course not," says Butch. "Boys his age don't listen. You've got to scream. When a kid gets a report card, do they look at the A's or at the one class where they got a C?"

"The C."

"Brett is an A player. If he performs lower than that, he's gonna hear about it. If he does his job, that's what I expect. If he goes beyond, he'll hear about it. But you need to stop with all the thumbs up for mediocrity, for just doing his job. Even for going above and beyond, until after the game, when he's yours. During the game, he's mine. That's what you signed up for. That's what being a Polar Bear means. Got it?"

Charlie's stomach hurts like he has eaten Caliente. More troubling, Butch is starting to make sense to him. Charlie makes a grunting noise that could be assent or a cough.

"Good," says Butch. "Now, let's get these boys to districts."

Chapter Twelve

 Piper Caldwell's Status Update:

Hockey Equipment, check! Suitcases, check! Case of wine, check!

#ThanksgivingTourneyWeekend
#LoveThesePeeWees #HockeyStrong

Justin and Piper always seem to get stuck with Tina and Bob. This makes no sense to him because Piper hates Tina, and Bob is a loser. Bob's skullet is hidden under a winter beanie hat, and their last name, CHURCH, is plastered over so much of Tina and Bob's bodies they could be evangelists. It's embarrassing to be seen with them. Not only that, but the conversation is insufferable. Tina is stressing out about Butch's "Indolence" Status Update, and is certain it was meant for them because Bobby's not seeing the trainer.

"We did the summer sessions," says Tina. "That should count for something."

"I'm sure it's fine," says Piper in a voice that is not at all reassuring.

"It's not like these boys are NHL-bound or anything, but I don't want Bobby punished or missing shifts."

"He can't play right now, anyway," says Bob.

"That's two strikes!"

90

"Once his foot is healed, we'll get him a trainer," says Bob. He rubs Tina's arms.

"We could probably start him now," says Tina. "There must be some exercises he can do for other parts of his body."

The boys have finished warm ups and run past them to the locker room, with Bobby bringing up the rear, limping in his boot. Tina stops him and gives him a protein bar. He argues with her for a minute, but finally takes it, leaving with a groan.

"He's getting so mouthy," says Tina. "Do you think it's Butch's influence?"

"It's the age," says Bob. "He's a growing boy. He's not your little fella anymore."

"Emphasis on 'little,'" says Tina. "That's why we've started a protein regimen."

"A what?" asks Piper.

Justin can see her competitive radar on alert.

"Protein regimen. I read about it on a Hockey Mom message board. Protein shakes, bars, and powder to sprinkle on their meals. I've been putting it in his Nutella sandwiches at school, and he hasn't even noticed."

Piper takes a hit from her mug that Justin is beginning to suspect holds more than coffee, and is about say something when Sal walks over laughing and scanning the crowd as if looking for someone.

"Hey guys," says Sal. "Wanna hear the latest?"

Sal doesn't wait for a reply. He gives the crowd another glance before leaning in and whispering.

"Did you notice Lucy isn't here?"

Piper looks suddenly interested. It figures.

"I heard Kip was seen at a dive bar outside of town with some slut who wasn't his wife."

"No," says Tina.

"Yeah," says Sal. "So ladies, watch out for fist bumps from that guy."

Justin looks at Piper, and she gives him a shrug.

Charlie and Kate have arrived. Justin makes a beeline. They are the only non-freak parents on this team. Unfortunately, the Millers seem just as tense as everyone else. They smile but it's clear they are having a heated discussion.

"Everything okay?" asks Justin.

The Millers look at each other as if silently conversing about whether to share their issue with Justin. Kate gives Charlie a nod.

"It's just Butch's bullshit," says Kate.

"What's the latest?"

"He basically told Charlie not to give Brett a 'thumbs up' when he finishes his shifts."

"What?"

"Yeah. God forbid we praise our son after subjecting him to Butch's lunacy."

"The man has issues."

"I kind of get what he's saying," says Charlie. "He praised Brett's playing, just said not to reinforce him until after the game, when he's ours again."

"Fine," says Kate. "I'll reserve all hand signals for Butch. Here's one."

Butch stands with his back to them. Kate flips Butch the bird. Justin laughs.

"I'm just trying to stay positive," says Charlie.

"Oh, Charlie. He's messing with your head."

"No, I've got a strategy. I've decided what I'll do so I can monitor Butch."

"What?"

"I'm going to work the penalty box more."

"Hank will not relinquish that duty," says Justin.

"I already took up the matter with Team Mom Tina, and she made a spreadsheet on the team Facebook page, with sign ups. I beat Hank to it, and I work tonight's tournament game. I'll be able to hear every word Butch says."

"Good," says Kate. "I like that you'll be close by. He's got something personal going with Brett. Is he like that with Aiden?"

"Getting information from Aiden is almost impossible. He's a space cadet. Totally oblivious."

"It's strange, but…it's like Butch is jealous of him—a child."

"Well, Brett is the leading scorer on the team," says Justin. "That takes away from Mike's grandeur."

"It's more than that. It feels personal."

"Like Brett has two parents who love each other, love him, and don't work at a dirty ice rink?" says Charlie.

"Exactly."

They are all silent for a moment.

"Hey, let's grab some coffee before the game starts," says Charlie, putting his arm around Kate. They nod at Justin and leave him standing alone.

He has a bad taste in his mouth, and doesn't know if it's from Piper's interest hearing Kip's name, the Churches and their protein regimen, or jealousy over Charlie Miller.

Chapter Thirteen

 Charlie Miller's Status Update:

Photo: Selfie, "Working the Sin Bin"

#GoPolarBears #HockeyStrong

It's artic sub-zero misery in the penalty box. The players arrive at the bench. The funk of their sweaty gear and the slurping of Hank's runny nose (he insisted on doing the score sheet so he could still be close by), in combination with the greasy slop of fast food he ate earlier, make Charlie feel as if he's going to puke.

Butch leans close to the boys, his voice deadly quiet. So quiet, in fact, Charlie cannot hear him. Butch gives him a sideways glance. Charlie pulls his phone out of his pocket and texts Kate.

--ASSHOLE IS WHISPERING. CAN'T HEAR A THING.

--NOT SURPRISED, she writes back.

The buzzer sounds, and the game begins. Competition in the extra tournament league is fierce. While the Polar Bears dominate their home league, playing teams from farther north is a whole new experience. Thirty seconds in, one of Hank's twins already has a penalty. Charlie opens the door for Franklin just as the kid flips off the ref, resulting in a game suspension.

"Hey, dickhead," shouts Butch. "Maybe if you'd keep your eyes on the game you'd see that kid was roughing Franklin up."

"Watch your mouth, or you're out," says the ref.

"Watch the game, or you are."

The ref shakes his head and skates away. The Polar Bears now have only four skaters to the other team's five, and they are barely hanging on as it is. The opposing team blows past the Polar Bear penalty kill lines, firing shot after shot. Viktor makes six impressive saves before the penalty ends and the teams are even. Franklin isn't allowed to play, but stays to watch. He joins his father in the score box, running his mouth off about the refs. Charlie is shocked at the language the boy uses, but Hank doesn't seem to care. At least Franklin's complaining covers up the awful sound of Hank's sniffing.

At the end of the first period, the score is tied zero to zero, but the other team has outshot the Polar Bears twenty to one. Butch is on a tirade.

"Polar Bears? More like Teddy Bears; you look like shit. This is a disgrace. Next year, I'll ban turkey on Thanksgiving if you all are going to play like you're drunk on tryptophan."

The boys look at each other. They have no idea what he's talking about.

Charlie recalls that it was Butch's word of the day. He feels a little sick that he "liked" it, as if it somehow supports what's happening now.

"Every game this season is an essential building block in the fortress we are erecting," says Butch.

Gordie giggles and hits Kyle on the shoulder. "Erect."

"What, you think it's funny to be a loser? Why don't you go join your asshole brother in the score box?"

"Sorry," says Gordie. He looks down at the ice.

"Maybe if you actually played defense instead of playing with yourself they wouldn't have gotten twenty shots on us. Twenty! You are the hunters—not the prey. Every time one of their players gets a shot off, it counts as a goal in my book, because you failed. You failed to defend the fortress. The enemy infiltrated. You were weak. If they were firing bullets instead of pucks, you'd be dead. Actually Viktor would be dead. You all would have let your brother in arms down. Semper Fi, boys."

Charlie cannot believe the nonsense spewing from Butch's mouth. And what's with all the military references? Butch was never a marine, though he loves to post soldier pictures on Facebook. Charlie recalls the times he has seen Butch drive the Zamboni, leaning forward, but always looking over his shoulder. He must see himself as a commander on an M1A1 tank, mowing down conquered villages. The thought makes Charlie laugh.

--WHAT'S HE SAYING? texts Kate.

--WAR SPEECH. HE'S A GENERAL SENDING TROOPS TO BATTLE.

--GOOD LORD.

--I KNOW. WHAT A LOSER. NOW I UNDERSTAND WHY BRETT CAN'T REMEMBER WHAT BUTCH SAYS.

--UH-OH. SNIPER HAS A VISUAL.

Charlie looks up and sees Butch glaring at him. He knows Butch can't see his phone, but the way Butch looks at him makes Charlie paranoid. He shoves the phone in his pocket and pretends to be interested in the scoreboard.

When the second period starts, Brett is not sent out with his line. He looks at Charlie. Charlie shrugs and quickly returns his gaze to the ice. He doesn't want Butch accusing him of coaching Brett from the penalty box or this will be his last time there. The clock moves at a snail's pace, with the other team firing another eight shots, all blocked by Viktor. Butch sounds like a man speaking in tongues, profanity the only decipherable words. Brett is passed over again, and Charlie feels his blood pressure rising. It doesn't help that Kate keeps messaging him.

--WHAT THE HELL? HAS BUTCH SAID ANYTHING TO BRETT?

--NO.

--I WONDER IF HE'S MAD YOU WERE TEXTING ABOUT HIM.

--HOW WOULD HE KNOW THAT?

--ESPIONAGE.

Charlie shoves the phone in his pocket. He can feel Brett's eyes on him, but he will not look at his son. He cannot compromise his fragile truce with Butch.

Kyle gets a penalty, and Kip snaps pictures of his son in the box.

"For the binder?" asks Charlie.

"Facebook," says Kip.

While they wait for the next period to start, Charlie sees that Kip has indeed posted a photo of his son in the penalty box. The hashtag reads: #ProudDad.

"Still tied!" says Butch. "When are you going to listen to me? I keep yelling 'Who's high' because one of you needs to be high in the slot in the offensive zone at all times. Do you think I scream for my health?"

--BUTCH DOESN'T UNDERSTAND WHY THEY'RE LOSING, texts Charlie.

--UH, MAYBE BECAUSE BRETT HASN'T HAD A DECENT SHIFT THIS WHOLE GAME.

--EXACTLY.

--ALL THE PARENTS OVER HERE WANT BRETT IN. THEY CAN'T UNDERSTAND WHAT BUTCH IS DOING.

--JOIN THE CLUB.

"And when I tell you to run the forecheck, do it," says Butch. "Don't stop and think about it. Just listen."

"Like we can understand him," whispers Mike.

"What? What did you say? You think because you're my kid you won't get benched? Keep it up, and you'll find out."

--INTERESTING DEVELOPMENT, texts Charlie. MIKE TALKED BACK TO BUTCH. BUTCH THREATENED TO BENCH HIM.

--I'LL BELIEVE THAT WHEN I SEE IT.

"I don't care if Mario Lemieux is on my team—he doesn't listen, he doesn't play! Now, get in there and win it!"

The Polar Bears have more fire going into the third period. They are skating harder, getting in more shots, and running Butch's plays. Butch continues screaming. He stands on the bench—adding to his considerable height—pacing and providing incessant commentary, like an inmate ranting down to the exercise yard from a barred window.

With only five minutes left and still no score, Brett gets more and more playing time. Just as his line is about to come off the ice, Mike dumps the puck deep into the offensive zone, and instead of Brett following Mike off the ice, he makes a split second decision to chase the puck. The goalie did not anticipate this, and has come far out of the net to knock the puck to the side, but Brett gets to it first. Butch screams at Brett to get off the ice, but he ignores him. He skates wide and shoots hard, scoring the first goal of the game.

Though he is not supposed to cheer from the penalty box, Charlie whoops and claps. Kate waves her fists wildly in the air. Team parents hug in the bleachers. As Brett comes off the ice, Charlie is careful not to give him a thumbs up, though he does nod his head and smile. Brett gives him such a look of excitement, Charlie finds himself strangely emotional.

The Polar Bears end up winning the game one to zero. They file off the ice, Charlie following, and as he and Kate join the mob, parents slap them on the backs, going on and on about how awesome Brett is. Charlie is proud and in total awe of his boy. They thank the team families and move toward the locker room. A hockey glove has fallen on the floor, propping open the locker room door, so the parents can hear Butch's post-game speech.

"You see," Butch says. "That's what does it. That's what makes winners. When you obey me, you play smart and you skate hard. You make it happen. You listen to me, and you'll make it all the way to districts."

The boys hoot and holler.

"Mike, you get the game puck," says Butch. "If you hadn't put that puck deep in the offensive zone, we never would have scored. Congratulations."

Chapter Fourteen

 Piper Caldwell's Status Update: ⚙

Heading to Wine 909 to celebrate the first big win of the tournament!

#ParentsNightOut #HockeyStrong

After last night's team parent outing at Wine 909, Justin can't stand to be around Piper. About three bottles in, her drunk dancing with Kip sent Justin over the edge. He left her at the bar and went back to the hotel, but couldn't sleep, especially after she stumbled in at one in the morning, stinking of cheap perfume and Russian cigarettes.

Piper has been trailing him all morning wearing her giant sunglasses—attitude ping-ponging between contrite and defensive—clearly not able to recollect why he left her at the bar, but unwilling to seek answers or forgiveness. She finally gets the message and stands about ten feet away from him, nursing her latte. Soon, Dawn approaches Piper from behind, slaps her ass, and pulls Piper into her massive chest for an embrace. Justin takes sick pleasure in watching Piper recoil; she hates public displays of affection. Unless she's drunk, apparently, and Kip is involved.

"You are one hot dancer!" says Dawn. "I never would have thought someone like *you* could be so much fun!"

Nikolai joins them, looking the women up and down and licking his lips.

"We smoke and drink more tonight; yes?" he says. "And disco dance?"

He does a ridiculous motion with his arms that makes Dawn giggle.

Piper's skin goes from pale to green. She excuses herself and crosses behind Justin, heading for the lobby, but crashes into Mee Maw, spilling the contents of her latte.

"Oh my God!" Piper says.

Justin knows Piper could cry over the pumpkin spiced (and possibly spiked) coffee puddle. She got up earlier than usual to visit the Starbucks next to the hotel—thirty minutes away—to get her caffeine fix. The rink café isn't open this early, so now Piper will have to endure a grande-sized headache.

Justice.

"My pants are soaked," says Mee Maw.

Piper hunts through her purse looking for a tissue.

"Never mind," says Mee Maw. "I don't think you'll find anything in that purse but cigarettes and loose one-dollar bills."

Loose ones? he thinks. *Did they go to a strip club after he left Wine 909?*

Piper apologizes and continues toward the lobby.

"And just a word of advice, dear," Mee Maw calls after her. "The next time you dance on a bar like that in a skirt, make sure you remember your underwear."

Justin feels like he's going to be sick.

#####

The game was a blur. The Polar Bears took the win, but only by one goal. Henry made a heroic lunge (that might have been a colossal trip) into a pile of defensemen, knocking the puck loose to Mario, who scored on a slapshot. Piper ended up sitting in the bleachers and never removed her sunglasses, while Justin stood with the Millers.

"It wasn't pretty, but I'll take it," says Charlie.

"A win's a win," says Kate. "I don't even understand how those boys could skate after all that travel, the game last night, very little sleep…"

"Tell me about it," says Justin.

The Millers didn't join the group who went to Wine 909 last night, and Justin wishes he'd stayed back with them. They were probably snuggling in the room with Brett under their #HockeyStrong blanket, watching *Miracle* and eating popcorn.

Helen and Louise interrupt them. They wear matching #HockeyStrong sweatsuits and scarves. Louise's stainless steel travel mug has the Polar Bears logo.

"They're in big trouble," says Helen.

"They deserve it," says Louise.

"Why?" says Kate.

"Weren't you here for the game?" says Helen.

"That they won?"

"Barely."

"If it weren't for [hashtag] Mario the Beast's goal, they'd be losers," says Louise.

Did she just do a hashtag with her fingers? thinks Justin.

"They didn't run the cycle," says Helen. "They didn't run the forecheck."

"They skated like they were asleep," says Louise.

"Which would make sense, since they've barely had any," says Kate.

"Whatever," says Helen. "If they want to be champions, they can't make excuses."

Justin can literally see Kate's temperature rising; her face turns bright red from the bottom up. Just as she is about to boil over, the locker room door bursts open, the boys jog in a line to the back of the rink, and head out to the parking lot.

"Where are they going?" asks Kate.

She hurries after the boys, followed by Charlie, Justin, and the other parents. When Justin exits the rink, he's blasted with a rush of icy cold air and freezing rain. Through the chilly fog, he sees the boys running up and down the massive, muddy hill behind the building. Every time they reach the bottom, Butch blows his whistle, and they have to go back to the top.

"They're going to get sick!" says Mee Maw.

"Half of them already are!" says Linda.

"They should at least have their coats on," says Mee Maw.

Over and over, Butch blows the whistle. Over and over, the boys run up and down the hill. Their sneakers tear up what was left of the brown grass, and some of them slip in the mud. Freezing rain falls harder, and their breath can be seen in puffs. David sobs; he should, since he didn't play one minute and he's getting punished anyway. Henry pukes, but resumes running when he finishes. Aiden begins to wheeze. Justin looks for Piper. She has Aiden's new inhaler, but she never came outside. He feels his lips curl in anger and doesn't know whom he'd like to strangle first.

"Enough!" says Kate, shaking off Charlie's grasp.

She charges toward Butch.

"He said only two more times," calls Charlie. "They're almost finished."

"Screw two more times; this is ridiculous!"

She walks past Butch—all five feet two inches of her—and yells up to Brett.

"Let's go!"

"He's not done," says Butch.

"The hell he's not," says Kate. "How do you expect them to play in tonight's game?"

"If he doesn't finish, don't bother coming to tonight's game."

"Bullshit. If Brett doesn't come, you can't win," says Kate. She leans closer to Butch. "And you know it."

Justin's mouth drops open. Butch stares Kate down, but the corner of his mouth twitches. Was that a smile? No, now he has a murderous look. Butch blows the whistle.

"Stop!" he says.

The boys stagger over to him.

"I would have made you run for an hour, but Miller's mother reminded me that you have another game today. Since I'm not interested in losing to a team my old nemesis coaches, I'll stay your execution. But hear this: if you all embarrass me this afternoon, you will run for an hour after every game until you learn to listen to me. Do you understand?"

The boys mumble yesses.

"Stand up straight!" Butch yells. "I said, DO YOU UNDERSTAND?"

"YES, COACH BUTCH."

Butch salutes Kate, and walks back to the rink.

Chapter Fifteen

 Kate Miller's Status Update: ⚙

Article Link: Standing up to Bullies

The Millers are cocooned in the warmth of their car—where they don't have to socialize with other hockey families—during the hour wait for the evening game. Kate reads through Facebook, while Charlie checks out Florida Keys boating and fishing sites on his iPad. Every few minutes he sighs and tilts the screen to show her another gorgeous scene of endless blue water, colorful fish, palm trees. They are already trying to plan their next trip. Kate returns her attention to Facebook, and clicks on the Polar Bears Public Page. There's a new post from Dawn.

"Oh boy," says Kate.

"What?" says Charlie.

"Oh my God, look at this! Dawn posted nineteen pictures from Wine 909 to the PUBLIC team page, tagging half the Polar Bear parents. LOOK at Piper!"

Charlie opens his Facebook app and finds the offending photos. As he scrolls, his mouth widens to a large O.

"In one hour, the album already has three hundred likes!" says Kate.

"Piper must not have seen because she hasn't untagged herself," says Charlie.

"How is that possible? She's never without her phone."

"Maybe she's taking a nap to sleep off her hangover."

"I can literally, actually see her ass in this picture!"

Kate enlarges the photo on her phone and holds it so Charlie can see. They burst into laughter. The pictures reveal the night's progress—or regress, depending upon how you look at it—and each time they scroll through the album it gets funnier and funnier.

"Oh, Piper," says Kate. "Intervention time."

"But let's discuss Dawn's impressive use of hockey terms in the captions."

They are laughing so hard tears run down their faces.

There is a sudden knocking at their window.

Piper!

Kate gasps, shoves her phone in her purse, and rolls down the window. Charlie flips his iPad over on his lap.

"Sorry to interrupt, but I need a phone charger," says Piper. She holds up her blank screen. "Nobody has one. Do you guys? You always seem super prepared."

Kate feels sweat form on her temple. She cannot look at Charlie or she'll lose it.

"Are you okay?" asks Piper.

"Yep, just fine."

Kate makes a show of looking through her purse and opens it to show Piper she doesn't have a charger.

"I'm going nuts," says Piper. "My phone died while we were at lunch. We didn't have time to go back to the hotel. Then we had to drive here—I can't remember the last time I didn't have my phone to entertain me in the car. Now we're stuck here the hour before the game, during the game, Butch's speech after the game, then the team dinner."

"Sorry we can't be more helpful," says Kate.

Piper pulls out her keys.

"It's fine," says Piper. "I have time if I speed. Will you just tell Justin I went back to the hotel to get a charger if he asks, not that he will. He's in a shitty mood for some reason."

"Will do," says Charlie.

#####

All the peace and humor from the wait in the car has vanished. Now, flanked by assholes, it's hard for Charlie to pay attention to the game. Butch is on the bench shooting Charlie glare-darts in the penalty box, and every time Butch raises his voice, he suddenly lowers it—as if remembering a sane parent is nearby. From the score box comes Hank's muttering under his breath about pushy dads, and his incessant slurpy nose sounds. Charlie feels as if he's being subjected to Guantanamo Bay torture tactics. The game will be over in eight minutes, he tells himself. Then he and his family can have a quiet evening. He has made the executive decision they will not join the team dinner later. He cannot spend one minute longer than necessary with these people. They are sucking the marrow from his soul.

The door of the other team's penalty box suddenly opens. Charlie has been so lost in thought he didn't notice that a Polar Bear kid is down. The sound of booing and shouting from the crowd reaches him.

"Come on, ref! This is getting out of hand!"

"He had it coming!"

"Misconduct! Get him outta here!"

That was Kate's voice.

Charlie leans forward and sees that it's his son writhing on the ice. It's general protocol to wait a minute and then let the coach walk over if the kid doesn't get up, but Butch just stands there with his arms crossed as the minutes tick by. Charlie forgets himself. He opens the door to the penalty box and walks over the ice to where Brett lies, slipping a little when he gets there. He crouches down.

"What happened?"

Brett can't speak. The way he holds his stomach, it appears the wind has gotten knocked out of him.

"Lose your breath?"

Brett nods and continues to squirm.

"Okay, buddy, I got you."

Charlie helps Brett to standing and the crowd claps. The ref talks to the other team's coach, explaining the penalty. Brett coughs and begins to take choking breaths. By the time Charlie deposits Brett at the bench, he's better.

"You all right to keep playing?" asks Charlie.

Brett gives him a grateful smile, then arranges his little face sternly, holds his stick like a spear, and gazes at the ice. A soldier awaiting his return to the front.

Charlie knows Butch does not approve of his intervention without having to look at him, so he proceeds back to the penalty box, keeping his eyes on the ice. When he gets there, Hank stands with the door closed, his arms crossed, blocking entry.

"Seriously," says Charlie.

Hank sneers. "I'm just doing what Coach says."

"Butch told you to take over?"

"Coach doesn't want people coddling the players."

"Then who's going to keep score?"

"Tina can do the score sheet and the clock."

"Come on, you have next game."

"I'm not getting out," says Hank. He wipes a drip of snot off his nose.

"I signed up for today, and I'm finishing."

"Excuse me." A ref taps Charlie on the shoulder. "You're holding everything up."

"But I'm working the penalty box!"

"Then why'd you get out?"

"Because my kid got gutted."

"You're too emotional for the box," says the ref.

"What?"

"Off the ice."

Charlie cannot believe this. He scans the faces of the players and coaches. All glare at him except for Brett, who gives him a pleading look. It's only because he doesn't want to embarrass his son that he proceeds to the door and exits the ice. As soon as he closes it behind him, the whistle blows and the game continues. Kate joins him and wraps their MILLER blanket around him.

"Is Brett okay?" she asks.

"I think."

"What happened with the penalty box?"

"Butch told Hank to get in there. The ref told me I was too 'emotional' to work it."

"Huh?"

"The inmates are running the asylum."

After two minutes, the kid who hit Brett is out of the penalty box and back on the ice, terrorizing the Polar Bears when the refs aren't looking. He punches Henry, trips

Dominik, and body checks Brett *again,* and never gets called. Kate screams at the ref to pay attention.

"That kid is going to kill somebody out there!" Kate says. "If he hurts Brett one more time, I'm going after him myself. I hope Gordie levels him when the ref isn't looking."

"Kate," says Charlie. "I need you. Stay with me now."

"We might as well put Gordie's evil powers to good use. I mean, look at that thug from the other team; he has a mustache. He probably drove himself to the game."

Charlie's relief is profound by the game's end, though his stomach is starting to churn. He has royally pissed off Butch, and hasn't felt this unsettled since waiting for his father to come home to tell him he decided to major in art in college. Charlie reminds himself that he is an adult and Butch is not in charge of him. He has the right to check on his injured son.

On his way out of the rink, Hank bumps Charlie's arm. Charlie turns, expecting an apology, but is met with a glare.

"I can't believe it," says Charlie, once Hank passes.

"What?" says Kate.

"Did you feel Hank bump me?"

"You don't think it was an accident?"

"Not based on the look he gave me," says Charlie. "It just reinforces my decision: we are not eating with the team tonight."

"Brett might be disappointed."

"I don't care. He'll be more disappointed if I end up in jail from getting in a brawl with Hank. If I have to hear him sniff his snot one more time, I'm going to lose it."

Chapter Sixteen

 #PolarBears Public Page

Photo Album: Team Parents' Night Out!

Tagged: Piper Caldwell, Dawn Cage, Hank Cage, Kip Howard, Mee Maw, Louise Gardenia, Helen Johnson

Justin wonders where the hell Piper is. She missed the whole game. She probably went back to the hotel to get her phone charger, but it shouldn't have taken this long. Aiden scored short-handed with a bar-down goal, leaving a satisfying ping ringing in the air. The kid had scanned the crowd for his mother after his point, and when he realized she wasn't there to see his goal, his shoulders slumped.

It occurs to Justin he's approaching a problematic threshold in his marriage. He ignores the stab of guilt over the amount of time he spends checking out other women and attending happy hours with co-workers, and instead makes a mental list of Piper's failings: phone obsession (off the charts), gossip (minor annoyance, but aggravating), drunkenness (alcoholism seems too strong a word, but getting close), vanity (but he likes having a hot wife, so…), flirtatiousness (a bullet point under vanity).

He knew what he was getting into when he married a girl who cared so much about her personal appearance—at least, he thought he did. Though when they were dating, he had no idea about the level of behind-the-scenes prep work that went into making Piper look like a natural beauty. Fraudulent, really. But he accepted it was foolish of him to think anyone could look like a movie star without an expensive and time-consuming beauty routine. The fact is, he is still attracted to Piper. He shows this attraction often, and just as often gets shot down. It's like having an Aston Martin in the garage and not being allowed to drive it. Is this why Piper responds to Kip? Because she just wants her engine revved in park, but doesn't want the mess of driving on dirty roads?

He feels a tap on his shoulder. Kip extends his fist for a bump. Justin looks at Kip's hand, but leaves him hanging.

"Come on; no hard feelings, dude," says Kip. "The pictures make it look way worse than it was."

"What pictures?"

Kip gets an '*oh shit*' look on his face.

A quick survey of the stands reveals most of the parents are either staring at Justin or pretending not to. Does the whole team know how Piper carried on last night? For once, Justin curses himself for not having a Facebook account. And for letting on that he hasn't seen the photos. It has cost him some power in this exchange.

"Look, we were just having fun," says Kip. "I'll tell you the truth man, I got my hands full of women. I'm not interested in taking yours, bro."

"That doesn't worry me. You're not in her league."

"I feel you," Kip says. "I'd be pissed, too, if Lucy showed that kind of attention to another guy, not that she ever would. I give her what she needs."

"Does she know about the slut you also give your attention to?" asks Justin. "Because I can arrange for Lucy to find out."

"Slow down, bro. We're on the same team, here."

"Fuck you."

Kip's face takes on a murderous look, and while Justin is not scared—the men stand eye to eye—he realizes he sees the true Kip now. The animal. The psycho responsible for the binder. The sociopath who cheats on his wife and tries to win the favor of other men's women. A guy who wants what other people have because he feels inadequate for never achieving what he wanted. Kip's veneer is off, and it's oddly refreshing because it's honest.

Justin raises his fist to Kip.

Kip walks away, leaving Justin hanging.

Justin needs to see those pictures. He spots the Millers, wrapped together in their #HockeyStrong blanket like a happy burrito, and strides toward them, trying not to run. Kate won't meet his eyes.

Shit.

"Show me the pictures," says Justin.

"What pictures?" says Charlie.

"I've got to go to the bathroom," says Kate. She leaves Charlie stranded.

He wears a pained expression.

"I know you know what pictures," Justin says through gritted teeth. "Show me what someone posted on Facebook that has made Kip apologize and my wife not show up to her son's hockey game."

"My phone is dead."

"Liar."

"Whoa," says Charlie. "Hold it, there."

"Put yourself in my shoes, dude. Are you going to make me crawl to Sal to see the pictures? To Butch? To some gossipy little team-mom bitch?"

Charlie exhales, pulls the phone from his pocket, makes a few swipes on the screen, and hands the phone to Justin.

Chapter Seventeen

 Kate Miller's Status Update:

Article Link: How CTE affects the brain.

Hoping to steer Brett toward full-time fishing before body checking begins.

Charlie hears Hank's sniffling before he sees him. He turns around, keeping himself between Hank and the door to the penalty box.

"Don't even try," says Charlie. His voice sounds strangely like John Wayne's.

"It's my turn," says Hank.

"I'm working the box for the championship."

"Listen, pal," says Hank, moving toward Charlie, the fluorescent lobby lights glinting off his shiny, wet nose. "I outweigh you by thirty pounds, and your eyes only reach my nipples. Don't make me regret what I'll have to do to you if you don't back down."

Charlie pulls the door open, but Hank swats his arm away and pushes him. Charlie catches himself before falling. Out of the corner of his eye, Charlie sees the flash from Butch's gallon-sized, stainless steel Polar Bears coffee mug. Sal stands with him, wearing a tee shirt that says, "OBAMA

CAN'T TAKE THESE GUNS," arrows pointing to his fat arms.

Charlie's not a fighter, but he doesn't want to look weak in front of Butch. He pushes back on Hank's chest. Hank returns the push with another that lands Charlie flat on his ass. Butch and Sal laugh. The hockey team files past. Charlie is humiliated to see Brett staring at him in horror or shame, he cannot tell.

"Get up!" Kate says. "Charlie!"

She looks blurry. He squeezes his eyes shut and rubs them, wondering if Hank somehow knocked his retina loose.

"Charlie!"

He opens his eyes, seeing nothing but darkness. Then a digital clock appears, red lit numbers reading 4:17. It takes him a moment to realize that he is in their hotel room. Kate shakes his arm.

"I'm awake," he whispers.

"You were yelling and thrashing in your sleep," she says.

Brett rolls over and mumbles from the other double bed in the room.

"Sorry," whispers Charlie. "Nightmare."

"You said Butch's name. Were you dreaming about him again?"

"I don't remember."

Kate doesn't respond to the lie.

Charlie's hockey dreams/nightmares are coming with alarming frequency. They confuse him by giving him false memories when he's in real hockey situations. And Butch is always there, watching. Judging. Provoking.

After a few minutes, Kate breathes deep and regular, but Charlie is unable to fall back asleep.

#####

"Sal's wearing the shirt," says Charlie, pointing.

"What shirt?" asks Kate.

OBAMA CAN'T TAKE THESE GUNS.

Charlie takes a long drink of his coffee. It's so hot it burns his tongue and so strong his heart races, but he has to do something to ward off the fatigue. His nightmare is coming to life on Sal's shirt. And to top it off, his father emailed him out of the blue:

"Your mother's retiring. You are all invited to the party. I know some good hotels nearby."

They've barely spoken over the past decade, since a horrible Thanksgiving fight when his father criticized Charlie for being an art teacher. Charlie's father was an officer in the army, fought in Vietnam, and was disappointed Charlie didn't follow in his footsteps. His entire life he had taken his father's criticism without saying a word, but that day, with his own infant son watching, Charlie snapped. The old man teased him one too many times about doing a "sissy job," and Charlie—drunk and at a breaking point—threw his wine glass, shattering it all over the khaki walls. He had been horrified at his loss of self-control, and grateful Brett was too young to remember.

His mother still religiously sends greeting cards and gifts for birthdays and milestones. She organized the trip several years prior for Brett to visit them in Florida and attend the Panthers game. She likes Kate's Facebook pictures, but never comments. She hasn't friended Charlie yet. His parents act as

117

if he has disappeared from the face of the earth, and he tells himself it's better this way. Still, occasionally, he wishes he could tell them about Brett's goals, or good grades, or the mahi he caught in the Keys, but he always stops himself. Maybe it is time to reach out.

"Fall in!" yells Butch.

"Why is he doing his pre-game speech here?" whispers Kate.

Charlie shrugs.

"Today's the championship," says Butch.

The lobby erupts in cheers, claps, and high-fives.

"Enough. You're lucky to be here. You've played like shit. This is Mile One. It's like nothing has happened before this moment. Both teams will come out fresh. Both want to win."

"Yeah, Buddy!" yells Sal. He punches his fist in the air.

"Think only of what I've taught you. Think of the plays I want you to run. Listen to everything I command from that bench. If you disobey me, slack, or screw up in any way, you'll run 'til you puke after the game."

"Semper Fi!" screams Amy.

"Your mission: Blitz attack. From the moment the puck drops, you are to push through enemy borders, mow down their villages, take no prisoners, and show no mercy."

Kate rolls her eyes.

"When we roll into our home rink, it better be with a banner to hang to show that we are the true conquerors; we are the victors; we will not be defeated! Do you understand?"

"YES, COACH BUTCH!" says the team.

"Louder!"

"YES, COACH BUTCH!"

The parents join the chant, even Charlie. Kate shoots him a glare, and he smiles, sheepish.

Once they file into the rink, they take their position at the top of the bleachers, where they can get a birds-eye view of the action. When Hank walks by, Charlie shudders and his eye twitches

"Piper's here!" whispers Kate.

Piper's sunglasses are large enough to cover half her face, and she holds Justin's arm like a blind woman with a guide. Justin's dark look parts the crowd around them and keeps anyone from standing near them on the boards. Charlie wishes he could convey such power with just a glance.

As Butch parades the boys in front of the stands to the whoops and cheers of the fans, Charlie's blood pressure and nausea level begin to rise. His mouth is too dry to cheer, so he gives Brett a thumbs-up, realizing his gaffe when Butch glares at him.

Damn! There goes a shift.

Fall Out Boy music blares from the speakers as the boys take to the ice to begin warm-ups. Charlie is having trouble breathing and fears a full-blown panic attack is about to start.

But then, the coach from the other team, the referees, and a man in a suit intercept Butch. Charlie can see that the conversation is becoming heated. Butch argues with the other coach. The ref shrugs. The suited man says something that makes Butch hurl his clipboard across the ice.

"What in the world?" says Kate.

The coach holds up a piece of paper, and Butch snatches it from him. His eyes bulge as he reads. His face becomes red. Charlie is no medic, but Butch looks like he could have a heart attack. With equal parts guilt and delight, Charlie finds himself elated at the thought. Butch glares at the stands. His menacing look touches each person, chilling their blood by the way they all flinch, until his eyes rest on Nikolai, who stands just outside the glass.

"You," he bellows.

Charlie thinks he might shit his pants if Butch addressed him like that, but Nikolai does not appear afraid. He remains motionless, standing on the other side of the boards near where his son blocks the warm up shots of his teammates. Butch marches across the ice. Charlie wishes the big bully would slip, but he doesn't, and when he reaches Nikolai, he slams the paper on the glass. Once Nikolai sees it, his face goes white. Soon, Butch is out the door, attempting to converse with the Russian. The refs and the other coach join them.

"The suspense is killing me," says Kate.

Louise and Helen have positioned themselves within hearing distance, and in a minute, they look at each other in horror. Tina scurries over and soon, they all return to the stands and start whispering to the fans. The voices of Butch, Nikolai and the other coach rise and become a mess of curse words and Russian. Kate runs down the bleachers to talk to Tina, and is back in a few minutes wearing a stunned look.

"Oh my God," she says.

"What?"

"Viktor's out."

"For the championship game?"

"For the season."

"What?"

"He's too old."

"What are you talking about?" asks Charlie.

"Nikolai never turned in Viktor's birth certificate because Viktor is thirteen. He should be playing up a level."

"Oh my God. We can't win without Viktor."

"I know."

"Could he get a reprieve?" asks Charlie, frantic. "Maybe Nikolai didn't understand. How can the kid—the team—be faulted?"

"That's apparently what Butch tried to say, but they aren't having it. Rules are rules."

Charlie runs his hand through his hair. He looks around and sees the sick looks on the families' faces. Butch storms toward the bench. Viktor is called off the ice by the ref, and the other coach grins. There's a war inside Charlie. As much as he enjoys anyone getting the better of Coach Butch, this is bad for the team. Only the back-up goalie David and his family seem happy. Tom has his son by the shoulder pads—forehead to helmet—giving him a pep talk. Viktor throws his stick, and Nikolai follows him to the locker room. Before they make it to the door, Amy comes from out of nowhere, screaming, "Cheaters never win!" She tackles Nikolai to the ground.

Chapter Eighteen

 Piper Caldwell's Status Update:

No Words.

#HockeyStrong

Piper's stomach is in knots. Justin hates her. They lost the championship game four to nothing, and they're stuck with an awful goalie the rest of the season. Tom actually patted David on the back when the kid got off the ice and told him how well he did under pressure. Praise for being a failure! What losers!

Justin slams on the breaks as an SUV stops short in front of him.

"Yellow light, asshole," he says, pounding the horn. "It's Kip. I should have rammed him."

Aiden cries quietly in the third row of the SUV. He stares out the window, sniffling, listening to his favorite hockey music on his iPod. Pitiful.

"This is a circle of hell," says Justin.

Piper has no idea how to respond. She senses she is part of that circle to him.

"All the money we spend, all the time traveling in the car, and for what?" he says. "A team that was supposed to get to districts that's now a laughing stock with a goalie who might as well not even be in the net. A kid who's miserable, crying in the back seat. A whole weekend wasted and ruined, and now we're supposed to eat with your parents because they watched the girls all weekend, which will be as insufferable as a team dinner."

"We can eat fast."

"No, you know what? Tell them I'm sick. It's true. I'm sick and tired."

"Fine," Piper says.

She's glad he won't go to her parents' for dinner. Justin is so much work sometimes. If he's angry, he can't hide it. It's ridiculous how he sulks. Then Piper has to deal with her mother's third degree the day after, and Piper just doesn't have the energy.

"Don't get an attitude with me," he says.

"I'm not."

"You sound bitchy."

"I have a headache."

"Less than twenty-four hours on the wagon and you feel this bad?"

She pinches the bridge of her nose. "Not now."

"Then when?" he hisses. "At your mother's dinner table? At home with kids everywhere? I have a work trip this week through Thursday that I have to be at the airport for at five thirty tomorrow. Did you forget?"

Shit. She did forget.

"No," she says.

"You're on duty all week, and unless you want your meddling mother in your ear, you'll need to cart the girls around with you to hockey."

"I'm fine to cart them."

"Will you be able to manage without the thought of your supersized wine bottle waiting at the end of every day?"

"You're being cruel. I told you, I'm done."

"I hope so, I don't want to have to worry about you-know-who while I'm gone."

"Are you serious?"

"Have you forgotten the Facebook photos?"

"You won't let me."

"No I won't. I'm humiliated."

"You? I can't apologize any more than I have."

"No, but you can act a little more contrite."

She crosses her arms over her chest, and is mortified to feel tears leaking out of her eyes. She swipes them away, but he notices. It's strange, but he seems to soften. She was crying over lost wine and single mom duty all week, but if he thinks she's crying because she's sorry, so be it.

Her phone pings from her purse, causing her to flinch. She cannot reach for it this quickly. She must show her self-control. It bings again twice in rapid succession. She folds her hands together in her lap.

"Aren't you going to check?" he asks.

"I didn't want to piss you off."

"I appreciate that," he says, "but this sounds urgent."

Thank God!

She leans down and rifles through her purse, lifting the phone like it's found treasure. Her hands tremble, and she wonders if it's from booze or technology detox. Piper groans as she reads through the group chat.

"What?" he asks.

"Tina already has a thread going about the next tournament."

"Are you serious?"

"Yeah."

"What does she want to know?"

"A team bus. Are we in?"

"Who else is in?"

"All of our favorites: Mee Maw and Poo Poo, Butch and family, the Gardenias—everyone. Oh, and Amy will be joining her family."

"What about Kip?"

"Yes, Kip. And Lucy."

Justin doesn't respond. Piper looks back toward Aiden and then at him.

"Justin, he grosses me out, seriously," she says. She means it…she thinks. "Any response to his attention was from the alcohol."

"I resent having to be a babysitter when you drink."

"You don't have to," she says. "Those pictures were a wake-up call. Wine and Piper don't mesh."

"It just sucks," he says. "It stifles my good time. I mean, if we could take a bus to the next tournament, neither of us would have to drive, so we could drink, which might make the whole team bus experience more tolerable."

"Champagne doesn't make me sloppy. I can drink loads of that before it has an effect. Just keep your hands on me, and pump the brakes if you see me getting messy."

The only way to break through to Justin is through seduction, and she'll do anything to ease this tension and get things back to normal. Well, their normal. Piper reaches for Justin's leg and squeezes his thigh. He jumps in his seat and swerves, running over the bumps along the side of the highway, smiling at her in surprise.

Score.

Chapter Nineteen

Three Months to District Playoffs

 #PolarBears Public Page

Photo Album: 5 pictures
Player development meet and greet
with Bob's company!
Tagged: Tina Church, Butch Johnson,
Piper Caldwell

#GoPolarBears #HockeyStrong

It figures Butch isn't at practice. Brett is killing it.

"Where is he?" asks Charlie.

Assistant Andy looks up from his phone.

"Who?"

"Your father."

"Oh, Coach. Islanders game."

He calls his father 'Coach.' Of course.

Andy's letting the boys—those who are here, anyway—scrimmage instead of doing drills. Missing are Mike—who must be at the game with Butch—Aiden and Bobby. Bobby's foot still isn't completely healed, so that makes sense (thought he hasn't missed watching a practice or game since his injury), but Aiden missing makes Charlie wonder. Does Justin and Piper's marriage drama have something to do with it? It's a darkly comforting thought to a guy with a hearty share of his own stress. Charlie's school had a wellness day earlier in the week, and Charlie was appalled to learn that his blood pressure was 152/94. The nurse told him he needed to follow up with his doctor as soon as possible to make sure he wasn't hypertensive. She said it could be a fluke, but if it continued to read high, he might need to go on medication.

"Can you get my kid's hockey coach fired?" he had joked.

The nurse looked at him as if he were crazy. She made a note in his file.

Since Brett's line-mates aren't at practice, he's playing with kids he doesn't normally pair up with to scrimmage. The boys seem charged by the freedom they have as a result of Butch's absence. Butch's practices run like this: ten laps around the rink, suicides, passing drills, play drills, and finish with ten more laps and suicides. If you screw up the plays, miss a pass, or make a noise that Butch didn't ask you to make, you do push-ups on your knuckles. On the ice. Without gloves.

For the first time all year, practice is fun to watch. The players take risky shots, pass backward and through their legs, high-five and cheer for one another after impressive dangles and snipes. Gordie and Franklin are coaching David on goal tending, and the kid shows improvement after twenty minutes. When David blocks a raging slapshot from the point, the boys pile on him in a giddy mass.

This is how it should be, thinks Charlie.

While the boys stop for a water break (which Butch NEVER allows when he runs practice), Charlie pulls out his phone to scroll through Facebook. He has found that a) he is becoming addicted to the site, and b) he doesn't know why.

His friends fall into one of several categories: political provocateurs, vague-bookers (non-specific complaints and barbs), philosophers (of the 101 variety), humble-braggers, those who want others to know they are working out, and those who want others to know they are eating. Charlie is drawn to the photographs, but those are what most often leave him feeling as if he's doing life wrong. Family trips to the zoo, pumped biceps, elaborate sushi platters, friends at bars, friends on vacation, friends at concerts, friends at sporting events: these photos seem less like a celebration of friendship or good health or nice weather, and more about showing off. What's worse, he has started sharing political posts, commenting on others' workouts, and just yesterday had an impulse (he suppressed) to take a picture of his pork barbeque sandwich. It's probably just a matter of time before he can't stop himself. Liking and sharing are the gateway drugs. It's like the stick figures on the car.

He continues to scroll and feels as if he has been sucker punched.

There is a photo of an Islander star forward with Brett's line-mates, Bobby and Aiden. And standing front and center with a big, hairy, burly smile—one arm around the famous athlete and the other around his son—is Butch.

Why wasn't Brett invited? If it was Bob's company, the Churches got to select their guests. Why would they take Mike (and Butch!) over Brett?

The answer hits him as soon as the question is formed. He's sick to his stomach.

--NICE OF THE CHURCHES TO LEAVE BRETT OUT, he texts Kate.

--I KNOW.

--SO, YOU SAW?

--YEP. TEAM PUBLIC PAGE.

--SICKENING. TINA IS SUCH AN ASS-KISS.

--I KNOW.

--WHATEVER. BRETT IS HAVING THE TIME OF HIS LIFE WITHOUT BUTCH AT PRACTICE.

--GREAT! Kate texts.

--I JUST HOPE BRETT DOESN'T SEE THE PHOTO.

--IS THE PICTURE ON INSTAGRAM?

--I DON'T KNOW. I DON'T HAVE INSTAGRAM.

As the boys continue to scrimmage, David blocks more shots than he lets in. Amy stands behind him outside the ice, clapping and cheering, slamming the glass instead of people's heads. Dominik and Brett have a sick shift, passing in and out of players with ease and agility, ending with Brett's goal and a chest bump from Dominik. Charlie sees Dominick's dad Jack, the quiet one. He has stopped typing and watches, a slight smile on his face.

Charlie's phone wiggles in his pocket.

--IT'S ON INSTAGRAM, texts Kate. BRETT WILL SEE.

Chapter Twenty

> **Piper Caldwell's Status Update:** ⚙
>
> Photo: Aiden, Bobby, and Mike, arms around each other, standing with Islander Super Star
>
> #BestBuds #MemoriesofaLifetime #Hockeystrong
> 🩶 💬

With Piper off the sauce for a week and the sexy greeting she had for him after work travel, Justin should have been in good spirits, but he couldn't shake the bad mood. He knew his guilt was a major factor. He'd crossed a line with a co-worker at the hotel bar, and ended up in her room in a hot make-out session before she put on the brakes and started crying. She was married, too. He left the room feeling dirty —his ego bruised—and he couldn't say which aspect of the rejection bothered him most. Justin told himself that if Piper hadn't messed around with Kip he never would have done so with his co-worker. What kind of guy was Piper turning him into?

"Is that Bobby Church on the ice?" asks Piper.

"Yes."

"He looks shaky."

Justin has a sudden memory of his make-out session, but shakes his head to clear it.

"I bet," he says.

Piper stares at him with narrowed eyes. He has the unsettled feeling she can read his thoughts.

"What's with you?" she asks.

"I'm tired."

"And I'm not? I had the kids for almost a week, alone. Without booze."

"Gold star."

She mutters something under her breath.

Kip walks by, but doesn't acknowledge the Caldwells. He begins setting up his filming station. Justin scans the crowd.

"I haven't seen much of Lucy lately," says Justin.

"I think their youngest started hockey."

"Isn't he like two years old?"

"Three."

"Did Kip tell you all this while I was gone?"

She glares at him.

A puck hits the glass where they stand, causing them both to jump.

Sal slams a large bottle of Mountain Dew on the ledge.

"This should be a cluster-fuck," says Sal.

"Tell me about it," says Justin. "David hasn't stopped one yet. Should be fun."

"I told Mario to play like the team has an empty net."

"That's what I told Aiden."

"Our record's gonna be shit. We probably won't even make the playoffs. It makes me sick when I think of all the money we spend."

"And time."

"Hey, Kip was telling me about a league he's taking Kyle up to see next weekend, for next year. It's in Boston."

"Massachusetts?" says Piper.

"Yeah, it's a hike, but it's just one practice during the week and then weekends. Driving would probably equal out, with the four practices we have each week here."

"I'm not going anywhere Kip goes," says Justin.

Piper lifts her coffee mug to her mouth and takes a long sip. Justin wonders if she's telling him the truth about being on the wagon.

"It's gotta be better than being on a team with a crap goalie," says Sal.

Slap!

Amy slams Sal in the back of the head and runs away crying.

Justin sees that Tina's bribery of Butch with the Islander game worked. Brett Miller has been replaced on the line with Butch's son, Mike.

"Whoa," says Justin.

"What? It's good to mix it up," says Piper.

"Says the chick whose son is now on the coach's son's line."

"Every man for himself."

Justin looks up at Charlie and Kate, and sees they are agitated. Charlie's face is the color of a beet. Kate looks like she's trying to get him to lower his voice about something. Justin wanders closer.

"I bet Butch thinks putting his son on the high scoring line will improve Mike's stats," says Charlie. "Asshole doesn't care to realize that BRETT is the reason they score so much."

"Shhh," says Kate. "People can hear you."

"I don't care."

The game resumes, and its clear Brett's new line-mates, Mario and Dominik, don't communicate. Mario (the beast) keeps trying to plow the puck down the center—through swarms of opposing players—resulting in confusion and turnovers. David is a disaster in goal. All of his confidence is shot, likely because his "pep talk" involved Butch saying, "Don't fuck this up."

The defensemen are working overtime and getting tired quickly. The Polar Bears are playing almost the entire game in the defensive zone, and losing 3-0. When Gordie goes to take the ice in the third period, Butch grabs him by the jersey and pulls him back. He whispers in his ear, and then shoves Gordie forward. Within the first minute of the third period, Gordie checks a kid so hard when the ref isn't looking the boy doesn't get up. The other team's coaches begin screaming at the refs, and the game is temporarily on hold while they sort out the penalty.

Charlie has ventured next to Justin, but Kate stays in the stands, fuming. Justin wonders if she's madder at Charlie for his loud complaining, or Butch for being an asshole.

"Did Butch just give Gordie a thumbs up?" says Charlie.

"I didn't see," says Justin.

"I guess when you make dirty penalties, you win his approval. Sicko."

Helen stands close enough to hear, and she'll report everything back to her husband. Justin feels the urge to quiet Charlie, but becomes distracted by Charlie's twitching eye. He doesn't look well.

Gordie is called to the penalty box, and instead of the usual two minutes, he is given a five minute major for boarding.

"You didn't see anything!" screams Butch. "You can't take a coach's word on something like this! Why don't you just give them the game?"

The refs ignore Butch and proceed to the ice to drop the puck. Butch makes a T sign with his hands and calls a time-out. The players skate to the bench, but Butch abandons them and leans over the boards to continue his tirade against the refs.

"He called a time out to yell at the referees?" says Charlie.

"I'm just glad my older son isn't here," says Dawn. "He'd be losing it."

"It was a penalty," says Charlie. "Gordie might have given that kid a concussion."

"Maybe, but Butch is right. If the ref doesn't see, it's not fair to call it," says Helen.

Butch continues his profanity-laced tirade.

"What a fine example for our boys!" says Charlie.

Justin puts his hand on Charlie's arm, but he shrugs it off.

"Back off," says Helen. "This ref has a long history of bad calls against Butch."

"It wasn't a bad call! That was a dangerous penalty."

"Whose team are you on?" asks Helen.

"I'm embarrassed to be a Polar Bear with shit like this happening," says Charlie.

"Right on," yells a fan from the opposing bench.

"Get over it!" yells Louise. "That's hockey!"

The boy who Gordie boarded starts puking in a bucket.

Justin has to get away from these people. Their insanity might be catching. He starts back toward Piper, but sees her laugh at something Kip says, and stops in his tracks. All of his guilt is replaced with anger.

On the next business trip, he thinks, he won't hold back.

Chapter Twenty-One

 Kate Miller's Status Update: ⚙

Article Link: Why Sports Parents Should Miss
a Practice or Game Every Now and Then
🖤 💬

The odor of diesel fuel fills Charlie's nostrils. He can see his breath in the pre-dawn air. Amy lurks in the shadows. There's no way he's getting on the bus until he sees where she sits, and plants himself as far from that place as possible.

Kate wasn't able to get off work, so she can't join them. She isn't happy that Brett will be missing two days of school for hockey, but there isn't much they can do. The tournament is on the US-Canadian border—eight hours away.

A bump from behind while he sips coffee makes him scald his lips. Hank has rammed his suitcase into the back of Charlie's legs.

"Sorry," says Hank, not sorry. "Didn't see you in the dark."

Charlie is about to give Hank a piece of his mind when Brett runs over, jumping up and down, and grabs Charlie's free hand.

"Come on, Dad! We can get on now!"

Brett was so excited about the trip he couldn't fall asleep last night. Charlie saw his reading light on at eleven o'clock, and when he went in to tell him to go to bed, Brett apologized but said he hadn't been this excited on the eve of something since last Christmas. It made Charlie feel better. How the kid could not be affected by Butch's negativity is beyond him, but he's grateful for it.

The players and their parents mob the door. Through the windows, Charlie sees the boys moving toward the back of the bus, forcing the parents up front. Brett looks at Charlie like he wants to join the players, but doesn't want to hurt his father's feelings.

"Go on," says Charlie. "It's okay."

Brett smiles and boards, scooting into a row with Dominik. Charlie feels a pang of disappointment, but shrugs it off.

"Sad, isn't it?" says Mee Maw. "They grow up so fast. One minute they're gazing at you with adoring eyes, needing you. The next, they're rushing to get away from you."

"I don't think he's rushing at this point," says Charlie. "He's not exactly a teenager."

Mee Maw pats his back and smiles a thin-lipped, *just-go-ahead-and-keep-telling-yourself-that* kind of smile.

Charlie climbs the bus stairs. Linda and Tom guide Amy to the middle rows, so Charlie selects the seat behind the bus driver. Since Kate isn't here, he will have a row to himself. He throws his backpack on the seat on the aisle and takes the window seat. Mee Maw and Poo Poo slide into the row behind him, which isn't ideal, but it's better than Amy. Kip, Lucy and their three-year-old file in after Kyle, and after some back and forth, Kip sits the little one next to him. Lucy occupies the seats behind them.

"If he sits with me, we can go through Kyle's binder and set some goals for his own binder," says Kip.

"You'll have to wait until his meds kick in for him to concentrate," says Lucy. "I forgot to give it to him at home."

Kip groans while Lucy forces the child—who climbs over the back of the seat—to swallow a pill the size of a horse tranquilizer. Kip puts him in a hold from behind and Lucy squeezes the boy's cheeks forcing the pill in his mouth, and near-drowning him with water. Charlie hears Mee Maw whisper to Poo Poo in the seat behind him.

"I cannot believe they are giving that child ADHD medicine. Aren't all toddlers active?"

"A sick society," says Poo Poo.

Mee Maw shuffles through her bag, rummaging and sighing, while bumping the back of Charlie's seat.

"What's the matter?" asks Poo Poo.

"I forgot Henry's allergy-free protein powder."

"I'm sure there's a drugstore near the hotel."

"They won't have the allergy-free kind; I had to special-order it."

David stands and cries out, "My Beats! I can't find my Beats!"

Amy starts to whine, and the bus is aflutter with people searching for David's missing headphones. Charlie checks the front of the bus, when something gleaming from the overhead light in the parking lot catches his eye. He runs out and back quickly, holding David's Beats.

"Here," he says.

David thanks Charlie and rushes back to his seat. Charlie wishes David could be as quick in the goal as he is when fetching headphones, then feels a pang of guilt for being so critical of a child.

The driver is the last on the bus, and when he closes the door, Charlie's nostrils are flooded with the unmistakable odor of garlic. He looks around, wondering if someone has opened a bag of flavored chips, but once the bus driver is seated in front of Charlie, he is dismayed to realize the odor is wafting from the man who will be within a foot of him for the next eight hours. As the bus begins to move, Charlie's eyes find the cup-holder filled with Zesty Garlic Slim Jims. The driver opens one and starts chewing. Charlie groans and pulls out his phone to send Kate an SOS text, but realizes he won't have her sympathy. Since she didn't support pulling Brett out of school for this tournament, she'd just be able to say, *I told you so*. He puts the phone back in his pocket, digs a scarf from his backpack to wrap around his nose, puts in his earbuds, and arranges a travel pillow behind his neck. Just as he's about to drift off to sleep, the seat next to him jostles. Amy has thrown his backpack on the ground, and squishes herself next to him. Charlie stands and looks frantically at the rows, seeing where he can escape, but every seat is full of a person, a child, or luggage.

"Linda," he yells. His voice sounds extra loud in the dark and the quiet that has settled over the bus.

"Sit down, sir," says the bus driver.

"Linda. Call Amy back!"

"She won't listen," says Linda.

"Why didn't you get a seat for Amy?"

"I have one across from me, but she won't stay there. Just give her something soft."

"What?"

"Soft! She likes to pet things. Like cotton. Do you have any cotton?"

"Sit down!" yells the driver. "You may not stand when the bus is in motion."

"Sit down!" Amy yells, hitting Charlie on the butt.

"Stop the bus!" says Charlie.

The driver veers sharply off the road, pounding over the rumble strips, and slams the breaks. Charlie falls into the partition dividing him from the driver. Amy clutches him.

"Are you hurt, my love?" she asks.

"Tom!" Charlie yells. "Get your daughter!"

Amy's face grows dark and she holds up her fists. "You wanna fight?"

Tom grumbles up the aisle and, with some force, is able to remove Amy from Charlie's row and guide her back to her seat. Charlie's relief expands the farther the girl gets from him. Linda has found a wooly lamb stuffed animal and shoves it toward Amy. Once she's seated, Dante slips in next to Amy, wearing a devilish grin.

Charlie drops into his seat and rubs his eyes. The bus again begins to move.

From a few rows behind him, Charlie hears Butch say in a hiss, "If we are late because of this sissy shit, Brett's missing his first shift."

#####

Charlie thrashes in his sleep. He's having another nightmare: he's trapped in a garlic-scented asylum with former sports parents mumbling all around him.

"Why should Henry eat protein powder?"

"Tina posted it on the Hockey Mom message board. It will help Henry grow."

"I don't care if you're three; I need you to focus. This is the path you'll need to skate to juniors, to college, and to the NHL."

"Effin' Libs. Just want to give a bunch of handouts, have people suckin' the government tit."

"Aren't you on disability?"

"Fuck you, Hank. I've got diabetes."

"…bagged an eight point buck last weekend. Here's the picture. Made Mike gut him. Gotta train 'em young."

"Thank God we packed the champagne."

He feels pressure on his arm; a hand rubs his leg. Charlie jolts awake, scaring Amy so that she slaps his face and runs crying toward the back of the bus. "Hate you, hate you, fuck you, fuck you!"

"Amy!" yells Linda. "Wherever did you get that language?"

A diabolical giggle emerges from Dante.

"He made me," says Amy, pointing at Dante.

Amy wedges herself in the seat between Henry and David and puts her head on her brother's shoulder. He pats her arm and tells her it's okay.

Louise climbs over Sal and yanks Dante by the arm into their row.

"Keep it up and you'll have no soda for a week."

Dante begins to scream. Sal turns red and searches the plastic grocery bags at his feet, pulling out a bottle of Mountain Dew and thrusting it in Dante's hands.

"What the hell, Sal?" says Louise.

"Just shut him up. We've got a long ride ahead of us."

Charlie hears the whoosh of the bottle being opened, followed by the unmistakable sound of a soda explosion.

Louise curses and stands, screaming at Dante for shaking the bottle and yelling at Sal for not opening it for him.

"Yo," calls Butch. "I'm starving."

"There's a McDonalds at this exit." says Sal. "You're gonna miss it!"

The driver hits the breaks and cuts across three lanes to a chorus of blaring horns. Charlie readjusts himself in his seat, at least glad that he has slept all the way to lunchtime. But when he glances at his watch, he sees that it is just nine o'clock. They have only been driving for three and a half hours. He could cry.

His phone buzzes in his pocket. It's Kate.

--HOW'S IT GOING?

Chapter Twenty-Two

 Piper Caldwell's Status Update: ⚙

Photo: Bus full of hockey players
Caption: Bonding!

#TournamentWeekend
#GoPolarBears #HockeyStrong

Justin was hesitant to leave the girls with Piper's parents again, but ultimately thought he and Piper could use some alone time—well, time alone in a sea of hockey families. Of course, Piper didn't take her eyes off her phone the entire bus ride. He spent half the trip dealing with work email and the other half in a semi-sleep state that has left him exhausted and irritable.

The bus ride took an hour and a half longer than they planned due to ice on the road, David needing to puke from getting car sick, and Amy having a screaming fit that required twenty minutes of pacing outside the bus to calm her. They are nauseous from the three fast food stops they made, and late. Very late. When they enter the lobby of the tournament rink, Butch's son Mike drops his hockey bag on the floor and slumps down on a bench.

"What the hell are you doing?" says Coach Butch. "Game starts in fifteen minutes."

"I don't feel good," says Mike.

"None of us do: we were just trapped on a bus for nine and a half hours with a bunch of assholes. Get over it."

"No, I'm really hot."

"Then drink ice water."

"I am, but…"

"No buts! Did we come all this way for you to pansy-out? Go AWOL? If we were in Afghanistan hunting terrorists, would you leave your platoon because you were a little hot? Pretend you're in the damned desert and get dressed."

Mike heaves himself off the bench and stumbles toward the locker room, struggling under the weight of his hockey bag. Butch insists the boys are not to have rolling hockey bags, only the carrying kind. He says rolling bags are for pussies.

Justin has never had a real problem with Butch. He respects Justin because Justin's taller than him, doesn't challenge him, and used to play hockey. Butch looks down on dads who didn't play the sport—especially when they try to critique his coaching methods. Justin doesn't like Butch, but he knows that a) a pack of wild boys are difficult to control, and b) hockey is an especially challenging sport.

When the game starts, Mike is back at center on Mario's line, likely the result of Sal's ass kissing. Mike doesn't look well, though. He collapses on the bench after each shift and suckles his ice water bottle until his next. David has let in three goals, and Butch has benched half the forwards for ineffective play. Brett is allowed out of jail for the second period and scores twice in a row. The other team starts

144

making stupid penalties, so the Polar Bears have a numbers advantage.

Early in the third period Aiden gets a wrap-around goal, tying it up. The stands erupt in cheers. His very tired line skates to the bench to rest, but Butch points back to the ice. There is some confusion—Butch usually doesn't keep the lines on for more than forty-five seconds, and Aiden, Bobby, and Brett have been on for two and a half minutes. Mike's line gets up to take the ice, but Butch shouts at them, and they sit down.

"Why won't he get them off?" says Piper. "They're exhausted."

"They keep scoring."

"But they won't be able to keep it up if he skates them to death."

"He's pissed at the other line, so he doesn't want to let them out."

The puck drops, and Aiden's line skates hard for another minute, but their legs are turning to rubber. Bobby is the first to try to get back on the bench—his foot has to be killing him—but Butch shakes his head in the negative. His arms are crossed over his chest.

"This is nuts," says Piper.

Sal storms over to them. "Mario has been sitting on his ass for like six minutes!"

"Butch is punishing them," says Justin.

"Lotta good that'll do! Look at Aiden. He looks like a geriatric patient."

"Butch won't let them off," says Piper. "Look, Aiden's trying."

Butch shakes his head.

Brett coasts until the puck comes to him, and flips it in the air over the boards, forcing the refs to blow the whistle and stop play. Butch calls a time-out, and when they skate over, he berates Brett.

"You are not in charge of stopping play in this game," screams Butch. "I don't care if you're tired. If you want to play triple A hockey, you need to dig deeper, skate harder, and sweat bloodier than those benders."

Tina cues the music to drown out his tirade. House of Pain. *Jump Around.*

Justin sees Charlie texting incessantly and shifting from foot to foot in the box. He does not look well. Charlie's skin is gray, dark circles hang hound-dog-like under his eyes, and the right eye twitches. His once meticulous appearance is untidy—three day old stubble on his chin, hair in desperate need of cutting. Justin should buy the guy a drink tonight. Explain how hockey goes. Charlie needs a reality check.

When the time-out ends, Butch makes the same line go out *again.* Brett, Aiden, and Bobby put their heads together, working out some scheme, and when the whistle blows, they shoot out like bullets. Bobby takes out a defenseman on the other team leaving Aiden and Brett against the remaining defenseman. They pass back and forth and around him. Aiden stops short and wrists a goal in the net, making the score 4- 3. Justin cheers and bangs the glass. Piper jumps up and down. Tina blares Beastie Boys, *Sure Shot.*

Butch finally lets them off the ice. The Polar Bears are able to hold onto to their lead for the rest of the game, winning the first round of the tournament. After they exit the ice, Butch tells them to get out of their equipment and into their running shoes for suicides.

Chapter Twenty-Three

 Charlie Miller's Status Update:

Photo: Sausage McMuffin, Hashbrowns, Styrofoam cup.
Caption: Fine dining on the road

#TournamentWeekend
#GoPolarBears #HockeyStrong

—BRETT MISSED THE ENTIRE FIRST PERIOD.

--OH GOD.

--ALL THE FRIGGIN' WAY TO NY FOR HIM TO SIT THE FIRST PERIOD.

--I'M SO SORRY.

--ON A BUS FOR 9.5 HRS, WEDGED BEHIND A GARLIC-SMELLING DRIVER AND NEXT TO AMY. SICK OF FAST FOOD. SICK OF PSYCHO PARENTS.

--CHARLIE.

--OUR HOTEL ROOM SMELLS LIKE A DOG AND I TOLD THE FRONT DESK AND THEY SAID IT WAS A PET FRIENDLY HOTEL. I TOLD HER I'M ALLERGIC TO DOGS AND SHE SAID THAT A NOTE SHOULD HAVE BEEN MADE WHEN THE ROOM WAS BOOKED, BUT WE DIDN'T HAVE THAT

OPPORTUNITY. TINA BOOKED THE ROOMS FOR EVERYONE.

--WOULD YOU LIKE ME TO CALL OTHER HOTELS?

--THEN BRETT WOULDN'T BE WITH HIS TEAM.

--I KNOW, BUT YOU SEEM FRAZZLED.

--I AM FRAZZLED!

--CHARLIE. WHAT DO YOU WANT ME TO DO?

--PUT OUT A HIT ON BUTCH.

…

--KIDDING. he texts. KIND OF.

--YOU NEED TO FIND YOUR ZEN.

--WTF DOES THAT MEAN?

--DEEP BREATHS.

--I AM BREATHING DEEP, BUT THE GARLIC ODOR IS STUCK IN MY NOSE.

…

--ARE YOU THERE? texts Charlie.

--YES.

--I'M LOSING IT.

--I KNOW. I'LL DO THE NEXT TOURNAMENT.

--THERE'S ANOTHER?

#####

Justin is practically begging Charlie to go out to the sports bar with him.

"Piper and Aiden would love Brett to join them for pizza," says Justin.

Charlie can't believe Piper would like that.

"I don't know," says Charlie. "I need to get Brett to bed early."

"I have a key, Dad," says Brett. "I'll put myself to bed at eight thirty."

"*I* need to get some sleep," Charlie says.

"Come on," says Brett.

"Yeah," says Justin. "One drink, some wings, some guy time, then we'll come back."

Charlie reluctantly agrees, and they walk to an Irish joint nearby. It has dark paneled walls, billiards and a smoking patio, and the clientele consists of a strange collection of college guys, business travelers, and what looks to be local wash ups, all facing a tiny television where two cage-fighters beat the tar out of each other. The patrons are as randomly matched as hockey team parents, but the heavy masculine vibe of the place feels like just the kind of draw for a guy needing a retreat from life. Justin orders a dozen wings and gets the first round of Guinness. When the beer arrives, he raises his glass.

"To hockey," Justin says.

"To cage-fighting," says Charlie. "Where I'd like to meet Butch, one of these days."

They drink.

"Look," says Justin. "I consider you a friend, so let me share something with you. Hockey is different from other sports."

"More like cage-fighting."

"I'm being serious with you, man. You don't seem to be handling the season very well, and I'm here to tell you that anyone who has played hockey understands the dynamic. You'll get used to it."

Charlie is sick of the way guys who played hockey act like members of a secret society. They're like dudes who honk at each other from jeeps or jacked up trucks.

"I'll never get used to an adult bullying children," says Charlie. "No one should. That wouldn't be acceptable under any other life circumstances."

"These aren't any other circumstances; this is elite travel hockey. Do you want it for Brett, or not?"

"I only want what Brett wants," says Charlie.

"Bullshit. You like that you can say your son plays for the best team in the area. You'll be posting on Facebook if they win districts like all those other parents."

Charlie begins to protest, but he stops himself. Justin is right.

"And that's okay because this is a big deal." says Justin. "I get on Piper for having Aiden play on this team, but the truth is, I'm proud. I like people to know Aiden is on the Polar Bears. Who knows whether these kids will get anywhere with hockey, but that doesn't matter. Right now, at eleven and twelve years old, they are in the NHL of Pee Wee hockey. And that's pretty fucking awesome, right?"

"I guess."

"No, *you guess*. You know! You get the thrills when Brett scores, the thrills from the music, the charge from the battle cry. Even the travel misery is a badge of honor. Nothing good comes without a price, my man."

"You have a point."

"Of course I do. Keep telling yourself, 'It's hockey.'"

"It's hockey."

"Even Butch is good for them."

"No way," says Charlie. "I will never agree with that."

"Butch prepares them for the asshole losers of life. And you and I both know our kids will have to interact with plenty of them. I had coaches like him growing up. If you survive them, you feel proud. You have war stories. Men want war stories."

"I'd like our war story to end with Butch's death."

"Easy, man. That means you're taking all this too seriously. Besides, it's hard to criticize a guy who gives so many week nights and weekends to coach kids."

"No way. He gives that time for the advancement of his son. He wants Mike to play the most, score the most, and make the best teams. That's why Butch coaches. That's why anyone coaches."

"You're very cynical, Charlie."

"That's hockey."

Charlie picks up the next round, and the wings come. While they eat, they watch the fight. It's bloody and brutal, and the guys around the bar cheer.

"I'm surprised Butch and Sal haven't wandered over to this man-cave," says Charlie.

"That would require exertion," says Justin.

"You'd think with all the skating, Butch wouldn't be such a pig."

"I think he spends a lot of time sitting in hunting stands."

"Yeah."

"But I'd do that too, if I could. No wife bitching at you. No kids. Just silence."

Justin's face now wears a deep scowl.

"Hey, I have an idea," Justin says after downing his second beer. "Can you have Kate give Piper lessons on how not to be a bitch?"

Charlie makes a sound like a laugh, but has a creeping uncomfortable feeling, like he's skating on untested pond ice. He should leave after this beer. He doesn't want to be hung over tomorrow, and at the rate Justin is going, he'll be in bad shape. Especially now that Justin is ordering shots.

"Ah, no, thank you," says Charlie. "I don't want to pay for this tomorrow."

"All we have is tonight, bro," says Justin. "The company sucks anyway. Might as well have a little fun between misery."

"I thought you said this is hockey."

"It is. And so is drinking to escape it. War stories."

Fireball shots arrive, and Charlie doesn't know how he can avoid taking it.

"Cheers."

It goes down surprisingly smooth. He feels as if he's stepping in a warm bath. Maybe he'll stay a little longer.

"I'm tired of people shirking their responsibilities," says Justin.

Maybe not.

"Piper's only responsibility in life is to look hot. And she's starting to drop the ball on that, too. Have you seen her lips? Freaky looking injections."

"Come on," says Charlie. "Piper's a beauty."

"If you knew how much time and money it took for her to look like that, you'd be disgusted. Not like Kate."

There. Justin brings up Kate again, and the icky feeling returns.

Justin orders more shots. The bar erupts in cheers for the ending of the cage fight. One guy lies on the ground covered in lacerations, clutching a broken rib, eyes swollen shut.

"To war stories!" says Justin.

Some of the college guys hear. They get in on the round of shots.

"To war stories!"

The bar grows blurred and hazy. Charlie feels mellower than he has in weeks. Maybe this is how he'll survive the rest of the season.

"To hockey!" says Justin.

"HockeyStrong!" yells Charlie.

As the clock hands move, conversation slips in and out of Charlie's ear. Everything is funny to him. Even Justin's argument with a local. He doesn't know what it's about, but he sees his friend stand and make a move toward a guy in the corner.

"Hey, bro," says Charlie. "No fights. Remember. We're in the man cave. No Butch. No trouble."

Justin sits down. He finishes another beer.

"I think I'm getting divorced," says Justin.

"To divorce!" yells a business traveler.

"Divorce!"

Shots.

"Hey, take it easy," says Charlie. "You'll make it."

"I'm bleeding money for her beauty treatments. Her shopping. Her boozing. Sports trainers. I can't keep up." The words slur together.

"You'll be fine. The season's almost done."

"My wife is a drunk."

"It's just the pressure," says Charlie.

"I don't know if we'll make it," says Justin. "I don't think I want to."

"Come on, man. It's just hockey."

"It's hockey."

"To Hockey!"

#####

The sun hasn't yet risen, but dance music blares through the hockey rink. Charlie's head pounds with the base.

"It's too early for Pitbull's *Fireball*," says Charlie.

"Especially after last night's Fireball," says Justin. "Piper was passed out cold when I got in."

"Drunk?"

"Yep. Champagne. She packed it."

At least there are no pictures on Facebook, Charlie thinks.

"Hey, man, sorry for going on like a blubbering mess last night," says Justin. "I just needed to blow off some steam."

"No problem," says Charlie.

Butch slams open the locker room door, and the team marches toward the ice. Once Butch has passed, Charlie gives Brett a sneaky thumbs up, and climbs to the top of the bleachers. His phone buzzes.

--I'M SO GLAD THEY WON YESTERDAY! texts Kate.

--ME TOO. I WAS AT ROCK BOTTOM. MUCH BETTER TODAY.

--YEAH, I WAS WORRIED.

--THERAPY WITH JUSTIN AT THE BAR TOOK OFF THE EDGE.

--DID PIPER JOIN YOU?

--NO, BUT APPARENTLY SHE FELL INTO CHAMPAGNE IN THE ROOM. PASSED OUT COLD WHEN JUSTIN GOT IN.

--WOW.

--YEAH. BUT I CAN'T JUDGE. I THINK I HAVE INSIGHT NOW. MEMO: I WILL BE DRUNK FOR THE REMAINDER OF THE SEASON.

--WHATEVER GETS YOU THROUGH. JUST DON'T FLIRT WITH KIP AND LET PEOPLE TAKE PICS.

--WHAT IF WE PROMISE NOT TO POST THEM ON FACEBOOK?

—:)

Both teams are running a little sluggish. It's common in mornings after travel, and frankly, it's a relief; they don't need the intensity of emotion to compound the stresses of the tournament. Even Butch is subdued. He rotates the lines for reasonable shifts, avoids screaming at refs, the opposing coach, and David, whose confidence when not being verbally abused visibly expands. Charlie allows himself to get lost in the fantasy of this being the new norm. Maybe it is. Maybe they've run the gauntlet and finally proven themselves.

On Brett's next shift—a penalty kill—he feeds the puck to Mike (who must be feeling better since he's back to playing extra shifts on defense) for a goal from the point. Butch nods at the boys when they come off the ice.

--BUTCH JUST NODDED AT BRETT FOR A GOOD PLAY!!!!!

--!!!!!!!!!!!!!!!!!!!!!!!!!!!!!!!!!!!!

--IF YOU NEED ME, I'LL JUST BE DEAD FROM SHOCK.

--LOL.

The Polar Bears win the game 2-1. Parents high five each other, there's laughter and joking. Charlie hasn't felt camaraderie like this since—well, he's never felt it, at least not with hockey parents. When he sees the smile on Brett's face when he emerges from the locker room, Charlie thinks that maybe they've finally turned the corner, and all will be well.

Chapter Twenty-Four

 Piper Caldwell's Status Update: ⚙

Photo: Selfie with Lil' Champs!

#TournamentWeekend
#GoPolarBears #HockeyStrong
🤍 💬

Following the win, everyone is in such high spirits, they consent to a team brunch at IHOP. Justin is especially glad, because the greasy food will be the perfect antidote to his hangover. Maybe Piper would be less of a bitch when she was hung over if she actually ate something.

Before they order, Butch stands to give a speech.

"We needed this," he says. "It's like we've been in the jungle fighting the enemy and swarms of insects and rainy season for months, and for one brief moment, the sun shined on us."

"Yeah, man!" says Sal.

"It's no accident that you played with such discipline today. My practices—as much as they bother some of you parents from the "everyone-should-get-a-trophy" school of thought—are best practices. It's only with the strictest mental and physical conditioning that you are able to withstand adversity and come out on top. I will continue to put pressure on you because you respond to pressure."

"HockeyStrong!" yells Amy.

"Now, onto business. First: carb-load at breakfast. The team you'll play this afternoon is number one in their division in Pennsylvania. Like you, they have excellent records and stats, and you will likely end up playing them in the championship. Second: they have a player—number thirty-six, Zung's the name—he's the size of a sumo wrestler with the speed and agility of someone half his size. He gets all their goals. Gordie, Franklin, you know what you need to do, but do it like a sniper. If the refs catch you, you're benched for the rest of the tournament."

Mee Maw raises her hand, but does not wait for Butch to acknowledge her before speaking. "It sounds like you're encouraging dirty play, and that's not appropriate, especially for kids this age."

Poo Poo elbows her, but she keeps talking.

"This morning was the first time this team has really played like a team and communicated, and it wasn't because of tricks or dangerous penalties."

"Mee Maw," says Poo Poo.

"I'm not finished."

"Any time you think my methods are too tough, you are welcome to put your grandson in one of the shitty programs feeding the future beer leagues of America."

"Mee Maw!" whines Henry, giving his grandmother a pleading look.

She slumps in her chair.

"If we are finished with the histrionics, I have one more order," says Butch. "After brunch, these boys are to go up to their rooms and lie down. No video games, no TV, no horsing around."

"No swimming pool!" shouts Kip.

"That goes without saying," says Butch. "You all better be rested and ready this evening, or you'll run so many suicides, you'll be pissing yourselves."

#####

Justin scoots closer to the snack machines to hear Kip's pregame speech to Kyle. He's curious to hear how Kip motivates his son—not because Kyle is better than Aiden, but because Justin enjoys hearing how nuts other parents are. It makes him feel more normal. His own father never seemed especially interested in Justin's playing unless he was criticizing, and Justin is determined not to be that way.

"Don't let me down, boy," says Kip.

"I won't, Daddy."

"You say that, and yet I find you running in the hotel hallway, chasing your little brother, when you're supposed to be resting."

"I swear, I'm not tired, Daddy."

"You depleted the energy you'll need for the game."

"I didn't! Mommy didn't give me my meds, so I'm wild."

"Good. I want you wild for the game. You heard Coach Butch. It's not just Gordie and Franklin who can be goons for him."

"I can be a goon."

"But don't get hurt. Don't be messing up your career to take out a few thugs."

"Yes, Daddy."

Justin peers between the machines at Kip. The huge guy is in his kid's face. He grabs Kyle's arm and pulls him nose-to-nose.

"If you let me down, I'll get you."

Kip lets Kyle go, and collects his tripod and binder.

Justin jumps from a tap on his shoulder.

"What's up?" asks Charlie.

As Kip heads into the rink, Justin shakes his head.

"I just watched Kip threaten Kyle. It was messed up."

"What did he say?"

"That if Kyle lets him down, he'll get him."

"What the hell does that mean?"

"I have no idea."

When they enter the rink, Justin joins Piper at the boards, and Charlie heads to the penalty box. Dante sits in the corner behind them, teaching Amy to parrot vulgar words and phrases. Linda is nowhere to be found. Kip and Lucy are within earshot, so Justin doesn't mention Kip's threatening behavior to Piper, though it would do her good to hear the guy she likes to flirt with is such a psycho.

Within moments of the opening whistle, it's clear that the intensity level is in a higher stratosphere than the morning game. Everyone's amped up: coaches, fans, players. The music ranges from Metallica to LL Cool J to Rage Against the Machine. Kyle, however, is playing scared, and Kip goes from hissing at his wife for allowing Kyle to roughhouse in the hallways before the game to screaming at his son.

"Act like you want to play," Kip yells. "You're killing me!"

The ample penalties are even between the teams. Gordie and Franklin have had two each on the Zung kid, but the boy is beast. He hasn't been knocked down yet. The Polar Bears are losing three to one. At the end of the second period, Kip pulls Kyle out of the huddle, and engages in such a tirade that Butch doesn't even call Kyle back. Kyle starts on defense in the third period. Within the first play, Kyle catches Zung in the corner with his head down, and blasts him with a helmet-crushing hit from behind. The fans are on their feet; the refs blow their whistles; Butch stays silent. Zung is on the ground, not moving.

"Do you think he's dead?" whispers Piper.

"If not, definitely paralyzed," says Justin.

The ref converses with Butch a moment before skating to the box and letting Kyle out again. He points to the door. Kyle has been ejected from the game.

Kip erupts, banging the glass, throwing his binder, and screaming about how ridiculous the call is.

"Zung had it coming! Did you see him knocking my son?"

When the referee points to Kip and to the door, Kip makes a sound like a growl and jumps against the glass, slamming it with his shoulder.

It shatters.

Each piece hits the ice—almost in slow motion.

The rink goes silent.

Chapter Twenty-Five

  #PolarBears Public Page

Photo, by Tina Church:
"Bobby and his best bud, Mike,
at Dave & Busters!"
Tagged: Butch Johnson

#TournamentWeekend
#GoPolarBears #HockeyStrong

Charlie stands in the dark on the balcony outside of the hotel room where Brett sleeps. In the name of preserving his own sanity, and much to the frustration of Tina, Charlie wouldn't allow Brett to attend the team dinner at Dave & Busters. Brett must have been exhausted because he didn't protest. They Ubered to a steak house, walked the half-mile back to the hotel, and Brett fell asleep at eight o'clock. Charlie is going to bed as soon as he gets off the phone with Kate.

"I was shocked it only took a half-hour to fix," says Charlie. "They have new panels on hand."

"I wonder if this is the first time a parent has shattered the glass."

"Based on the amount of psychos we've come across, I doubt it."

"I'm surprised Kip was the one who lost it. I could think of a handful of other parents I could see going postal before him. Including some I know very well."

"Ha. It doesn't surprise me at all. Kip's a snake, coiled and ready to strike."

"You're right. Anyone who manages his kid the way he does Kyle must be crazy."

"Thank God we're still sane."

"Thank God."

Through the steamy cloud of his breath in the frigid air, Charlie can see the team bus pull into the hotel parking lot. He sees Butch's lion-like outline in the window, and imagines threading an arrow into a bow and firing.

"The inmates have returned," says Charlie. "I can see them from the balcony."

"I saw Tina's Butch ass-kissing post on the team page. You were smart to avoid the team dinner. You would have been miserable."

"I know. I don't connect to any of these people."

"Aliens."

"They live for these tournaments and all of the ridiculous group outings. Don't they have lives at home? Jobs? The championship game is tomorrow morning, but the bus isn't scheduled to depart until Monday, so we're stuck all day again. I'm hoping we can just leave when it's over."

"Did you say anything to Tina?"

"Yeah, but she said the bus is contracted through Monday and the conference made you book hotels through the weekend, so they want to get their money's worth."

After they wish each other goodnight, Charlie creeps into the room as quietly as possible. Brett's breathing is deep and regular. He is envious; he can never sleep at these tournaments. Hoping to help with his allergies and get a decent night's sleep, Charlie takes three Benadryl tablets he bought at the Hotel Mini Mart. He passes out before he has finished checking the online tournament rankings and team Facebook page.

#####

"Dad! Dad!"

Charlie feels as if he's swimming in mud.

Someone bangs on the door. Brett shakes him.

"We overslept! The bus is loading!!"

Charlie bolts up and grabs his phone. In a few swipes, he realizes he set his phone alarm for seven *p. m.* instead of seven *a. m.*

"Oh shit!"

He jumps up, and runs to answer the door. It's only after he throws it open that he realizes he's only wearing boxer briefs. Justin gives him a once over.

"Dude. The bus is about to leave."

"Tell 'em five minutes."

Justin nods and hurries away.

Charlie and Brett pull on the clothes they wore last night and left on the floor. They run around the room stuffing Brett's equipment left out to dry into his bag. Charlie has no time to pee, shower, or brush his teeth before they're out the door, and it's only when he and Brett fall into their seats and the bus is in motion that he realizes he has forgotten his phone, his jacket, and his wallet. He will not be able to text Kate, stay warm, or pay for coffee.

Butch stands at his seat, glares at Charlie, and clears his throat.

"Since the irresponsible among us can't bothered to get to the bus on time, we are not going to have our full hour to warm up before the most important game of the tournament, nor will I have time to give the entire speech I prepared in the locker room. I don't usually like to give my speeches in front of parents for a variety of reasons, but Miller has left me no choice."

"Dick," hisses Sal.

Charlie clenches his fists.

"How's Kip, Lucy?" says Butch.

"Miserable," she says. "Embarrassed."

"Crazy!" yells Amy.

"He hurt us with that episode," says Butch. "Kyle, if you're caught doing anything like that again, you could face a multigame suspension."

"Notice, Butch doesn't reprimand Kyle for that dangerous play," whispers Mee Maw from the seat behind Charlie.

"You have to play the tough team this morning," says Butch. "Zung's out. He has a concussion."

"Sweet!" says Mike.

"That shouldn't make you happy," says Butch. "You should want to return to battle with him to redeem yourself from that defeat. Do not be satisfied with inferiority. If you win today, it will be a cheap victory because they are down their best player—and win, you better."

"YES, COACH BUTCH!" the boys scream.

"I want that tournament banner," says Coach Butch. "I need that banner. If we take this tournament, our names will be immortalized, hanging from the rafters of the home rink as a reminder to everyone who skates on the Polar Bear ice, forever, who the real champions are. Do you hear me?"

"YES, COACH BUTCH!"

Charlie slides down in his seat. He takes deep slow breaths to control the pounding of his heart, but that only brings wafts of garlic into his nose. He tells himself that he only has to survive *this game*, and then he can go home.

Just this game.

And the rest of the day in company with the team.

And tomorrow's eight-hour bus ride home.

And four more months of hockey.

Chapter Twenty-Six

 #PolarBears Public Page ⚙

Photo, by Piper Caldwell:
"Aidan and his bestie, Mike, at Dave & Busters!"
Tagged: Butch Johnson

#TournamentWeekend
#GoPolarBears #HockeyStrong

Justin pops ibuprofen and regales Charlie with tales of last night at Dave & Buster's.

"I went all out," said Justin. "Drank about five pitchers of beer. Piper snapped a dozen pictures. Posted them to Facebook, I'm sure, but whatever. She doesn't care about embarrassing me, so I don't care about embarrassing her."

"I would check the pictures for you, but I left my damned phone in the room. And my wallet. Hey, can I hit you up for a coffee. I'll owe you one later."

"Sure."

They stand in the coffee line—which is fifteen exhausted looking parents deep.

"I'm happy to tell you that I didn't dance suggestively on any bars without my underwear on," says Justin. "But Bob Church and I might have been kicked off the skee ball lanes. And Sal and I might have arm wrestled."

"Who won?"

"Sal was winning but had to stop when he got chest pains. Louise determined it was only because of the large pepperoni pizza he ate for dinner by himself, but I think it might have been the six burritos he had earlier at Taco Bell."

Charlie laughs.

"Oh, and I must have switched clothes with Bob at some point. I woke up wearing head to toe CHURCH 99 #Hockeystrong apparel. Good thing Bob packed a suitcase-full."

Brett appears, tears running down his face, and tugs Charlie's sleeve.

"What's wrong?" asks Charlie.

"I forgot my skates."

"What?!"

"In the room—when we were hurrying to pack."

"Oh shit."

"Coach Butch says I'm benched the whole game if I don't find a pair of skates in five minutes. This is the championship! They need me!"

Charlie runs a hand through his hair and steps out of line.

"This is all my fault," he says.

Justin sees the lights of the proshop flicker neon red at the other end of the rink.

"There," says Justin. He hurries with the Millers to the store. The kid working the cash register has his eyes closed, headphones on, and his shoes on the counter.

"Excuse me," says Charlie.

No response.

Charlie bangs the bell with one hand and the counter with the other, and the kid startles.

"I need skates. Pronto. Can we borrow a pair?"

"From the pro shop? No."

"But he forgot his skates at the hotel. A half hour away. And I forgot my wallet, so I can't buy new ones."

"Then you can't rent them either. It's twelve bucks to rent a pair of skates."

"I can find twelve bucks. You just fit him. ASAP. His coach won't let him play in the championship if he doesn't have skates in five minutes!"

Justin checks his wallet, but he's broke.

"Sorry, bro. Used all my bills at Dave & Busters."

Charlie looks like he's going to be sick. He glances around, just as Poo Poo walks out of the bathroom across from the proshop, fastening his belt.

"Poo Poo!" yells Charlie. "I need twelve bucks. I left my wallet at the hotel. Do you have any money? It's a long story, but I'll fill you later."

Poo Poo digs in one pocket, but comes up empty handed, and reaches in the other, struggling to get the wallet out of his pants, tight against his old man ass. He licks his finger and counts through the money.

"I only have eight, but you can have it. Sorry, Charlie."

Poo Poo laughs at his own stupid joke.

While Charlie runs back to the pro shop, Justin heads to the rink. Charlie's anxiety is making him jumpy. Not only does he not want to miss any of the game over some other kid's skate drama, but Justin doesn't want to be seen with Charlie. Butch might punish Aiden.

#####

By the end of the second period, the Polar Bears are winning 2-1. In spite of Brett tripping and falling from the lousy loaner skates as much as he's upright, he has managed to assist one goal for Aiden and score one himself. After Brett's goal, Charlie runs over to Justin and Piper, and asks Piper to text Kate. Piper pulls her phone out of her purse, and scrolls through screens of texts.

"Oops," says Piper. "Kate has been texting me frantically. I can only check my phone at certain times. Justin is sanctimonious about my usage."

"Addicts are always the last to admit their dependency," says Justin.

"You're one to talk."

Piper makes a dozen or so clicks and hits send.

"There," she says. "She's all filled in."

"Did you tell her about Brett's goal?"

Piper stares at him a moment, then pulls the phone back out and clicks so fast her fingers are a blur. The phone buzzes almost immediately.

"What'd she say?" asks Charlie.

"It's not Kate," says Piper. "It's my mother. Girl drama."

Justin groans.

Piper heads for the lobby to call her mother.

Charlie chews his nails.

"Dude, relax," says Justin. "You're making me nervous."

"Sorry, I'm just frazzled, uncaffeinated, freezing my balls off."

"Hey, man, bummer on the skates," says Sal.

Charlie gives Sal a cool look.

"Good thing Butch is goin' easy on Brett," says Sal.

"What do you mean?"

"He told Brett because of the delay, he'll have to skate suicides at the next practice."

"What? Where did you hear that?"

"When the boys were in line to get on the ice."

"You can't be serious."

"At least Butch is letting Brett wait for his punishment until we get home."

"It wasn't Brett's fault we forgot the skates. I set my alarm for the wrong time."

"Doesn't matter," says Louise, leaning over Sal. "Kids these days need to stop blaming their parents for everything. This generation is spoiled and entitled. Consequences make 'em better."

Justin looks at Charlie. The guy looks like he's about to have an aneurism.

There is a sudden war of shouts and cheers as the other team scores—tying up the game. On the next play, Franklin boards the kid who scored, bringing a major penalty on the team. Within the first twenty seconds of the penalty kill, the other team scores, putting them in the lead. Butch kicks the door. He screams at the ref about a forward from the other team being in the goal crease, so the goal shouldn't count.

"We saw no such thing," shouts the ref. He's a huge guy —hairier and meaner looking that Butch—and he's not taking any of Butch's bullshit.

"That's because you have your head up your ass."

"Say one more disrespectful thing, and I'll have you thrown out."

When the ref's back is to him, Butch mumbles under his breath. The ref turns and makes a big sweep with his arm to show Butch is out.

"What?" Butch screams.

The ref points toward the door, and when Butch doesn't obey, the guy skates over in an impressive and aggressive motion that sends Butch slamming out from the bench and into the locker room. Assistant Andy looks like he might crap his pants.

The boys take charge of the remainder of the game, rotating in and out in an organized fashion. As the clock ticks down in the championship game, the noise begins to grow in the stands. The fans yell louder and louder, and with fifteen seconds left, the opposing team claps and cheers as if they've already won.

Aidan's line is up, and with lightning speed, Bobby cycles the puck to Aiden, who spots Brett in front of the goal. With two seconds left in the game, Brett slams the puck into the goal, tying the score and sending them to a shoot out. Without Butch there to berate him, David is impenetrable, but the first two shooters for the Polar Bears—Mike and Mario—are unsuccessful. There is some back and forth about who the final shooter will be, and though the fans are screaming for Brett, Andy passes him over to let Gordie have a go at it. Gordie goes all out, skating fast and furious, and stops within ten feet of the goalie to fire a slapshot that goes bar down and wins the Polar Bears the championship!

The crowd goes wild! Justin cheers and looks for Piper, but she is on the phone in the lobby. She missed it. The worst thing is, she'll probably be more upset about Tina posting about the win on Facebook first and getting more likes than actually missing her son's game.

The parents celebrate around him. Sal bear hugs Charlie, Helen and Louise high five, Mee Maw and Poo Poo kiss, and Lucy fist bumps Linda and Tom. Bob Church runs circles around the boards with his CHURCH 99 blanket flapping behind him like a flag. Butch exits the locker room and surveys the scene, motioning Andy over for the report. He slaps his son on the back and joins the team in the high five line. *We Are the Champions* blares over the loudspeaker.

Piper finally runs in and toward the ice to snap a photo, but she comes to a halt. The cheering sounds have been replaced by something else. The other team is having some kind of collective fit. The boys are throwing off their gloves and helmets, banging sticks on the ice, crying and screaming about their loss. The big, hairy ref tells the other coach he better get control, but the guy just shrugs, as if he approves of such poor losing. The other team's parents stand around with their arms crossed glaring at the Polar Bears, doing nothing to reprimand their sons for acting like assholes. The big ref is finally able to corral the team into some kind of line, but once they are halfway through handshakes, an all-out brawl erupts. Their team attacks the Polar Bears, and while most of the boys hurry off the ice, Gordie, Franklin, and Mike remain, throwing punches, pushing, and kicking the losing team.

The head of the tournament, who was waiting to hand out banners and trophies, takes the microphone and yells about poor sportsmanship. By the time the kids are separated and subdued, he announces that while individual players not engaged in the fight will receive trophies, the fighters will not. Oh, and one more thing. Because of the unsportsmanlike conduct of Coach Butch Johnson of the Polar Bears setting the bad example, the team will not take home the much coveted tournament banner.

Chapter Twenty-Seven

  #PolarBears Public Page

First Episode of Tina & Bob Church's new podcast #SportsTaxi is live! All you sports parents need to listen and SHARE!

#GoPolarBears #HockeyStrong

BOB CHURCH: Hey Sports Fans, Bob and Tina Church here with a new program called hashtag SportsTaxi —the podcast for all of you sports parents intent and focused on helping your son--

TINA CHURCH: Or daughter!

BOB: --succeed on a team. We'll cover everything from the highs of winning to the lows of losing, to sports fundraising opportunities--

TINA: --Hashtag HockeyStrong!

BOB: --to best sports' parent practices--

TINA: --and worst!

BOB: --marriage tips, family tips, conditioning tips, and most important...

BOTH: Team building! Ha ha ha...

TINA: In all seriousness, youth sports are a huge part of family life today--

BOB: --more than ever before.

TINA: And we, as parents, need to take our roles as managers—Bob, is that too strong a word?

BOB: No, Tina. It's not.

TINA: That's what I thought. We need to take our roles as managers, or even ambassadors--

BOB: Ooh, good one.

TINA: Thanks. We need to take it all very seriously. It's not like these kids are heading to the NHL, but if by chance there are a few out there who just might go pro, we need to ensure their mental and physical conditioning are in top form for the rink, the field, and for life.

BOB: Well spoken, Tina. You know, as a businessman, I can tell you, when I look at a resume and see that a candidate has played team sports for any number of years, I know they have an edge, something unspoken, unnamable--

TINA: A *je ne sais quoi.*

BOB: Ooh, La, La. Yes! Did you like that, Canadian listeners?

TINA: It was Coach Butch's Word of the Day once.

BOB: Yes, as I was saying, team sports lead to success in all areas of life.

TINA: And your child's life success is certainly something all parents should invest in.

BOB: While we are talking investments, my company, Globeforce 5 is available for all of your financial planning needs. Please see our website for an inquiry.

#####

Charlie switches off the podcast; he cannot believe he listened as long as he has. What insufferable nonsense. They are four hours into the bus ride home, but by his estimation, they aren't even close to halfway.

Aside from random shouts from Amy and burps from Butch, it has been silent the entire ride. Brett sat with Charlie, in spite of Charlie's insistence that he was all right, but Brett seemed to sense his father needed an ally. His son now rests his head on Charlie's shoulder and is making snoring noises in his sleep. Brett took off his shoes because his blisters were so bad from the loaner skates, he couldn't bear to wear them unless absolutely necessary. He has his feet curled up underneath him, making him appear even younger than his twelve years.

Charlie watches the steadily falling snow with increasing concern. They should have been home by now. When they finished the game yesterday afternoon, Tina had called a meeting with all the team families because some said they wanted to leave immediately. After a solid half-hour of bickering, which escalated to name calling, Tina had a vote. It was split about fifty-fifty—with whackos like Sal wanting to hang around—"We'll get our money's worth, at least!"— to those disgusted by the team families like Piper wishing to leave—"I have a life at home I need to attend to." Charlie had voted an emphatic LEAVE, but Hank was the last to vote, and Charlie was sure Hank voted to stay to spite him. Hank claimed it was because he had purchased tickets for his family to attend the Red Wing's game, and didn't want to have to eat them.

There is a sudden popping sound, followed by the unmistakable flapping of a huge bus tire gone flat.

"Fuck me!" shouts Louise.

"Language!" yells Mee Maw.

"Hate you! Hate you! Fuck you! Fuck you!" yells Amy.

Dante giggles.

Of course. Of course they would get a flat, in a snowstorm, on the most miserable sports trip ever taken.

--FLAT TIRE, texts Charlie.

--YOU MUST BE JOKING.

--I WISH.

--WE'LL BE ABLE TO LAUGH ABOUT THIS ONE DAY.

--I'M LOOKING FORWARD TO THAT DAY.

The only good news is that the driver has to get off the bus, so Charlie is given a temporary reprieve from the garlic odor. But the bad news quickly follows when the driver gets back on and radios for support.

"Over, we got a flat on 80. Texting coordinates. We need support."

"Negative. Closest crew sixteen miles away."

"Snow falling steady, over. We'll get stuck if we don't get moving soon."

Charlie feels as if he's going to have a panic attack, or a heart attack. He does not want to die with these people. Brett stirs.

"What's wrong?" he asks.

"Flat tire." His voice comes out wavering.

The conversations and Amy's hysterics are rising, so Charlie can no longer hear the back and forth of the driver and dispatch. After a few minutes, the guy hangs up the walkie talkie, takes a bite of his garlic Slim Jim, and addresses the group.

"Don't panic, but it's gonna be awhile. Apparently we aren't the only bus in trouble."

"Can we change the tire?" asks Kip.

"Negative. Not on a bus this size. Plus, I gotta follow protocol, and the company isn't letting any passengers change tires. You'd probably get killed and sue."

"I'm starving!" yells Sal. "And I'm outta snacks."

There is a general murmuring about hunger, until Helen holds up her phone.

"McDonalds is one point six miles from here, if you want to walk."

"Hell no," says Louise. "No way. We don't have boots or anything. Sal, you're in flip flops, for Christ's sake."

"I'd walk barefoot. Let's go."

Louise curses and rounds up coats for her boys. Sal pulls a sweatshirt on over his "Celebrate Diversity" tee shirt, covered in different gun models.

"Bring me back something," calls Butch.

Helen smacks his arm, and he grumbles for a moment, but stands to join the Gardenias. Other families begin to follow, until only Charlie and Brett are left with Mee Maw, Poo Poo, and Henry.

"Dad, I'm hungry," says Brett.

Charlie sighs and pulls on his coat and scarf.

"What can we bring you," he says, turning back to Mee Maw.

"Oh, bless you. Poo Poo shouldn't be out in the cold. Just a couple of chicken sandwiches, please."

"What can Henry eat?"

"I think the nuggets are just made of chemicals, so I don't think he's allergic to anything in them."

"Does he want to come with us?"

"Please, Mee Maw!" says Henry.

"Absolutely not! You could get killed by a car or sick from the cold."

Henry continues to protest, but Mee Maw will not let him go.

Charlie and Brett join the team on the long, cold trek to McDonalds.

They arrive forty minutes later and near hypothermic, only to see the golden arches have gone dark. No power.

Chapter Twenty-Eight

  **#PolarBears Public Page** ⚙

Episode 2 of Tina & Bob Church's
podcast #SportsTaxi is live!
Join the conversation!

#GoPolarBears #HockeyStrong
💙 💬

TINA: Welcome back to #SportsTaxi. I'm TeamMom Tina.

BOB: And I'm SuperFanDad Bob.

TINA: And today's podcast is about budgeting for youth sports.

BOB: Some of you with younger kids might be surprised that budgeting is necessary but here's a run-down of our hockey-related expenses this year so you understand how serious it is. Now, our son is on an *elite* travel team with an *extra* tournament league, but if your child shows promise, this can happen before you know it.

TINA: It really can, Bob. Our Fees: Try outs: $450, 3 Summer Camps—one at an exclusive Minnesota boarding school: $3,600, New Equipment: $880, Season Fee: $4,800, Extra League Tournaments (4--including registration and travel-related fees): $2,100, Non-League Games (6): $120, Visiting Coach at Skills Practices (3): $75, Personal Off-Ice

& Skating Trainer (monthly fee, year-round ideally): $4200 total. Not included, but must be accounted for: Fundraising and Team Dinners. Also, all of this supports our goal: district playoffs, which will be held in Florida. That cost is not included, but will run about $1600 with flights, hotel, and tournament fees.

BOB: For those of you keeping count, that's over $12,000 *before* the personal trainer, fundraising, team dinners, and play-offs. Trainers are, of course, optional, but if you want to be competitive, you have to keep up.

TINA: It's true, Bob. Even though most of these kids will never make the pros, it's important to invest in their immediate success and happiness.

BOB: And can you really put a price tag on happiness?

#####

Justin watches practice with Sal and Charlie. Sal pumps his fist to Ozzy Osbourne's *Crazy Train*, and takes big gooey bites from his second Snickers bar. Justin is beginning to find Sal and his antics strangely endearing. It happens with team family relationships over the course of a hockey season—attachment or hatred, unhealthy levels of either. Sal might be rough around the edges, but at least he's amusing, unlike Charlie. Aside from having won the wife lottery, Charlie has become a total drag, and looks like he could use some time in a sanitarium.

Sal looks around and sighs.

"Good to see it's all men here, today, brothers. I'm sick of the hens."

"Amen, dude," says Justin, giving Sal a high-five.

"Bitches mess shit up!" says Sal. "It's gotten to where I can't even watch Sports Center without some chick doin' a feel-good story about some guy who overcame adversity to play in the NFL. That same loser will be arrested next week for knocking his woman around in an elevator."

"True," says Justin.

"I don't know when it got all pink shoelaces and one-on-one interviews. At least the NHL keeps that shit out. It's about the game."

Justin finds it somewhat troubling that he agrees with Sal, but dismisses the thought.

"I've pretty much banned Piper," says Justin. "She's a pain in the ass."

"They all are," says Sal.

They both look at Charlie for agreement, but Justin knows they won't get it from him—not with a wife like Kate. Justin would actually prefer Kate to Charlie. At least she doesn't take any of this too seriously.

"Hey, did you hear about those losers we beat at the tourney?" says Sal.

"What do you mean?"

"Louise stalked their team page on Facebook and saw that their goalie had been playing with a broken hand."

"How do you stalk a Facebook page?" says Justin.

"Sometimes people forget to mark their posts private, so anyone can see 'em. Even if they don't have a Facebook account."

Good to know, thinks Justin.

"But anyway, some of the hens from that team were bitching right on a public conversation about how this kid's dad saw his son's hand swollen after the boys were playing football at the hotel, and he didn't tape it or anything. He just made the kid shove his hand in the glove and play."

Justin thinks of Aiden's asthma, Bobby's foot; he wonders if he'd make his kid play with a broken hand. Probably.

"The dad jumped in the conversation," continues Sal, "and said they weren't complaining when they were winning, and maybe if their sons would have done their jobs on defense, they would have won. One of the moms bitched back that it was abuse to make a kid play with a broken hand. Then the dad said, when you drive six hours and pay all that money, people should have to play unless they're dying."

Quiet settles over the group for a moment.

"I hate to admit it, but I can see his point," says Justin.

"Yeah, me too," says Sal.

When the song ends, Butch can be heard screaming, "Who's high?" He stops the scrimmage, skates toward the goal, and drags Mario by the jersey to the place he wants him to stand.

"Here, you idiot," says Butch. "This is where you stand. How many more times do I have to tell you?"

Sal shakes his head, crumples his candy wrapper, and throws it on the floor.

"What a retard," says Sal.

Butch or Mario, wonders Justin.

"How many times does Butch have to tell Mario to stay high so he can be ready for the shot," says Sal.

Justin looks at Charlie, who widens his eyes.

Okay, Sal's a freak. If Butch manhandled Aiden, Justin would get in his face.

"Mario the beast. More like Mario the dipshit," says Sal.

Justin can almost feel the air around them starting to buzz. Charlie's hand trembles on his coffee mug. He tries to lighten the mood.

"So, Piper found a deal on the skating treadmill we've been looking at for Aiden for Christmas."

"No way, man. Those are like fifty grand."

"Nope. We found one on an NHL used items website. The Predators used to train with it, but they got a new model. This one even comes with a warranty."

"Shut up," says Sal. "How much?"

"Twelve thousand."

"Wait." Charlie grabs Justin's forearm. "Twelve thousand dollars? For a Christmas present?"

"It's a hell of a deal," says Justin. "And we're calling it a Christmas present, but he'll be able to use that thing until he moves out to play juniors somewhere."

"Louise would never go for that," says Sal. "We settled on doing the synthetic ice flooring in the basement. It'll be for both Mario and Dante."

"What is that?" asks Charlie.

"It's like fake ice. And it's not cold. You can skate right on it. Cool, huh?"

"What does that run?"

"All in with installation, it'll be four grand."

Charlie chokes on his coffee, splattering it all over the glass. He uses his sweatshirt to wipe it off. Justin and Sal start the side-shuffle away from him.

"Did you hear what Kip and Lucy are doing?" asks Sal.

Justin clenches his jaw. Sal doesn't seem to notice or care that Kip is a sore spot with Justin.

"Getting their whole yard graded," says Sal. "For a real ice rink! And they live in one of those house-on-top-of-house communities. It'll be the whole damned back yard."

"Are you serious? What an eyesore," says Justin.

"Yeah, and that's going to be twenty-four grand. The company grades your yard, builds the box, puts up boards, lines it, and fills it with water."

"What if it doesn't get cold enough this winter for them to play?"

"Tough luck."

"How do you clear the ice? Does this company provide Zamboni services?"

"No, you have to buy a little machine separate. It heats water, and you drag it across to smooth the ice."

"And what do you do with it when it's not winter?"

"Kip says you can just roll up the liner and store it."

"He's insane."

"Dude, what's with your eye?" says Sal.

Justin follows Sal's gaze to Charlie, whose twitchy eye is working overtime. Justin wonders if he has any aspirin, because this guy is going to have a heart attack.

"It just started a couple months ago," Charlie says. "I don't know why."

Justin looks at Sal, who takes a long drink of his soda, and burps. Charlie walks away, climbing to the top of the stands, alone.

"What's his problem?" asks Sal.

"Might as well have a hen around, with that guy," says Justin.

"Seriously."

Chapter Twenty-Nine

 Charlie Miller's Status Update: ⚙

Shared Post:
Butch Johnson: Word of the Day: Dysfunctional
Not operating normally or in a productive way.
Often used with families, but can also be
applied to other systems.

#HappyHolidays #HockeyStrong

♥ 💬

"You shared his 'Word of the Day'?" says Kate.

The Millers are driving to Kate's parents' house for Christmas Eve dinner. With Kate's two brothers and their families, her parents, and her crazy grandpa, there will be sixteen people. Sixteen sporty, competitive people. Kate knows Charlie doesn't feel up for it, but Brett loves to see his cousins, and they won't be able to see the family on Christmas Day because Butch scheduled a non-league game. Butch had put out a survey over email to see who could show up Christmas night to play a Canadian Lower A Pee Wee team down for a tournament that didn't start until the twenty-sixth, and all the other families (except Mee Maw and Poo Poo) responded with an immediate and enthusiastic YES! Mee Maw's reply was wordy, judgmental of sports on holidays, concerned about kids not being allowed to just be kids, but ended with an affirmative response.

"It's an easy way to strengthen our relationship," says Charlie.

"Do you think sharing a post really does that?" says Kate.

"It was a moment of weakness. I saw a bunch of team parent likes and piled on. And the word certainly fits the holidays."

"Would you rather go to your parents' house?"

"No, but at least there I wouldn't suffer physical injury. Your big brother can't seem to give up his old football days. I still have the scar from the Thanksgiving game."

"Pete means well."

"Let's make a bet on how long before he starts asking about Brett's team wins and losses, and telling me about Pete Jr.'s football success? Four minutes? Six?"

He has a point.

"Did you ever answer your father about the retirement party?" she says.

"No. I have to work myself up for it."

"It's your family. I'll do what you want."

"What do you think we should do?"

"I think we should go. You could you use the sunshine. It's only a weekend, and they would like to see Brett."

"Go where?" says Brett.

"To Florida. To see Dad's parents for your grandmother's retirement."

"Cool!"

"Don't we have games that weekend?" says Charlie.

"Actually, no," says Kate. "We were supposed to play in that MLK Day tournament, but Butch has some kind of reunion."

"Who told you that?"

"Louise. I got roped into a conversation with her because Helen was home sick, and Sal had Dante at *his* hockey practice."

"Where do those people get the money for two hockey players?"

"Between freebies from Butch and Sal's settlement, I think they're pretty set." says Kate. "Ugh. I still cannot believe everyone wanted a game on Christmas night."

"I thought that at first, but really, what are we doing that late, anyway? Listening to your sister-in-law spout off about the pressures of her girls' Irish Dancing? Sitting on the couch, watching *A Christmas Story* for the sixth time in less than twenty-four hours? Having the same conversation with Grandpa over and over again?"

"Nice," says Kate.

"What? I'm just being honest."

"Why are you guys so grumpy?" asks Brett.

There is a collective sigh from the front seat.

"Sorry, bud," says Kate. "We have no reason to be grumpy. We are healthy, and happy, and have plenty of friends and family. Adults get weird on holidays."

"Adults are weird all the time," says Brett.

They pull up to the two-story colonial—its yard peopled with various inflatable reindeer and Christmas characters, and eaves decorated with multi-colored lights. They are the last to arrive, and Kate can see her family in the windows, talking and laughing like actors in a Christmas commercial. Brett leaps from the vehicle—blinky lights on his ugly

Christmas sweater flashing—and runs toward the house. Kate reaches for Charlie's arm.

"Sorry," she says.

"Me too. I need to chill."

"Same."

They get out of the car and, as they enter the house, Kate's brother, Pete, is the first to spot them. He hurls himself at Charlie in a tackle, crushing Charlie against the wall in the foyer.

"Merry Christmas, Bro!" says Pete. "How's hockey season going?"

#####

The volume of the Christmas music, warring with the football game on TV, warring with the noise of humans and the incessantly barking Goldendoodle named Doodlebug, the intense aroma of garlic mashed potatoes and deep-fried turkey, and the heat of his ugly Christmas sweater (a Snoopy and Charlie Brown covered cardigan) make Charlie feel as if the walls are closing in on him. If Amy were here—subjected to this level of sensory abundance—she would be attacking every male in sight.

"I love the ugly Christmas sweater idea," says Kiera, Kate's brother John's wife. "When will we vote on the winner?"

"After dessert," says Colleen, Pete's wife. "The winner will get a gag gift that I hand-selected."

"What if you win?" says Kiera.

"I'm happy to receive this one."

"Can somebody turned that freakin' music off?" says Grandpa. "I can't hear the goddamned game."

189

"Dad," says Kate's mom. "Language."

"Do you know what my father used to say in front of me? He owned a bar in Baltimore—a speakeasy," he leans into Charlie, who somehow always ends up next to Grandpa at family events. "He used to have a lot of sexy dancing girls around…"

"Dad! That isn't true. Great Granddad was a barber."

"That's what you think."

"Hey, Pete," says John. "I hear your boys are going to the championship."

Oh God, here were go, thinks Charlie. He looks at Kate. She rolls her eyes.

"Yes, sirree—fourteen and one was our final record. We won County. Now we're going to States. Right Pete, Jr.!"

"Yeah, dad," says the sixteen-year-old without looking up from his phone.

"We don't allow phones at the table," says Kiera. "It discourages conversation."

"Wait'll you have a teenager," says Colleen. "Then we'll see how that goes."

"Charlie, how are districts looking for Brett's team?" says Pete. "I saw they won that tournament in Detroit, but they had a tough loss recently in their league."

"Where did you see this? Is ESPN covering the Pee Wee Polar Bears hockey team?"

"It's on the Facebook page," says Pete.

"You check the Polar Bears record on Facebook?"

"Well, yeah. Don't you check out Pete Jr's stats?"

"Um…."

"He's new to Facebook," says Kate. "But truly, don't you think this obsession with youth sports out of control?"

"You are all crazy," says Grandpa. "Our kids went to school, did chores, and went to bed at reasonable times. I never had to take a second job to pay for sports travel."

"Who took a second job?" says Kate's dad.

"John did," says Kiera. "And I don't care what any of you say about hockey or football; Irish Dancing costs a fortune."

"The fake hair, the costumes," says John. "The trips to Ireland. Year round."

"You wouldn't complain if it were a boys' sport," says Kiera.

"We're not having this conversation again," says John.

"None of you have any free time," says Kate's mom. "And I can't keep up with your games. If I went to one, I'd have to go to seven, and I just don't have time for that."

"While we're talking about this, ma, it would be nice if you and dad made an effort to get to a championship or two," says Pete.

"Excuse me. Most of your championships are in other states. I'd have to travel, and get a hotel room, and pay for meals, board Doodlebug…"

"She's right, Pete," says Kate's dad.

"Serious competition can only be found when you go outside your market," says Pete. "You've got to travel. But, whatever, if Facebook videos are enough for you…"

"I think it's healthy that Mom and Dad don't feel the need to be at every game," says Kate. "We have a set of helicopter grandparents on our team."

"They go to games in a helicopter?" says Grandpa.

"No, it means they hover," says Colleen.

"It's outrageous," says Kate. "The time spent on youth sports, the trophies, the panoramic posters, the clothing, the fatheads—it's making these kids legends in their own little minds."

"Well said, Katie," says her dad.

"And you don't buy into any of that?" says Pete.

"I do buy into it. I can't fight it. It's the culture. It's like, if you don't do all this for your kid, you're leaving them at a disadvantage, but for what? How many of our kids are going pro?"

"If you had been to one of Pete Jr.'s games," says Colleen, "you'd see it's a possibility."

"Or Kelly and Mara's dancing competitions," says Kiera. "They place in the top thirty almost everywhere they go."

"And what's the future in that?" says John.

"Don't even get me started," says Kiera.

"At least none of you has been jailed," says Grandpa. "I saw a thing on the news last week that a teenaged referee for ten-year-old soccer was attacked at his car after the game by a coach."

"I believe it," says Charlie. "I was reffing a soccer game, and two moms got in a fist fight."

"And don't forget recruiting," says John. "A nine-year old football player just signed with a college team. His trainer was quoted in the article."

"Trainer?" says Kate's father.

Charlie raises his eyebrows at Kate.

"Madness," says Kate's mother.

Grandpa's cheers pull the attention back to the football game on TV. While the table is briefly occupied, Charlie is able to catch his breath.

"You want a beer?" Charlie asks Kate.

She shakes her head no, and starts to argue with John and Pete, while Colleen and Kiera compare their sports expenditures. Charlie rubs Brett's hair on the way out to the garage, but Brett is engrossed in a conversation with Pete Jr's younger brother about the game of Minecraft he's playing at the dinner table.

The garage is cool and pleasant. Charlie stands outside drinking his beer, reveling in the peace. Pete is so intense. He worries he will become that way as Brett gets older. Is he starting to put too much pressure on Brett? Is Brett being negatively affected by the anxiety his hockey team inspires in Charlie, and even Kate? So often they assume Brett isn't listening in the back seat, but every time he pipes up, Charlie is reminded that kids are always watching, taking their cues from the adults around them. And what will that mean when Brett gets older if his whole life he has seen his dad ignore his own parents? They can't be much worse than Kate's family; can they?

Charlie kills his beer, pulls his phone out of his pocket, and calls his father.

"Charles."

"Hey, Dad."

"Are you coming to the retirement party?"

"Yeah, I think so. I just have to check with work. Hey, I was calling to wish you and mom a Merry Christmas."

Charlie's dad makes a grunting noise.

"I know it's been a long time—too long. But I've been thinking about you, and all the time that has passed, and how silly it all was. Is."

Silence.

"And anyway, Merry Christmas."

"You'll let me know if you're coming to the party, right? I need to give a headcount to the caterer."

"Yeah. I'll email you next week."

"Here's your mother."

"Charlie? It's so good to hear from you!"

He feels sick with guilt, and from the lingering dissatisfaction of every conversation with his father.

"It has been too long," he says.

"Did you get the present we sent for Brett?"

"Yeah, he loved the drum set. Well, he will, once I put it together."

"We would love for you to visit."

"We hope to, soon."

"I have to run, Charlie. The turkey's coming out of the oven. Our neighbors are celebrating with us. They're Jewish but their kids don't visit them either, so we're making a new holiday together."

He emits a laugh-like sound, but doesn't know if this is the appropriate response.

"Okay, Happy Holidays," he says. "Bye."

Charlie puts the phone in his pocket as Grandpa throws open the door. "Here he is! He's checking his phone in the garage so Kiera doesn't bitch at 'em for doing it at the table. Charlie, let's go. It's time to vote on the best ugly sweater!"

He doesn't have the energy to protest, and joins the family in the dining room. They fill out their slips of paper, and Kate's mom counts the votes. Kate wins with her vest of fuzzy Christmas balls. She opens the gag gift and unrolls a sheet to reveal a life-sized fathead of Pete Jr. in his football uniform.

"I know you don't approve, but I thought it was funny," says Colleen.

Kate gives a tight smile, and rolls her nephew back up. "Here, Colleen. I know you'll make good use of this."

Colleen takes it without smiling.

Over the next two hours, they go through the ritual of opening presents (*I have a hand mixer; is there a gift receipt? Skullz? Those are lame. Kids only wear Beats. How many pairs of socks do you think one old man needs?*), to stuffing their already full stomachs with pie, to watching *A Christmas Story*, which gets interrupted by an argument between Pete and John about the best college football team, which gets further interrupted by an argument between Pete, Kate, and Charlie about tough versus lenient coaches.

"That Butch guy just sounds 'Old School,'" says Pete. "You coddle Brett too much."

Charlie can tell by his blinking that his eye is twitching, and feels a similar surge of anger to the night he smashed wine all over his parents' dining room. He stands, upsetting Grandpa and Brett's game of chess.

"Damn it!" says Grandpa.

"Dad!" says Brett.

"Sorry. We've got to go."

"Why? The cousins aren't leaving."

Everyone glares at Charlie. Kate must sense that he's about to blow. She stands.

"That's enough," says Kate. "It's getting late, and you have a game tomorrow."

"Games on Christmas," says Pete. "Who's crazy now?"

Charlie rounds up Brett's gifts, ignoring his son's grumbling, and gives his mother-in-law a quick kiss on the cheek.

"I wish you didn't have to run," she says. "I haven't even made coffee yet?"

"And Kelly and Mara were going to do a dance for everyone," says Kiera.

"In that case, you better run," says John.

Charlie persuades Brett to help him load the car, while Kate says her goodbyes and makes her apologies. Charlie fumbles for his keys with shaking hands. His heart races and he feels as if he's going to get sick.

"Look, dad," says Brett. He points to the flip flop family on the back window, where the top of Charlie's shoe likeness has worn away. "You're falling apart."

Chapter Thirty

 Piper Caldwell's Status Update: ⚙

Video: Aiden Skating on Hockey Treadmill

#NHLPrepHasBegun #HockeyStrong

🤍 💬

Justin glares at Piper. She has been drunk for the last forty-eight hours from the series of family and neighborhood holiday parties they have attended. Justin is now faced with carrying around his exhausted daughters—who were supposed to be babysat by Piper's parents until the big Christmas Dinner Fight—at a fucking Pee Wee hockey game on Christmas Day. The icing on the shit cake is watching Piper flirt with their kiddie hockey bully coach to advance her son's place on the team.

Agreeing to this game was a mistake. Canadian lower A hockey players are heads and shoulders above kids at the highest US level. The Canadians are big; they are smart; and —running counter to cliché—they are mean. Bitches like Tina probably thought this would be a fun, little exhibition game they could brag about to their families and post pictures of on social media—BOBBY PLAYING CANADIANS AND HOLDING HIS OWN!—but it has become an old-fashioned ass-whooping.

The second period just ended, and the Polar Bears are losing seven to nothing. His girls are whining and crying. They won't let him put them down, and quite frankly, he doesn't want to. He's afraid they'll toddle over to where their mother mans the music in the scorebox, and realize something is wrong. The three-year-old has started saying, "Why Mommy sick?" when Piper is at her worst. The other kids are silent about it.

How Piper is able to cue up her iPhone hockey mix is beyond him, but he thinks Helen—who's keeping score—must be helping her. When the music plays, Piper dances and twirls around, making a spectacle for all the fans to see. She clearly loves the attention, and seems to think people are laughing with her. Every once in awhile, Piper turns on the microphone to announce another goal, but Helen has wrestled that duty from her after the last goal when Piper had this commentary: "Fuckin' Canadians scored again. Take off, 'eh?!" It was hard to say if Dawn's crazy son or Dante enjoyed Piper's language more. Aiden buried his helmet in his hands.

Justin catches Piper's name in a conversation behind him, and turns his head to see Tina and Bob huddled together near the vending machines. They clearly don't notice him standing there, because Tina is going off about Piper.

"I asked Piper what she was getting Aiden for Christmas, and she never mentioned that treadmill," says Tina.

"So?" says Bob.

"She was clearly hiding it. She doesn't want Bobby to be better than Aiden."

"I don't know if that's true."

It is, thinks Justin.

"It is," says Tina. "She didn't tell me about the special trainer, either. I had to find out from Charlie, of all people."

"Take deep breaths," says Bob. "The upcoming assistant captain announcement has you flustered."

"I just want Bobby to have the very best."

"But aren't those treadmills like twenty grand?"

"I'm sure she got a deal. Besides, the boys can use them through adulthood. Not that they'll necessarily be in the NHL, but you know what I mean."

"Bobby's birthday is in February. I'll put the feelers out."

Justin rolls his eyes.

"Bro," says Sal, joining him. "It doesn't look like everyone's holiday was very merry."

"Why?" says Justin.

"Have you seen Kip's eye?"

"I don't pay attention to Kip."

"Total shiner!" whispers Sal. "The shit must have hit the fan."

"What do you mean?" says Justin, before he can stop himself. He shouldn't encourage Sal.

"I can't be sure, but I'll do a little covert op and circle back with you later."

Shortly into the third period, a Canadian girl who has been chippy with Mike all night boards him, drawing a major penalty for her team and a major tantrum from Mike. Mike charges after the girl, but is held off by the ref. He must have cursed at the guy because now Hank is opening the penalty box door for Mike.

"She has been playing dirty all game!" screams Butch. "She has no skill, so she just throws her weight around. And there's plenty of it!"

The Canadian fans mock him.

"What? Your boys can't take it from a girl?"

"That bitch is no girl," yells Dawn's crazy son.

Dawn holds his shirt when the Canadian parents start yelling back at him.

As the language and the potential for fighting worsens, Justin takes the girls up to the warming room. He climbs the steps and enters the room that overlooks the rink to find Jack—the quiet dad—alone and typing. He briefly glances at Justin, but goes back to work without speaking.

The girls let Justin put them down to play with the disgusting, germy box of toys that has probably been here since the nineties, but he doesn't stop them; fatigue overwhelms his concern for their health. Piper blares The Offspring's *Keep 'em Separated* over the loudspeaker while the ref leans in to tell Helen how to mark the penalties. Justin sits at the window and rubs his face with his hands.

"Wears you down, doesn't it?"

At first Justin thinks he's hearing things, but when he opens his eyes, he sees that Jack is actually speaking to him.

"Yeah," says Justin. "Is that why you don't engage?"

"Yep. Self-preservation. I have an older son, and I went through the whole "team culture" thing with him."

"And you're back for more?"

"It lets us spend time together, so it's a trade off. I'm trying to find the right balance."

The teams have settled down, and the game continues.

Jack's laptop keys begin clicking. Justin finds the sound annoying, but it's better than the cacophony of assholes in the bleachers. He thinks he'll bring earbuds next time. He'll listen to music while he watches.

When Mike gets out of the penalty box, he skates to the bench, and Butch pulls him close, his nose touching Mike's helmet cage. Butch screams at Mike—whether it's for the retaliation and referee name-calling or for getting flattened by a girl, Justin can't be sure. On the next shift, as Mike is about to take to the ice, Butch grabs him by the jersey, whispers something in his ear, and pushes Mike forward. Within the first play, Mike skates toward the girl at lightning speed and checks her—head-first—into the boards.

"Jesus," says Justin.

The girl writhes as her coach crosses the ice to help her. The players take a knee. The Canadian parents scream from the stands.

Mike has to serve a two-and-ten major. The girl is half carried to the bench, her helmet is removed, and an assistant coach looks into her eyes with a flashlight. Within minutes, he motions to her parents and she is escorted from the rink. Soon, the game concludes with the Canadians beating the Polar Bears twelve to zero. Justin gets up to leave.

"See you later," says Justin.

Jack looks up, glasses blue from the screen. "Yeah, see ya."

Justin picks up his girls and starts to go, but his curiosity gets the better of him.

"What exactly do you do that requires you to work so much?"

He can see by the way Jack's face turns red that he's struck a nerve. Jack closes the laptop as if he doesn't want Justin to see, and clears his throat.

"I'm a writer."

Chapter Thirty-One
Two Months to District Playoffs

 #PolarBears Public Page

Photo Album: Elite All Stars Showcase
(#MariotheBeast, Mike, Aiden)
Tagged: Sal Gardenia, Louise Gardenia,
Butch Johnson, Helen Johnson, Piper Caldwell

#HockeyStrong

Charlie can't get out of bed. Every muscle aches, his throat is raw, he burns with fever. The illness has reached its fourth day, and Charlie's worry that he wouldn't be able to go to the New Jersey games is now a reality.

"It has to be the flu," says Kate, sitting on the side of the bed and feeling Charlie's head. "Have you had any ibuprofen lately?"

"I can't remember."

"You need to write it down. You're delirious."

Charlie has a coughing fit.

"If it's the flu, why aren't you sick?" he asks.

"I got a shot, and Brett got the mist at school."

"It's probably tuberculosis from that damned Hank."

"Is he sick?"

"He always has snot running out of his nose. It was worse than ever on Christmas. I'm sure I got it then."

"Your body is telling you to take a break," says Kate, rubbing his arm. "You can use the time off hockey."

"I don't want you and Brett to be alone in Jersey with a psychopath."

"No, you don't want to miss any games."

Charlie doesn't respond. She's right.

"It's only two games: one tonight and one tomorrow morning," says Kate. "It will be good for your mental health to miss them. I promise, I will keep you up to date with texts. But I want you to make a serious effort to rest. And stay away from anything remotely hockey related—including Facebook."

"I will. I'll try."

Brett enters the room holding up his iTouch and trying not to cry.

"What's wrong?" asks Kate.

"I didn't make the All-Star Team."

Charlie sits up in bed. "What All-Star Team?"

Kate tries to usher Brett out of the room.

"Kate, what is he talking about?"

A minute passes, and then she slowly turns. He can see that she doesn't want to tell him, but knows it's inevitable that he'll find out whatever it is she wants to hide. Kate nods at Brett and lets him take the iTouch to show his dad the picture. Mike, Mario, and Aiden are tagged in Mario's Instagram post. The boys wear "All-Star" jerseys and shit-eating grins at an ice house in Rhode Island. Caption: Elite All-Stars Showcase!

"What is this?" says Charlie. "Did you know anything about it?"

"First I've seen it," says Kate.

"Is that why you didn't want me on Facebook?"

"No, Charlie. I just said it's the first time I've seen it."

Charlie thinks Kate might be lying to him. She just told him to stay off social media. She must have known, and knew it would send him over the edge.

"He's not going to Jersey," says Charlie.

Brett starts to cry. Kate grabs the iTouch with a shaking hand. Her face is red.

"Number One: I knew nothing about this "All-Star" Game," she says. "Clearly Butch didn't tell people because he knew it would spark outrage. Number Two: Brett, this is a good life lesson: sometimes it's who you know, not what you can do. Number Three: We have paid for this season in full and like it or not we will see through our commitment, if for no other reason than to show that asshole Butch that we refuse to be broken by him. It eats him alive that you are better than his kid—that's why he chose Mike for this. He chose Mario because Sal is his neighbor. He chose Aiden because his mother flirted with him. Whether he chooses you or not makes no difference. You will never be his underling and after this year, you will never play for that animal again. Do you understand?"

Brett nods. Charlie feels guilty for thinking Kate was lying. He has never seen her so angry—except the time in the parking lot when she went after the mom. That's twice this season that the calmest woman he knows has lost her shit. He feels comforted to know he isn't alone in his spiral into sports parent madness. It's as if Kate has picked up the other side of a heavy weight so he doesn't have to carry it alone.

"I'm sorry," says Charlie. "Brett, your mother is right. Don't let it get you down, buddy. It would have sucked to have to travel with Butch and those people an extra weekend anyway, right?"

Brett shrugs.

"Even if you don't think it would suck, trust me. It would."

"It's not fair," says Brett.

"No, it's not. But we'll learn from this. You keep doing what you're doing. Your worth is clear to the rest of the team, even if it isn't to Butch."

"It's especially clear to Butch," says Kate. "That's why he boxes Brett out every chance he gets."

"It's not basketball, Mom."

"Beside the point."

Brett still scowls, but he has stopped crying.

Charlie kisses his family goodbye, and watches them leave, feeling a new sadness in him. These lessons mark the receding of childhood, the killing of innocence. Charlie wonders if kids this age should even be allowed to play on youth teams if the culture steals the very thing it proposes to support.

#####

TINA: Hard topic on #SportsTaxi today, folks.

BOB: We debated whether we should do it.

TINA: But we decided to. The sad truth is, the ones who should be listening won't be.

BOB: And we can't shy away from the dark underbelly of youth sports.

BOTH: Favoritism.

BOB: Our team had the experience of playing a Canadian Team. It was a privilege to see how a country so enmeshed in the history of hockey approaches the sport at the youth level. Team spirit was contagious.

TINA: Full support on display—in signs, clothing, food and drink.

BOB: There was a real unity there. Something we strive for here in the US, but haven't yet been able to attain. Tina and I have been mulling why this is, investigating, digging around, asking questions, and we've found something interesting.

TINA: We have, Bob.

BOB: Based on our unscientific polling, we have found the satisfaction level of teams where parents are *not* allowed to coach is much higher than those teams with dads—

TINA: Or moms—

BOB: On the bench. Like the Canadian team. The coaches weren't parents; they were paid.

TINA: Parents should support their kids, but only from the stands, separate from coaching.

BOB: It leads to nepotism. Decision-making based on ego and a wish to give an edge to one's own offspring. I've felt guilty for years that my background in football and my high-powered job has prevented me from coaching my son in hockey. But not anymore. I see how it can lead to trouble.

TINA: It requires real self-control. If I could play hockey, I probably couldn't stop myself from sharing my talents with my son and his team through coaching, but I'd like to think I would go the extra mile in trying to be fair to all the kids on my bench.

BOB: You would, Tina. Because it's all about "team" with you. There's no "I" in team.

TINA: And that's a good place to end this podcast.

Pause.

TINA: I can't believe that piece of shit made an Elite All-Star Team and didn't even tell me—the team mom!—or pick our son. All the time I put into arranging tournaments, travel, fundraising. I guess if I don't flirt with him like Piper does, Bobby suffers. That slut probably had sex with Butch to get Aiden on the team.

BOB: Honey, we're still recording.

TINA: Make sure you edit out the end before you post it.

Chapter Thirty-Two

 Piper Caldwell's Status Update:

Merry, Merry!
Upcoming ski trip at peak season,
$5K. New ski equipment for 5 people,
$3K. Wardrobe, $1K.
Time with friends and family: Priceless!

#Blessed

Before Justin can hide, he is caught in Sal's radar. He groans. He and Piper just had a fight about the ski trip with her college roommates and their families she's desperate to join on their only weekend off from hockey. Not to mention the fact that the couples are awful.

"I'm not spending all that money and flying all the way to Utah to be with people I can't stand," he'd said, "and get stuck on kid duty because you're wasted half the time."

"We do this every other year," said Piper. "I'm the only one who hasn't confirmed yet. These are my best friends."

"You haven't seen them in two years. Their husbands are dicks. It's a cock fight over whose wife is the hottest, who makes the most, who has the most beautiful children."

"Well, we win all those categories, so what do you care? Have you seen Rachel's ass since she had Baby #3?"

"I care because you bitches just want the kids to show off at dinner in their matching, monogrammed sweaters, but you have no plan for watching them during the day. The ski trip includes me having to deal with kiddie breakfast and lunch every day, the kiddie pool, kiddie tubing, kiddie sledding, and kiddie skiing lessons while you and your roommates groom yourselves, shop, and drink."

"Then we'll take a nanny with us. Callie and Rachel are bringing theirs."

"We don't have a nanny. We have your mother. And she is not going with us."

"I know someone at the club whose daughter could travel with us."

"No. Even if we had a nanny, I'd have to spend my day with the douchebag club."

"Just out of curiosity, why do you think you're so much better than them? It's not like you lead such a different life than they do."

Justin had told her fuck off at that point. She was still packing herself and the girls for Jersey—and they were running late. Without spending too much mental energy on the decision, he found Aiden, ushered him to the car, and left without saying goodbye. Piper had been blowing up his phone since. He finally had to turn it off and shove it in the glove compartment. His only concern was that Aiden would be upset that Piper wasn't going, but when Justin told him that they would be late if they waited for the girls, the kid actually looked relieved that it was just the two of them.

"Hey, Buddy," says Sal. "You gotta hear this. Remember Kip's Christmas shiner?"

"Not really," says Justin.

"So I get to talking with this Jersey dad—a guy from a team Kip wants Kyle on next year…"

"Wait," says Tina Church, who has wandered over. "Kip is going to drive all the way to Jersey every week for Kyle's hockey?"

"Yeah, who knew Jersey was a hockey hub? It's a triple A team that only practices one week night and does camps and game days all Saturday and Sunday. Juniors scouts come. Big time."

Justin can see Tina's wheels spinning.

"Anyway, this dad knows Kip. Played hockey in college with him. Said he was just as much of a dick then as he is now. He heard through a mutual friend that Lucy gave Kip the black eye."

"What?" says Tina.

"Shhh," says Louise.

"Why did Lucy punch Kip?" whispers Tina.

"He has been having an affair." Sal pauses for dramatic effect. "With a stripper."

"No!" says Tina.

"Not surprising," says Justin.

"And not only that, but Lucy makes the big bucks, and he was using her money to keep this slut in an apartment where they could meet. Have their little trysts."

"Where the hell did you get that word?" says Louise.

"Butch's 'Word of the Day'."

"How did Lucy find out?" asks Tina.

"That retard mixed up Christmas presents. He bought some tacky piece of shit necklace with two hearts. One heart said Kip, the other said Mercedes. Had it all laid out on some lingerie that was about six tit sizes bigger than Lucy's."

Louise stifles a laugh, but Justin can't find any of this funny. That sleezeball has made inroads with his wife. It's humiliating.

Amy creeps up from out of nowhere and smacks Sal on the head.

"Secrets are bad, tattoo man! Fat man!"

"Someone needs to chain Amy to a wall," says Sal.

"I'd cut off Kip's balls," says Louise. "With an ice skate blade. Unsharpened."

Justin moves away from the group while they continue to speculate about how they would handle such a betrayal. He is tired of these people and they haven't even played their games yet. He searches the stands for an ally, but he sees only Henry's grandparents. Kate stands at the far end of the rink. He wonders where Charlie is. Before he can walk over to her, Poo Poo spots him. Justin curses himself for making eye contact—again!—with someone he can't stand.

"Hey, there," says Poo Poo. "Have a minute?"

"Sure."

"Mee Maw saw that pretty hefty piece of training equipment you got for Aiden, and wondered how much one of those things costs."

"Where'd she see it?"

"Facebook."

Fucking Piper. What a show off.

"We got ours used," says Justin. "It was over ten grand."

Poo Poo whistles. "That's what I thought, but Mee Maw said, no way. So my second question: Could Henry get in on that?"

"Excuse me?"

"Look, Henry wasn't chosen for the Elite All-Star Team. Aiden was. Maybe Henry needs a little extra skating practice,

211

though how that could be true is beyond me. I drop him off for hours every weekend. Sometimes he eats his breakfast from the waffle truck and his lunch and dinner from the café! Ha!"

"Doesn't he have food allergies?"

"Yeah, but Mee Maw met with the manager to go through the menu item ingredients and order things Henry could have. You know, women. Overprotective."

Justin remembers the time Piper got drunk at the country club, their littlest fell in the pool, and the lifeguard had to save her. He thinks of how Piper ignores her girls during practices and games, and pushes them off on her parents as much as possible. He might actually loathe his wife. He also loathes this guy who's raising his daughter's kid.

"Did you hear me?" asks Poo Poo. "I wouldn't expect it for nothing. I mean, I trade services with the rink manager to let Henry hang around on the weekends. Does your place of work need snow removal? Does Aiden need rides to practices or games? We can make some kind of deal."

Justin walks away without answering.

Chapter Thirty-Three

 Charlie Miller's Status Update:

Photo: Chicken Soup, crackers, hot tea.
Caption: Sick. Missing Brett's NJ games. Sad.

#GoPolarBears #HockeyStrong

--WHO DOES BUTCH HAVE ON BRETT'S LINE?
texts Charlie.

...

--KATE! I KNOW THE GAME HAS STARTED!
WHY AREN'T YOU KEEPING ME POSTED, LIKE
YOU SAID YOU WOULD???????

--IT STARTED ONE AND A HALF MINUTES
AGO.

--WHO'S ON BRETT'S LINE? DID BUTCH KEEP
THE "ALL STARS" TOGETHER?

--YEP.

--I KNEW IT!

--YOU AREN'T LISTENING TO THE DOCTOR'S
ORDERS.

--YOU AREN'T KEEPING ME POSTED.

--<<Eye-roll Emoji>>

...

--BRETT IN SECOND SHIFT OF THE GAME WITH DOMINIK AND BOBBY. Texts Kate. BRETT IS SKATING WELL. OFFSIDES BY BOBBY. BRETT CHASES PUCK BACK TO DEFENSIVE ZONE. BUTCH SCREAMS AT BOBBY. BOBBY SKATES LIKE FOOT STILL HURTS. BOBBY BENCHED. BRETT DIGS OUT THE PUCK AND SKATES IT DOWN THE ICE. BUTCH WANTS HIM TO DUMP AND CHANGE.

--BRETT JUST GOT OUT THERE!

--33-SECOND SHIFT. THE ALL STARS ARE BACK IN THE GAME.

--ASSHOLE!!!

…

--WHAT'S GOING ON? texts Charlie. KATE. KATE!

--I DO ACTUALLY WANT TO WATCH THE GAME.

--MAYBE YOU COULD CALL ME. REAL TIME IT.

--LIKE AN ANNOUNCER?

--YEAH.

--MAYBE I COULD TAKE VIDEO AND SEND YOU BRETT'S SHIFTS. OR MAYBE THE LOCAL CABLE ACCESS CHANNEL CAN STREAM THE GAME.

--NOT NICE, KATE.

--YOU NEED TO CALM DOWN. I'LL UPDATE YOU WHEN SOMETHING INTERESTING HAPPENS.

…

--ALL STARS JUST SCORED! MIKE WON THE FACEOFF. AIDEN TOOK THE PUCK TO THE CORNER AND CYCLED IT TO MIKE FOR THE SCORE! 1-0 POLAR BEARS!!

--DAMN.

--WE SCORED, CHARLIE.

--I'D RATHER LOSE THAN HAVE BUTCH'S SON
SCORE.

Chapter Thirty-Four

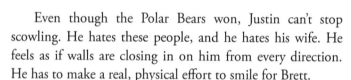

 Piper Caldwell's Status Update: ⚙

Photo Album: Mommy-Daughter Salon Day!
Caption: Mani-Pedis! Smoothies!
Sugar & Spice and everything NICE!

#LoveMyGirls #GirlsWeekend #Blessed
💜 💬

Even though the Polar Bears won, Justin can't stop scowling. He hates these people, and he hates his wife. He feels as if walls are closing in on him from every direction. He has to make a real, physical effort to smile for Brett.

"In celebration of our win," says Tina. "I took the liberty of scouring Yelp for close restaurants with good ratings, and narrowed it down to ones with back rooms we could reserve. Unfortunately, the sports bar back room within walking distance of the hotel is booked for a birthday party, leaving a very fancy Italian place that is probably not a good idea for our boys, and a bit of a risqué establishment that isn't ideal, but will have to do."

"Risque?" says Mee Maw.

"It's just a little sexy, but they have great wings."

"What's it called?"

"The Tilted Kilt."

Sal laughs and high fives Hank. "Yeah, Buddy!"

"Do they have their allergy information online?" asks Mee Maw.

"I don't know," says Tina.

"Do they have a light menu?" asks Helen.

Justin notices that Butch's wife—who is usually make-up-less and clad in #HockeyStrong sweatpants—wears a sparkly sweater and tight, tight jeans. She has long fake nails, blonde highlights in her ashy hair, and her lips appear swollen.

"Um, I don't know," says Tina.

Justin can't stop staring at Helen's plumped lips. What could this new interest in her appearance mean? Is it that reunion they're going to over MLK weekend? Or has Helen noticed Butch ogling Dawn and Piper, and she's now trying to keep up? He shudders.

"Anyway, we have the back room," says Tina. "But the reservation is in ten minutes, so we need to get moving the moment the boys get out of the locker room.

"Aiden and I aren't going," says Justin. "I'm tired."

"Us, too," says Mee Maw. "We don't need a "risqué" establishment with a menu full of things that could kill my grandson."

"Same," says Jack. No explanation needed.

"The Tilted Kilt can't guarantee the room if we don't have at least twenty-five," says Tina, trying to keep the shrillness out of her voice. "Then we'll be stuck out waiting for a big table in the main restaurant. That could take hours."

"We don't want to go either," says Kate. "It's not my scene."

"Come on!" says Dawn Cage. "It's not about you. It's about the team."

She and Hank glare at Kate.

"Thank you!" says Tina. "I don't mean to be rude, but this team has a little trouble coming together. I think all of our stress levels would be lower if we weren't always warring with each other. Sometimes you have to look for the greater good of the group before you look out for yourself."

"We did a podcast about this," says Bob. "I'll have Tina link it up."

Butch walks out of the locker room scratching his crotch.

"Let's eat," he says. "I'm starving."

"There's a little back and forth going on," says Tina. "The team can't agree on a venue."

"Did you make a reservation somewhere?"

"Yes, but not everyone wants to go."

"Where is it?"

"The Tilted Kilt."

"We're going."

There are some mumbles in the crowd, but Butch holds up his hands.

"How about this: If you want your kid to play tomorrow, you'll go. Now, who's gonna be a pain in the ass?"

#####

Justin scans the bar and dining areas of The Tilted Kilt. The place is meant to resemble some kind of sexy Scottish Ale House, with waitresses clad in white collared half shirts, short plaid kilts, and thigh high boots. Three-fourths of the girls have muffin tops lopping over their kilt buckles and chunky thighs bulging over their boot tops. Sal doesn't seem to mind.

"Dude," he whispers. "How can I get Louise outta here so I can…"

He does a pelvic thrusting motion.

Louise slaps him. "I can hear you, jackass. Like any of these chicks would give you the time of day."

"I'll remind you I was quite the catch in my day."

"About a hundred and fifty thousand candy bars ago."

The boys giggle in the corner, where Dante has stuck two hockey gloves up his shirt. He shakes his giant pretend boobs until Mario squeezes them, eliciting a punch in the gut from Dante. They begin to wrestle, and Louise runs over to intervene.

"Sheesh," says Sal. "Next time, dads only!"

A girl with long blue-streaked hair, triple D boobs spilling out of her shirt, and a Rolling Stones mouth and tongue logo tattoo on the side of her ample midsection grabs a pile of menus and tells them the room is ready. Hank wipes his nose and motions for her to go first, nudging Sal and Butch, and pointing to her ass. Helen and Dawn waddle after the men, jeans screaming across their backsides. The rest of the group follows, leaving Justin and Kate in the rear.

"This is awesome," says Kate.

He laughs. If feels as if a thousand pounds of pressure are released from his chest.

"I don't know if I have an appetite," he says. "The visual feast is filling enough."

"There's something to be said for a well-placed tattoo."

"Yeah, and Butch probably likes it. Classic rock. Rolling Stones lips."

"If he can tear his eyes away from Helen's. They're just as plump. And red."

"I thought something was different there. And not in a good way."

They share a laugh and take seats at a table in the corner.

"I'm sorry," says Kate. "I hate to be so nasty, but these people are freaks."

"You don't have to apologize to me," he says. "Hey, why are you solo?"

"Charlie's sick and needed a break, even if he didn't want it. Is that why Piper's not here?"

"No. *I* needed a break."

"Got it."

The waitress gives them menus and mentions that haggis is the special. Tina corners the girl and explains the ordering system with a party this large, and the girl looks thoroughly confused. She finally hands Tina the ordering pad, and Tina takes everyone's order using the jersey number system.

"See," says Tina. "Easy. Then you just have to enter the separate checks at the end."

The waitress rolls her eyes. The beers arrive quickly, thank God, and Justin takes a long drink.

"So what do you think's up with Helen?" says Justin.

"I heard Butch has a high school reunion in PA."

Butch belches from across the room. Beer foam rests in his wooly beard, and his stomach hangs over his sweatpants.

"It's a shame Butch isn't making more of an effort," says Justin.

"I wonder if he'll dress up?" says Kate. "You know he's from the 'If I can't wear camo, I'm not goin' school."

Justin laughs.

"Seriously," says Kate. "I just want to finish this season and get the hell out of here."

"Same. Do you think you'll have Brett try out for the Polar Bears next year?"

"Absolutely not."

"Didn't you and Charlie say that last year?"

"Yeah, and Butch kissed up to Charlie at the very end, and got him fired up about the extra tournament league and districts."

"Same with Piper."

"And then Brett didn't want to leave his line mates."

"Yep."

"And here we are."

"Here we are."

"Eating dinner at The Tilted Kilt."

They knock their glasses together, and take a drink.

"We should coordinate trying out for a new team," says Justin. "Aiden loves playing with Brett."

"Yeah, it's a shame about the lines being changed every other week."

"I don't know what that's all about, but I have a feeling Butch liked the attention from my wife. Piper was drunk and flirting on Christmas."

Kate goes silent. She appears uncomfortable when he disses Piper. He switches tack.

"Is Charlie going to make it through the season?" he asks.

"I hope so," says Kate. "Between Butch's bullying and Hank's nutso behavior in the penalty box…"

"Assaults from Amy…"

"Sal's gossiping…"

"The competition between the parents…"

"I don't know if any of us will make it out alive."

A new waitress appears. She is as skinny and sexless as the other is voluptuous. She has a splattering of pimples across her forehead and her eyes are rimmed in heavy black eyeliner.

"Big Arse Burger," she says in a flat voice.

Justin raises his hand, and she plops it in front of him.

"Fish 'N Chips."

Kate takes the basket and thanks the woman.

Justin is glad he left Piper at home. She'd be complaining about the venue, the greasy food, the cramped quarters. Kate looks over at Brett to see if he's all set, and he gives her a thumbs up. She smiles and turns back to Justin.

"This isn't so bad," he says, lifting his burger.

Kate takes a bite of fish. "Surprisingly tasty."

"I don't mean the food," he says. "Hanging with you. You're laid back. I like that."

"Ah, surely you remember me going after the woman in the parking lot whose kid called Brett a cherry-picker."

"Okay, maybe not laid back, but cool. Just the right kind of crazy."

#####

Justin noticed that Kate got quiet during the rest of the team dinner, and she clearly wanted to go up to her room when they got back to the hotel, but Brett begged her to stay up a little longer so he could join his teammates in some knee hockey.

"Please! Just one game!"

"Don't you ever get tired of hockey?"

"No!"

She checks her watch.

"ONE game. ONE. And you are to give me no crap when it's time to go up."

"Thank you! Thank you, thank you!" He kisses her and joins his teammates in front of the broken fireplace."

Justin and Kate join an assortment of team parents at the hotel bar. The bartender—a guy with an earring, a mullet, several missing teeth, and a Bon Jovi tee shirt ripped at the sleeves revealing disappointing arms—plays eighties hairband music. He vapes between pours and launches into air guitar at random intervals.

"What are you all doing here?" he asks.

"Our boys play for an elite travel hockey team," says Tina.

"Bantams?"

"Pee Wees," says Justin.

"They have you all traveling at their age?" says the bartender.

"Oh, yes," says Bob. "It starts earlier and earlier."

"Huh."

Kate holds out her hand to the bartender, and he shakes it. "Kate," she says.

"Hull," he says.

"Like the famous hockey player?" says Justin.

"Yeah, my dad named me after Bobby Hull."

"We have a Bobby, but he's named for Bobby Orr," says Tina.

"Mario the Beast was named after Mario Lemieux!" says Sal. "Come to think of it, most of our kids are named after hockey players!"

"Or brands," says Bob. "Franklin."

"Ha!" says Sal.

"Wild," says Hull.

223

"Did you play?" asks Justin.

"Yeah," says Hull. "Still do when I can, but I had a couple of knee replacements, so not as much as I'd like."

"Oh my," says Bob. "Not quite the padding back then the way they have now, eh?"

"Padding was okay, but my body just shut down after that third year in the NHL."

The group goes silent.

"Wow," says Kate. "Who did you play for?"

"New Jersey Devils," says Hull.

Justin's underarms begin to sweat. He is suddenly parched. He drains half his beer.

"Awesome," says Kate.

"Awesome until that knee replacement," says Hull. "Then I got hooked on narcotics. Then heroin. The rest is history. Clean and sober now for seven years."

"Yeah, Buddy," says Sal, high-fiving Hull. "I was using some of the fun pharma back in my day, too. Bodybuilder."

"No way! Win any belts?"

"Sixteen. You all wanna see what I used to look like?"

Justin's mind stutters over the fact that an ex-NHLer is tending bar at their crappy motel. All the time his parents must have spent. All the money!

Sal holds his phone so they can all see a picture. There is a Schwarzenegger-like, rat-tailed, leathery man whose only resemblance to the portly bald guy sitting with them are the tattoos. Kate leans in and squints, then looks at Sal.

"Huh? Huh? What do ya' think?" he asks, toothy grin extending from ear to ear.

"Look at you, you hunk!" she says.

Louise snorts.

Justin sees that Tina Church is flustered. Her face has turned red and Bob whispers in her ear. He requests a water from Hull. When the water arrives, Tina drinks it so fast dribbles run down her face and onto her Polar Bears CHURCH 99 rugby-style shirt.

Sal calls the boys over to meet Hull. He finds an NHL picture of him online, and the boys ooh and ahh and start asking a million questions.

"Did you score any goals in the NHL?" asks Brett.

"Forty."

"No way!"

"Cool!" says Mario.

"Why'd ya stop?" asks David.

"Injury."

"I have an injury," says Bobby. "I'm playing on a broken foot."

"No you're not," says Tina. "It's healed."

"Mom, it still hurts. I have to take four ibuprofen just to get through each game."

"Enough."

"Any concussions?" asks Aiden.

"Six."

"Whoa."

"Yeah, but I don't think it really did anything bad. They were spaced out over a couple years."

Bang Your Head starts playing.

Hull and the kids do just that.

With each beer, the mood lightens. In Kate's company, Justin is able to forget Piper, Butch, and the troubling feelings stirred up by hanging out with a loser who used to play for the NHL. Because Brett and Aiden have *just-one-*

more-gamed them to death, they are the last parents left at the bar. Skid Row's *I Remember You* plays.

"This one seems to really touch Hull's heart," says Kate.

"His eyes are closed, while he mouths the lyrics," says Justin.

"One of the all-time great rock ballads. I can remember Friday nights at the ice rink, couples skate with Matthew Simpson, thrilled that he didn't know I'd written his name in a heart on my forearm because my bomber jacket covered it up."

"Wow. You and Hull are both going to start singing."

"I'd need more beer for that."

"Buy you one more?" asks Justin.

"No, thanks. I don't want any pictures on Facebook tomorrow."

"Hey, easy there."

"Your dancing with Bob on the skee ball lanes pictures were my favorites," she says.

"Better than *body shots* with Bob."

"Did it get to that?"

"I was about one pitcher away."

"And Charlie thinks these things are no fun."

Brett cheers when he scores. Aiden tackles him, and they begin wrestling.

"It's great for Aiden to have a guy to hang with," says Justin. "Our house is so friggin' female. No offense."

"I understand."

"We have white carpet. White countertops. White walls. It's like a museum. Aiden is only allowed to play hockey in the basement."

"At least it looks nice for company. In our house you can't walk five steps without tripping over hockey gear, soccer balls, running shoes, art books."

"That sounds awesome."

Kate laughs, but not easily. She grows quiet. Justin wonders what she's thinking. Maybe that it's not awesome with a neurotic mess like Charlie around? He reaches for her arm. She pulls back.

"Just trying to check the time on your watch," he says.

"Sorry," she says. "I was lost there for a minute."

"I'd like to get lost with you."

It's out of his mouth before he can stop it, but he's glad. There is definitely something vibing between them. He doesn't know if he'll act on it, but he's more than willing to take it to the line. Justin turns his gaze from her arm to her face, expecting to find his sentiment matched. Instead, Kate sits up straight; her eyes are narrowed. She looks as if she's on alert. Did he misinterpret her? He should down-shift.

"Have you talked to Charlie since the game?" he says.

"Yes. He wishes he could be here. How about Piper?"

"She's been blowing up my phone. The girls were all supposed to come but we had a big argument, so Aiden and I bailed."

Kate doesn't ask what the argument was about. He keeps talking.

"Piper is trying to get me to commit to this damned ski trip she takes with her bitchy friends and their dickhead husbands every other winter. Four miserable days with people I can't stand."

"Oh my."

"It's horrible. It's like a photo shoot of a Vineyard Vines catalogue."

She laughs, relaxes her posture. Good. He continues.

"Corduroys, bowties, monograms, martinis. Fancy dinners."

"Yeah, who would want all that when you could have warm up pants and fast food and Hull—at the Days Inn Motel—pouring your drinks?"

"Hey, beers with a cool girl beats the ski trip any day."

She's quiet again. Stiff.

"One more drink. Come on," he says. "The boys are happy. The beer is cold. Skid Row's on. We're free from our spouses."

Kate stands.

"Brett," she says. "Time for bed."

"Oh, man," says Brett.

"Now."

Chapter Thirty-Five

 #PolarBears Public Page

SportsTaxi Episode #6:
What's Your Backup Plan?

#GoPolarBears #HockeyStrong

TINA: Hey, #SportsTaxi fans, Tina and Bob here, and we're going to be discussing a very important topic today:

BOTH: The back-up plan.

BOB: Even though Junior might appear to be on the NHL track, he can get derailed.

TINA: Things can sideline your child's sports career any step of the way.

BOB: Injuries, missed chances, bad team politics…

TINA: Drug abuse, coach abuse, being accused by females of roofie-ing their drinks…

BOB: Car accidents, bus accidents, plane crashes…

TINA: At any moment, all the hard work, time, and money can be rendered useless, and if your child doesn't have Plan B for what to do with his spare time—

BOB: Or his life—

TINA: If he gets sidelined, it will all be for nothing. The sports trainers. The extra lessons. The team dinners and travel expenses.

BOB: Tina, I can see you're getting emotional. Don't fight it. The struggle is real.

TINA: Sorry, fans. Tough week of seeing tough things. But the good that has come of it has led me to think hard about budgeting for other areas of interest outside of sports.

BOB: Everyone you meet—from a former bodybuilder, to a coach, to a bartender—is put in your life for a reason, if you are willing to learn.

TINA: And we have learned. In fact, this afternoon our son is meeting with a science tutor.

BOB: And not because he struggles in school—quite the contrary.

TINA: No siree, he's working with a leading scientist from the Smithsonian Institute to help stimulate his inborn affinity for all things science related.

BOB: He's starting with physics as it relates to hockey, but soon, he'll take on other subjects.

TINA: Biology is up next, and you never know where that could lead.

BOB: Pre-Med anyone?

TINA: Sports Med, for sure.

BOB: The point is, no matter what happens, Bobby will come out on top because we have made a back-up plan.

TINA: Have you made a back-up plan for your child?

#####

The Millers finish an episode of #SportsTaxi in the rental car just as they're pulling into the hotel for Charlie's mom's retirement dinner. The podcast has become their new obsession. They love it. They live for it. It has helped them immeasurably because it is a reminder not to take one minute of all this seriously. Kate has taken to egging on Bob and Tina, thanking them for the podcast, telling them how much they enjoy it. The Churches don't seem to understand they are the butt of a joke.

"Have we made a back-up plan for our twelve-year-old?" says Kate.

"They are so weird," says Brett.

"Totally," says Kate.

"What is your back-up plan, *Junior*?" says Charlie. "If you don't make it to the NHL."

"Easy! President."

"Quick, Charlie," says Kate. "Start calling Capitol Hill. Get him an internship."

Charlie laughs.

Kate was pleased that Charlie admitted the break from hockey was just what he needed. Kate and Brett were able to spend quality time together, and once Charlie felt better, he used the free time to exercise, cook healthy meals, and catch up on the household chores he had been neglecting. He had clean gutters, a lawn free of the leaves he had never raked, and almost a cord of firewood chopped. Charlie also grew a beard, which Kate thinks is hot, and he reported that his eye hadn't twitched in forty-eight hours.

"We need to listen to the last episode," says Kate.

"I think we're caught up."

"No, we missed the one about favoritism."

"How'd we do that?"

"Because we have lives outside of hockey and Facebook."

"Not really."

Kate's phone buzzes. She checks it and suddenly feels as if someone has opened an ice rink door in her face.

"What's wrong?" Charlie asks.

"Nothing," she says. "Brett, your grandparents are going to be really happy to see you. It has been so long."

Charlie keeps trying to catch her eye, so she turns her gaze out the window.

"Kate?"

He will find out eventually, but why did the text have to come now—when they just arrived in Florida, and the sun is just beginning to thaw them out? Kate waits a few moments before answering. When she does, her voice comes out with a false note of brightness.

"It's fine. Butch has just set up a game this weekend."

"What? Doesn't he have that reunion?"

"The reunion is on Saturday. He got free ice time on Sunday, and wants to use it."

"Aw, man," says Brett.

"Who cares," says Charlie. "I've seen the benefits of breaks from hockey."

Kate wishes it were so simple. She stays quiet for a moment.

"What?"

"He mentioned that anyone who doesn't make the game a priority will miss the first period of their next league game."

There is a pause. Kate waits for the tirade against Butch to begin, but Charlie remains strangely calm.

"So what," he says. "I'm not going to let Butch get to me anymore. He has way too much control over our lives. So what if you sit out a period, Brett."

"I hate getting benched!"

"I know, but he didn't say it would be for a whole game. He's just being a jerk because he knows we're away. I forbid anyone in this car to allow Butch to make us miserable. How can any of us be grumpy in all this sunshine? In January!"

"Wow, Charlie," says Kate. "I'm impressed."

They turn their attention back to the present, and as they turn up the palm tree lined driveway to the hotel, they ooh and ahhh over the grounds. The place is beautiful. The people are beautiful. The sunshine glinting off the water flowing from fountains and swimming pools—there are three—is beautiful. They find a parking spot near the lobby. They step out of the car and into the warm embrace of the tropical afternoon. In January!

"This is heaven. We're moving," says Charlie.

"I'm in," says Kate.

"Can I play hockey here?" says Brett.

"Yes," says Charlie. "I was looking up teams online. They have tons!"

"Really?" says Kate.

"Coached by ex-NHLers, nonetheless!"

"Ah, people who have made it, so they won't take out their unrealized sports fantasies on children," says Kate.

"Exactly."

"I'm in," says Brett.

As the Millers walk to the lobby to check in, Charlie's phone buzzes. He looks at it and holds it up so Kate can see.

Butch.

--CALL ME ASAP.

#####

233

The Boca Room of the restaurant for Charlie's mother's retirement party overlooks a glassy bay reflecting a waxing gibbous moon. The tinkle of forks on plates, clinking glasses, and laughter run like an undercurrent to the soft jazz piano playing in the corner. Brett has made fast friends with distant cousins, and they are off having adventures.

"Crab puff, sir?" asks a waiter.

Charlie's mother motions to him from across the room to meet yet another group of strangers. It seems that Charlie's parents have gone on with their lives without him in it, and though he knows he should be glad for them, he has the jealous pang of a peevish child. His parents had moved down to Florida when his dad retired from the military, but his mother quickly learned that being with her tightly wound spouse—twenty-four seven—wasn't going to work. She found herself a part-time job as an admin at a law firm, but is now ready to surrender her days to golf and Bunco.

Charlie finishes his crab puff, picks up his beer, and scans the crowd for Kate. In a midnight blue sleeveless dress and sparkly earrings, she is easy to find. He joins her by the piano, kisses her cheek and puts his arm around her waist.

"You are beautiful."

"You're not so bad yourself," she says, running her hand over his new beard.

"I hate to interrupt the romance, but my mother beckons," he says.

"Happy to join her."

"Why do you sound so pleased to meet more strangers?"

"I'd be pleased to meet an alligator. Florida is heaven. Why don't we live in a place that feels like this all year?"

"I don't know."

They join Charlie's parents.

"I'd like you to meet our Bunco friends," says Charlie's mother. "Ruth and Daniel, Christina and Jim, Lilith and Walter. This is our son, Charlie. He's an art teacher, which keeps him very busy since he never comes down to visit us."

"Well, that and youth hockey," says Kate.

"We were just discussing moving here," says Charlie.

"My kids always say that," says an old lady. "Then they leave and forget us."

"Kate works for a recruiting firm," says Charlie's mother.

"A recruiting firm," says one of the old men. "What's that?"

"It's some group that finds professionals for job openings," says Charlie's dad. "One of these middle men outfits, where a company pays a guy to find a guy to pay."

"Hmmm…"

"Then there's Charlie. Teaching art. Did you ever hear of a guy teaching art to middle schoolers?"

The old men shake their heads.

The temperature in the room seems to have spiked. Charlie pulls at his tie and takes a drink. He looks at Kate who, mercifully, remains calm.

"When I retired from the armed forces," continues Charlie's dad, "I told Charlie he needed to seriously look at his contribution to the world. Who wants to spend most of their waking hours working for a place that doesn't manufacture anything or keep societal order or prepare you for the hard stuff of life."

"I think we can all agree that passionate educators motivating our youth and inspiring their creativity is an extremely valuable contribution to society," says Kate.

"And it makes me happy," says Charlie.

"Happy," says his father. "Your generation is all about doing 'whatever makes you happy.' Happy isn't a destination: it's a state of mind."

"Which is why your mother was such a treasured admin all those years," says one of the old ladies. "She kept the partners at her firm positive, organized, and productive. The same way she keeps us on task at Bunco and our Ladies Book Club. I don't know how we'd get along without her."

"You are too kind, Ruth," says Charlie's mom. "Charlie and Kate are very independent. They like to do things all alone. No help from anyone."

"Just wait," says one of the old men. "The independent ones are the first who'll come calling when they need money. Like our boy, right Lilith?"

Charlie motions for another beer and notes with dismay that they are only one hour into the four-hour event. Kate squeezes his hand.

"It's so lovely to be in Florida during the winter," says Kate. "We spend most of our week nights and weekends in ice rinks. I've been shivering since October. We might actually get back here in March if our son's hockey team makes it to district playoffs."

"So much time and money," says Charlie's dad. "Kids sports have become outrageous!"

"Their parents need to get their own interests," says an old lady.

Charlie's eye begins to twitch.

"What's with your eye?" asks his father.

Charlie's phone rings.

"And technology!" says an old guy over the ringing. "You can't have a whole conversation anymore without someone's phone going off. I miss the old days when you couldn't carry these damned things around everywhere."

"My daughter made me get on Facebook to see pictures of my granddaughters' cheerleading competitions."

"Made up like little prostitutes, if you ask me."

While the Bunco group continues to complain, Charlie looks at his phone. It's Butch. He hits "decline."

"You never called him?" whispers Kate.

"No. I'm not at his beck and call."

"I support that. As long as you're prepared for Brett suffering the consequences."

"What, you think I should have called him?"

"I don't know; maybe. I mean, any personal contact has the potential for improving your relationship."

"What?"

"If he made an effort to call me, I might have picked up the phone."

"Don't confuse me, please. I'm not in the mood."

"I'm not trying to confuse you; I'm trying to figure him out."

Charlie's eye twitches. His phone rings again.

"Answer," says Kate.

"Isn't he supposed to be at a reunion?"

"Find out!"

Charlie groans, but answers. The connection is bad and it's hard for him to hear.

"Wait, I need to step outside," says Charlie.

He makes his way outside, where Brett and the other kids at the party run up and down the deck. Brett waves at Charlie.

"What's up, Butch?"

"I need a headcount for tomorrow's game."

"Aren't you supposed to be at a reunion?"

"I am, but I also have responsibilities that need taken care of. Will Brett be there?"

"No, I'm in Florida for my mother's retirement party. We've had this planned since we saw the open schedule."

"In the letter I gave you on the first day of pre-season camp, bullet point six said to be ready at a moment's notice. That to play triple A hockey means to be on call. Even if a weekend appears to be open. Did you miss that?"

"No, I didn't. But family comes first."

"The Polar Bear family comes first," said Butch. "I've made that clear. Brett is the only one who won't be there."

"Aiden won't be there. The Caldwells are on a ski trip."

"Justin just texted me. He and Aiden are flying home early to make the 3 PM game."

Charlie's stomach clenches. He has a fleeting thought that they could switch his flight to get Brett home on time, but then he shakes his head. No. He told his parents they would join them for breakfast. It would be wrong to cancel. He is not Butch's bitch.

"How do you think it will make Brett feel to be left out on Sunday?" says Butch. "Did you know that the local television news will be coming? They are doing a story on the rise in popularity of youth hockey, and they picked the Polar Bears to showcase. How do you think Brett will feel to see the Instagram posts and videos from the news? How do you think he'll feel to be benched for the first period of the following game because his father doesn't have his priorities straight."

"Just you wait a minute…"

"No, you wait. From day one, I have had nothing but attitude from you—a guy who has never played hockey, who has never been in the trenches, yet who thinks he can lead better than a man who has been on skates as long as he could walk."

"I don't presume to tell you how to coach because I think I know more about the game, but I sure know about kids, and…"

"Kids! I've raised two boys, and they are upstanding citizens who respect adults. You have no respect for anyone. You bitch with Hank over the penalty box, you judge other parents for their investments in their kids' talents, and you hate me because I am the head coach of the most successful youth hockey club in Polar Bear history."

"If you think I am jealous of *you* in any way…"

"There it is again: your judgment. You think you're better than me because I don't wear a tie to work, but let me tell you, I do more good for families by leading sports programs than you'll ever do in your little finger-painting class."

Charlie trembles with rage, but he cannot erupt because Brett's eyes are on him.

"Charlie!" His father is at the door. "If you can tear yourself away from your cell phone, your mother is about to make a speech."

His father leaves, and Brett motions for Charlie to follow. Charlie puts up his finger to show he'll be along in a minute. Once Brett is inside, Charlie begins to speak again.

"Butch. This call is finished."

"Fine. You be done. But make sure you're man enough to explain to Brett that YOU are the reason he's missing out on the TV news and the first period of the next game."

Charlie feels like he's going to be sick. He cannot give into Butch. He cannot leave when he told his parents he'd stay for breakfast, as miserable as that is shaping up to be. But Brett would want to go home—he would want to be with his team—the team whose success he is such a part of. Charlie rubs his face with his hands.

"Charlie," says Kate from the doorway. "Your mom wants us up there for her speech."

He hangs up, shoves the phone in his pocket, and returns to the party.

Chapter Thirty-Six

 Piper Caldwell's Status Update:

Fire roaring in our cabin, toasted marshmallow martinis, gentle snow, good friends.

#Blessed

"Come on, Justin. Just one picture of the five of us together," says Piper.

"No. No more pictures."

"We don't have any of the family in front of the fireplace!"

"We got pictures at the airport, the ski slopes, the reindeer breakfast, the bonfire. We don't need one in front of the fireplace."

"Everyone is wearing their coordinating sweaters."

"You aren't wearing a sweater!"

"My blouse matches the colors."

"I'm tired of posing for your Facebook feed."

"Come on! Callie will be here any minute to take the picture."

Piper thrusts the sweater at Justin, but he refuses to take it.

"I'm not posing for any more of your fake happy life photos."

"It's not fake! We are in a winter paradise with beautiful, successful people!"

"This trip has been misery from the two-hour airport delay that started it, to the first night at dinner when we couldn't get a reservation at "the" restaurant until 8:30 and the kids were melting down, to the hangovers, to the shithead husbands who think nothing of getting handsy with you, especially that nasty banker, Cortland. Where do people even get names like Cortland?"

Piper groans. "Give me a break. What? You'd rather be in a foul, smelly hockey rink with rednecks and freaks, freezing our asses off, in an endless cycle of taking the girls to pee in disgusting public bathrooms."

"At least I wouldn't have to get dressed up for cocktails in premier lodge suites, where we'll have to continue to hear about the wildly successful businesses of your sorority sisters' husbands, the perfect academics of their children, and the pro athletes they all think they're raising."

Since she doesn't react well to wine, Piper has been avoiding it, but it's all they have left in the liquor stash, so she's diving in. She just opened her second bottle of sauvingnon blanc, and she dares him to say a word, especially after his whiskey bender last night.

"Oh, great!" he says.

"What now?"

"Butch scheduled a fucking game for Sunday, and anyone not there will get benched at the next league game."

"That isn't fair! That game wasn't on the calendar!"

"You know he said to be ready at a moment's notice."

"Whatever. Who cares?"

"Who cares? Aiden, that's who cares. If we hadn't gone on this trip, it wouldn't be an issue! You don't care about hockey—only glory. Notoriety. Likes on Facebook."

"That is not true. I have taken Aiden's career very seriously since he was a mite!"

"Career?"

"Yes, career. I want our children to be successful people."

Piper's phone pings.

"Ugh, Callie's on her way. Please!"

"I'm not wearing that goddamned monogrammed plaid sweater."

"Come on!"

"What don't you understand about "no"?"

She types a message on her phone, and glares at him when she finishes.

"I told Callie never mind because you're not feeling well," says Piper. "I'm sure she sees right through the lie. You're such a child."

"That's because I've been on duty this whole fucking trip. Just like I knew I would."

"That is not true! I took the girls for chocolate pedicures yesterday!"

"Are you serious? Spa treatments for yourself when you allow the girls to tag along is your definition of duty?"

"They were a handful, Justin. It's not easy to keep two girls quiet in a spa! You should have seen the looks we got from some of the older women."

"Poor Piper," he says. "How do you manage? And not a nanny in sight to help."

"Fuck you."

She is taken aback by the look of pure hatred on his face. She steps toward the settee for balance, while he pulls off his bowtie.

"What are you doing?" she says. "You at least need to keep that on for the cocktail party. Cortland said you have to wear a tie and jacket tonight!"

"Screw Cortland. He's all I've heard about this trip."

"Please, Justin."

"No, it sounds like you are spending more time with Rachel's husband than you are with your so-called best friend."

"That's ridiculous! I'm trying to get to know him. I told you they're moving to our area."

"If you think I'm going to socialize with him once he moves close to us, you are sadly mistaken."

"This new jealousy thing is so unattractive. Where is Old Justin?"

"He's looking for Old Piper. Can you point him in the right direction, or are you too drunk to see straight."

"I'm not drunk!"

"Yet. A half hour in the lodge suite with Cortland should be enough time."

"Do you ever think maybe I drink because you make me so uncomfortable? You've been such a drag this trip. I'm so tired of making excuses for you."

"You won't have to tonight. I'm not going."

"What?"

"I can't take it any more."

"You know what. Good. I'll just tell everyone you're sick. Then I won't have to deal with you sulking, embarrassing me."

"You don't have to deal with me anymore at all."

"What are you talking about?"

"I want a divorce."

Piper stares at him in shock. A moment of sadness passes over her like a wave, but leaves only rage in its wake. She throws her wine glass at him. He moves just in time for it to shatter against the wall of their master suite.

Chapter Thirty-Seven

 #PolarBears Public Page ⚙

LOOK WHO MADE ASSISTANT CAPTAIN:
#MARIOTHEBEAST
Tagged: Louise Gardenia, Sal Gardenia

#GoPolarBears #HockeyStrong
💜 💬

The Millers arrive during the National Anthem. Charlie leans over and places his hands on his knees to catch his breath, while Kate presses Brett's helmet on his head and pulls his skates out of his bag. When the song ends, Brett opens the door and skates across the ice to join his team on the bench. Charlie and Kate walk over to the boards where Tina and Bob stand. They collapse against the glass and exhale.

"Just made it," says Kate.

"It's a shame you couldn't get here an hour ago for warms ups," says Tina. "You know how Butch is about people missing that."

"I would think he would appreciate the effort we made to get home from Florida."

"It cost us five hundred bucks to change our flights," says Charlie.

"And we couldn't sit together," says Kate.

"And I'm pretty sure my parents will never speak to us again for hurrying through the big breakfast they planned for us this morning."

"Stupid idiots!" yells Amy.

Amy's right, thinks Kate.

The game begins. Bobby and Aiden head out with Brett following, but Butch puts out his arm, blocking Brett. He motions for Mike—who now has a large C stitched on his jersey—to take the ice.

"What the hell?" says Charlie.

"Calm down," says Kate.

"All the trouble we went to get him here and Butch is benching him!" says Charlie.

He starts forward but Kate holds him back.

"Just wait a minute," says Kate. "What are you going to do now that the game has started? Butch might just have the lines mixed up. He's been doing that."

"No, he's fucking with us."

"Charlie!"

"After all we went through. And where are the fucking TV cameras?"

Sal meanders over, clearly drawn by the stink of controversy.

"They cancelled," says Sal.

"What?" says Charlie.

"Picked the Ice Dogs instead. Butch thinks the coaches' wife has an in at the TV station. He's pissed."

"*He's* pissed! Do you know what we went through to get here today?"

"Take a chill pill, dude," says Sal. "It's only youth hockey."

"Only! You're one to—"

Kate shushes Charlie.

"I see Mike has a C on his jersey," says Tina, interrupting in a trembling voice. "When did Butch make him captain?"

"After the All-Star game," says Sal. "Mario and Aiden have A's. You see? They're his assistant captains."

Tina's face turns red and she squeezes her hands into fists. She's shaking all over.

We are all losing it, thinks Kate.

"Butch has a lot of nerve," says Tina.

"Honey," says Bob.

"No, I've been silent for too long," says Tina.

Sal and Louise stare at Tina with barely restrained amusement.

"This may seem funny to you," says Tina, "but that's because your kid has the A. Why does Mario get an A over Bobby?"

"Tina."

"No, Bob. I'm serious. Where are the criteria? Why does Butch get to decide? Was there even a vote?"

"There was, actually," says Louise. "The boys voted for it in the locker room after practice one night."

"Oh, you expect me to believe that the boys voted Mike —the kid who hurts the team over and over again with his dirty penalties and unsportsmanlike conduct—the captain? No way."

"I'm sorry," says Bob. "Tina's a little tired today,"

"I am tired. Sick and tired. You know, I have judged the Millers all season for their aloofness."

"Hey!" says Kate.

"But you're on to something," she continues. "You see this club for what it is."

"And what is that?" asks Sal. He leans in, eager.

Kate can see that Tina is losing her nerve. Sal will report every word back to Butch and it will hurt Bobby's playing time.

"Never mind."

"No, go on," says Sal. "Get it out."

"I think what Tina is experiencing is the classic late-season slump," says Bob. "It's common in players of all levels —where they hit a bit of burn out, which unmoors them. It must be true for parents as well. Especially at the triple A level. Especially when they are as passionate and dedicated as Tina is."

Louise snorts and turns her attention back to the game.

"Come on, honey," Bob says, massaging Tina's shoulders. "Let's sit down. Maybe the air will be less charged if we get a little further from the ice. Right, Sal?"

"Yeah. Buddy." Sal's voice holds none of the usual enthusiasm.

#####

In spite of what she initially thought, Kate realizes the hockey break wasn't good for Charlie, nor was escaping to warm weather. It was like being in remission from cancer: it's much worse when it comes back.

Kate leads Charlie to the smelly, concrete stairwell beneath the warming room.

"I can't believe this," Charlie says, ranting the whole way. "Brett benched! After all we went through to get here!"

"We were fools to go through all that."

"If we'd bagged the breakfast, we would have been here earlier. I could have gotten the eight a. m. flight. And much cheaper!"

"You are not going to blame me for this," she says. "Your parents invited sixteen people. We were the guests of honor. It was rude enough we had to leave an hour into it."

"Like I said—we should have bagged it altogether. Then we wouldn't have had to deal with their disappointed stares and nasty sports parent comments."

"They have a point, Charlie."

"You told me to take the call from Butch! Don't pretend you didn't want to come home when you heard about the TV news."

He's right. But it was a lapse in judgment.

"It gave me pause," says Kate. "For Brett's sake. But it was a mistake."

"This is all for Brett's sake!"

"Is it? Do you think Brett enjoys watching his parents argue? The constant tension. Rushing from hotels to airports to ice rinks—where he might not get to play—when he could be playing on the beach?"

"We asked him and he said he would be sad to miss the game."

"He's a kid! He would eat ice cream for breakfast, and pick his nose, and watch horror movies until three in the morning, if we let him!"

"But if he saw the pictures on Instagram--"

"We should have decided for him: family first. Even if that family is crotchety and difficult. Everything about this team is crotchety and difficult. What kind of message are we sending?"

'Loyalty. Commitment. Hard work even when it isn't fun. All the things you said before Jersey."

"You don't believe any of that with regards to these people."

"Well, there's not a damned thing we can do about it at this point. Brett would be miserable not playing hockey. I should have switched him to the Ice Dogs earlier this year."

"If you think the culture at the Ice Dogs is any better, you're crazy. Do I need to remind you of the goalie's mother?"

They get a glimpse of Amy rushing toward the door to the stairwell through the small, diamond shaped window, and flatten themselves against the wall in the shadows so she doesn't see them. Amy puts her eyes up to the window and glances left and right before hurrying away.

"This has to be a new low," says Kate.

"It can always get worse."

"No, hiding from an autistic girl and arguing in a dark stairwell is pretty bad."

"Worse than you confronting the woman in the parking lot?"

"Yeah. We were on the same side then."

Charlie rubs his face and exhales.

"Less than two months," he says. He takes her hand.

"We can do this," she says. "And when we finish, we'll be stronger for it."

"Or we'll be in jail."

"We'll take Brett on a vacation with no hockey families or dysfunctional families or maybe people of any kind. The Galapagos."

"Maybe he'll want to become a marine biologist."

"I can ask Tina who they got from the Smithsonian to tutor Bobby."

Charlie lets go of her hand.

"Kidding, Charlie. That was a joke."

Chapter Thirty-Eight
One Month to District Playoffs

 #PolarBears Public Page

#SportsTaxi: Favoritism
Tagged: Piper Caldwell, Butch Johnson
468 Likes, 110 Shares

#HockeyStrong

Justin is surprised to see the decorating committee has done an admirable job of making the rink Butch has managed right into the gutter look somewhat presentable. From the grimy ice panels to the rusty bleachers to the cinderblock walls, white lights hang from every available stringing surface and are reflected in the glassy sheet of ice. The row of broken vending machines is covered with a plastic wall mural of the Las Vegas Skyline, and the area by the pro shop is full of tall cocktail tables covered in black, red, and white tablecloths, with playing cards sprinkled throughout. There are bacon sliders, clams casino, steak and chicken kabobs, seven layer dip, cupcakes decorated with card suits, and a martini bar. Frank Sinatra croons over the sound system.

Still, nothing can distract him from the fact that he is here, in a place he hates, with a drunken woman he's about to divorce. When Piper and the girls returned from the ski trip, she said nothing about the fight. She pretended as if it never happened. But she has been wasted ever since. He has already set up a meeting with a lawyer. He's only here tonight to keep up appearances for the kids. Making the announcement will happen after hockey season. He doesn't want to jeopardize Aiden's performance.

"Pretty amazing," says Piper, hiccuping and pointing to the décor.

"I must give Pinterest credit where credit is due," says Tina.

Piper drains her plastic wine cup.

Hockey parents multiply like glove bacteria. There are raucous conversations and laughter, remarks over how strange it is to be at the rink without Junior, jokes about starting a motel behind the facility for all of those who practically live there. At quarter after seven, Butch rolls in wearing camo pants and a hunting jacket. His hair and beard are already growing out from his pre-reunion trim. A crowd —mostly dads whose sons didn't make Butch's team last year but who are angling for a spot next season—encircles him.

Piper's phone pings. It must be a voicemail notification, because she wanders away to listen. Justin is left within earshot of a group of hockey moms, drinking his beer, silently hoping Kate Miller will soon arrive.

"They say he's already fighting with our coach because he wants the upper slot next year," says a nearby mom.

"No way is my kid playing for that animal."

"Who's starting the petition for Butch's removal?" Tina says, joining them. "I'll be the first to sign. In blood."

She nudges one of the moms who just stares at her with a strange look on her face.

"You are talking about Butch, right?" says Tina.

They eye her as if she's a lioness just wandered into their pride from the wilderness. Hockey parents have a tendency to get tribal.

"You know, our number one ranking might lead some to believe Butch is a good coach," Tina continues, "but I'm here to tell you, we've done well *in spite* of him. Not because of him."

"He's been an asshole since I've known him," says one of the moms. She extends her hand. "Jenny."

"Tina Church. Team Mom, #HockeyStrong sales rep. Here's my card."

"Wow, it's shaped like a hockey puck," says one of the women.

"I try to stay on brand."

There's a tittering.

"Look," Tina continues, "I don't want lead the charge— politics, you know—but if the club director wants our very talented son and his teammates to remain in this program, he's going to need to get Butch out of here. I've heard of several families looking into other clubs for next year."

"I'm married to the club director," says Jenny, puffing up her chest. "I'll give him your card. Wilson has been trying to oust Butch for years—especially since Butch kicked our niece, Zoe, off the team—but the problem is the guy's employed as a rink manager by our operating company. Even if he isn't coaching, he'll be around all the time. Not to mention the fact that there aren't many parents who can give so much time to coaching, or who even know how to ice skate."

"I've heard Butch steals from the vending machines. Can you use that?"

"Wilson's been talking to a guy about installing cameras, but it's so costly, I don't know."

"And Butch has a following," says a mom. "Look."

The men around Butch continue to grow like fungus.

"It's a good ol' boy network, for sure," says Tina. "But it's time for a new order."

"Here, here!" says Jenny.

Piper emerges from the hallway, teetering in her knee-high suede boots, wearing a homicidal look. Her skin is as pale as her winter white mink coat, shirt and leggings. Sparks could shoot out of her eyes the way she glares at Tina.

"You bitch!" Piper says.

The song has ended, and Piper's words echo throughout the building. The women around Tina recede into the crowd, leaving the team mom alone, clutching her martini. Bob is nowhere in sight.

"How dare you," Piper says.

"What are you talking about?" says Tina.

"That podcast. Seems you forgot to edit out the ending."

Tina has a question on her face, until Justin sees a slow dawning. A realization, followed by horror. He wonders what Tina could have possibly said.

"Hockey is an intense sport," says Tina. "It stirs passions, even inappropriately."

"Bullshit. That has nothing to do with your vicious insinuations."

"You have to understand my perspective. I do so much for this team, without appreciation or reward. And *you*, doing little to nothing, working the system, hiding Christmas present ideas from me—"

"What do you mean, hiding?"

"I asked you about what you were getting Aiden for Christmas and you never once mentioned that skating treadmill."

"It was last minute! I had to convince Justin. He was being cheap!"

Fuck her.

"No, you want Aiden to be better than Bobby. That's why you keep secrets from me, undermine me, flirt to advance your son's career."

All true.

"You're sick," says Piper.

"Me? I'm not the drunk."

Piper's face contorts into an ugly sob. She blubbers, wiping her black mascara on the sleeve of her white mink coat. She looks around and finds Justin's eyes—her gaze pleading with him—but he turns his back on her. Whatever is going on, Piper has dug her own hole, and he will not help her out of it.

"At least I'm not like you," says Piper. "Some loser-mom pedaling tacky shit on Facebook."

"Excuse me," says Tina. "I sell #HockeyStrong because I enjoy supporting my team. At least I'm contributing something."

"Ladies," says Bob, sliding over. "I hate to break this up, but Tina, you are needed."

Bob guides Tina away.

Justin looks back at Piper, and sees her searching her bag with the intensity of a TSA screener. She finds the coveted object—a flask—and drinks from it. Humiliated, he throws his beer in the trash, storms over to Piper, and pulls her out of the rink.

Chapter Thirty-Nine

 Charlie Miller's Status Update: ⚙

Check-In: Las Vegas Strip
Photo: Showgirl! Tagged: Kate Miller

#ThingsWeDoForHockey #HockeyStrong
💜 💬

In the lobby of the rink, the Millers step into a storm. As it turns out, they had just caught up on their missed #SportsTaxi episodes on the way over and were laughing hysterically about the unedited ending, only to walk in and find Piper and Tina going at it. It didn't take long for Justin —red-faced and trembling—to yank his drunk wife out of the rink, peeling wheels on his way out of the parking lot.

"I'm glad they're gone," says Kate.

"Why? Aside from the obvious," says Charlie.

"I've been getting an uncomfortable vibe from Justin."

"Like flirting?"

"Yeah."

"Sick."

"I know. He was being way too friendly on the Jersey trip."

"Why didn't you tell me?" says Charlie.

"I didn't think of it until now."

"Why didn't you text it to me from Jersey?"

"And give you a stroke? No thanks."

"Now that I think of it, he makes me squirmy when he talks about you. He must have a crush. I can't blame him. Have you met his wife?"

"Seriously," says Kate. "I guess Piper heard the podcast."

Charlie pulls out his phone. "Look, someone tagged her and Butch."

"I wonder who?"

"Probably a Gardenia. Trouble makers."

They take their positions at the money wheel, hoping to get through their hour of team service as quickly as possible so they can grab dinner alone at a nice restaurant—one that doesn't smell like funky hockey equipment and sweaty children. Charlie ties on the ridiculous apron provided, while Kate puts on a sequined, feathered headband. She stares at him with a flat expression, and he snaps her picture with his phone and posts it to Facebook.

"What is this music playing? Britney Spears? Toxic?" says Charlie.

"They must be featuring singers with Vegas acts," says Kate.

"Great. Lionel Ritchie will be up next."

"Better than Butch's playlist. We'd need a black light for that."

"Maybe next year's theme can be 'Butch's office.' We'll have shell casing decorations, venison, beef jerky. We'll wear camo, and listen to Lynyrd Skynrd."

Hank and Dawn walk up to the table. Dawn wears a low cut, sleeveless, short green dress that may or may not have fit her ten years ago, dangling hockey skate earrings, and sparkly silver shoes. Hank wears a brown sateen suit, and has a drip of snot hanging from the tip of his nose, threatening to drop on the felt covered table at any moment. Charlie does not conceal his disgust.

"What are the odds for this game?" says Hank.

"I have no idea," says Charlie.

"Could you ask someone?"

"Could you not use that tone with me?"

"Don't start with me, Miller. The kids aren't here, so I'm not holding my temper."

"Whoa, Big Guy," says Dawn, pulling him back. "We're just having fun, K?"

Hank's face is red as the blocks on the money wheel. He breathes heavily. Charlie cannot believe this loser has come out ready to fight. Hank stares at him for another minute before digging in his pocket and throwing a pile of ones on the table.

"Put 'em where you want," says Hank.

Dawn spreads out the bills, covering all but the $1 and $5 bets. Charlie spins the wheel, and it lands on a $5. He smiles and pulls the bills off the table.

"You don't have be so fucking gleeful about it," says Hank.

"Shut up," says Dawn.

She places ones on the $1, $5, and $10. Kate spins the wheel, and it lands on the $20.

Charlie moves to collect the dollars, and Hank grabs his arm.

"Hands off," says Hank.

"You better let go," says Charlie.

"Just leave that money there and spin again."

"What the hell are you talking about?"

"Maybe I can forgive you for being such a neurotic fuck, if you don't take my money with so much joy."

"Get out of here, you cheater."

"Who you callin' a cheater?"

"Big man you are, stealing from the hockey program."

Butch joins the table, and Hank releases Charlie's arm.

"Ladies," says Butch. "What are you bitching about? I got team moms cat-fighting by the bleachers, parents of fucking benders trying to kiss up to me for next year, and now you penalty box dads going at it. Can't we all just get along?"

Sal laughs and high five's Butch. Butch lays down stacks of quarters on the $10 and $20, and Hank follows his lead with one-dollar bills.

It is all Charlie can do to keep himself from exploding. Butch is the epicenter of every one of the cracks in this ice, and he's an asshole to pretend otherwise. He has created this culture of paranoia and animosity. Charlie's eye twitches, his jaw trembles, and his heart races. Kate puts her hand on his back and pulls him away from the table.

"Can you get me a beer?" she says.

Charlie knows she doesn't trust him to keep from erupting; he doesn't trust himself. As he steps away, Kate turns the wheel. When it stops, Charlie hears Butch and Hank cheer. He turns to see them high five, and a crowd draw near. He has a momentary, irrational anger at Kate for spinning the numbers that would let Hank and Butch win anything. He is also close enough to hear Hank say, "I knew that asshole was fixing it."

Charlie is about to confront Hank, when he is stopped by Mee Maw and Poo Poo. They are dressed like a couple of high rollers from the nineteen eighties at The Golden

261

Nugget. Mee Maw has a heart drawn near her eye with eyeliner pencil and clown-like red lipstick. Poo Poo wears a shiny tuxedo with a spades covered bowtie. Seeing them so decked out for an event at a dirty hockey rink stuffed with manic parents fills him with an unexplainable sadness.

"Hello, Charlie," says Mee Maw. "We were hoping you wouldn't look as anxious without a game going on, but here you are, rattled as ever."

"Hush, Mee Maw. Can't you see the man is in distress? What is it, Charlie—the clams casino? They've already done a number on my stomach, too. Allow me to give you a hint: don't use the nearest men's bathroom for at least an hour."

He nudges Charlie's arm and winks.

"Young people don't know how to have fun anymore," says Mee Maw. "Everyone takes themselves so seriously!"

"You're right," says Charlie. "I don't know what's wrong with us."

Charlie is having flashbacks of his parents and their friends, and wonders at what age he'll become completely oblivious to the social cues of others, and feel the need to express his opinion on every subject. He excuses himself, and continues making his way to the bar. It's staffed by Helen and Louise, who wear matching snide smiles that don't reach their eyes.

"You look like you need something stiff," says Louise.

"Did Hank start up with the penalty box?" says Helen.

"He's a real asshole," says Charlie.

"Not if he likes you," says Helen.

Charlie grits his teeth.

"Two Miller Lites," he says.

"Just like you and Kate, ha!" says Louise. "Miller lites."

"What's that supposed to mean?"

"Nothing, sheesh. You need a lite: lighten up!"

Helen snorts.

Charlie turns, and runs into Kip. Beer splashes down the front of his shirt.

"Sorry," says Charlie.

"No problem, man," says Kip. "Hey, I want you to meet Mercedes."

Charlie nods and slips between groups of parents, desperate to get back to Kate. He prays Butch and Hank have moved on, but when two enormous Bantam hockey dads part, Charlie sees that the terrible two are still at the money wheel, and are—by the crowd gathered and their creepy grins—on a hot streak. He starts toward a group, but sees Linda showing photos of David in goal, praising him to parents from another team who don't know any better. He rolls his eyes.

Slap!

As Amy lunges at Charlie with a bear hug, he drops both beer bottles, shattering them on the ground. Linda turns and shrugs, then goes back to her conversation. Tom is nowhere to be found. Charlie feels a stinging on his leg, and looks down to see red in the fabric of his khakis.

"Sorry!" Amy says. "Sorry. Not sorry."

What the hell is Amy doing here?

Charlie tries to pry off her arms so he can find a broom, but he's having no luck. He calls to Linda, who looks thoroughly annoyed to be interrupted. She saunters over and reaches in her purse, pulling out a wad of cotton.

"Here, Amy. See. Soft. It's okay. Get away from that angry man."

"He's angry."

"Always, dear."

Chapter Forty
One Week to Districts

 #PolarBears Public Page ⚙

CHAMPIONSHIP GAME!
WINNERS GOING TO DISTRICT PLAYOFFS
LOSERS: GAME OVER

#GoPolarBears #HockeyStrong

GROUP TEXT:

TINA: Good Morning, Polar Bears. In case you haven't looked out your window, you'll need to build in extra driving time. The roads are covered in snow.

BUTCH: If you're one minute late for early arrival, your kid will be benched.

SAL: #MariotheBeast made us leave at 6 AM for an 11 o'clock-er. LOL. Leaving the IHOP near the rink now.

DAWN: Just got off the night shift. Trees down. Accidents everywhere. Leave now.

PIPER: Now? I just got out of the shower.

KIP: :)

MEE MAW: Henry's parents are driving us. I'll tell them to pick us up ASAP.

LOUISE: We're five minutes away, and there's a major crash at the intersection near the rink. Huge back-ups starting.

TOM: David is in the car.

LUCY: Leaving with Kyle now.

PIPER: I'm not worried. My SUV can beat any snowstorm.

KIP: Already at the rink. Setting up cameras with my assistant.

LUCY: Pig.

KIP: Group text. Hello?

BUTCH: While I have your attention: if they don't win today, there will still be practice this week: Punishment Practice. Suicides. If we win: Conditioning Practice. Suicides.

HANK: You can count on us, Butch. Loading up the car now.

TINA: Us, too. We won't let you down.

#####

Justin has been so preoccupied with keeping the divorce news from his kids that he hasn't fully thought about the importance of today's game. A work convention kept him out of town for two days, and he came straight from the airport. He's exhausted, but glad he took the red-eye. He can't let Aiden down, especially not before he's about to upset the kid's whole existence.

After Casino Night, Piper agreed their marriage was over, and they would wait to tell the kids until the season's end. Justin found a rehabbed brownstone within his price range and walking distance of his office, but he got physically sick in the toilet while the listing agent banged on the door, and he's too embarrassed to call the guy back.

Maybe he should just suck it up and stay with Piper. Divorce is a lot of work. And money. Laziness and greed are hardly reasons to stay with someone you despise, but they must count for something. Who really has a happy marriage, anyway?

He parks, and makes his way through the crowd of Ice Dog parents tailgating in the parking lot. Who the fuck tailgates for Pee Wee hockey? In the snow? In the morning? Piper would fit in with this crew. When he enters the rink, he sees Charlie and Kate standing with an agitated group of old people—must be Brett's grandparents. Justin thinks about joining them, but Charlie's glare stops him. Kate must have said something to Charlie about his flirting. Great. His only semi-ally on the team is lost.

A quick scan of the crowd is disappointing as ever. Kip sets up his camera equipment behind one of the goals, and a chick with butt length black hair and two inch blue fingernails stands with her hand on his ass the whole time. Must be the stripper. Lucy scowls from the top of the bleachers, making no effort to hide her gawking. Mee Maw and Poo Poo have Henry's parents with them; this must be a big deal for them to take time out of their busy lives to watch their son play. Dante uses a roll of friction tape to bind the opposing team's sticks together in the holder outside the locker room. Jack types on his laptop in the warming room.

One big happy fucking hockey family.

He smells Piper's perfume before he sees her. She walks into the rink looking gorgeous and sober. He feels a pang until he sees who follows her.

Cortland.

What the fuck? What happened to their agreement to wait? He didn't even mess around with any women at the work convention. Now she's banging Cortland? He thinks he might be sick again.

"What's he doing here?" says Justin.

"Nice to see you, too, pal," says Cortland.

"I told you," Piper says over her shoulder to Cortland. She turns back to Justin. "Cort is here scouting houses for his family. I took him by the one for sale in our neighborhood that he really likes. I'm going back to work. He's actually using me as his realtor."

"I'm sure he's using you," says Justin. "Has he been through our house? I'm sure he's seen the master bedroom already."

"For your information, Cort's son is interested in playing hockey, so I thought I'd give him a taste of the madness."

God, how he wants to punch the smug, white-toothed smile off this douchebag's fake tanned face.

"Poor Justin," says Piper. "So paranoid."

She pats the side of his face, and motions for Cortland to follow her to the stands. She stops before climbing the stairs, and turns back to Justin.

"By the way, I'm not going to have to sell the house, because I'm reactivating my real estate license. Cortland's purchase will get me started nicely."

She tosses her long blonde hair and walks away from him.

Justin runs his hands through his hair and turns back to the ice, suppressing the urge to scream. Is he becoming as unglued as Charlie Miller? How has this happened?

"I told you, bitches ruin everything," says Sal. It took him no time to hone in on Justin. "Don't let her fool you. She's miserable. And a drunk. You're not missin' nothing there."

Justin feels worse getting props from a guy like Sal. He feels dizzy. He turns away, looking for a water fountain, and spots Aiden. His son runs over and hugs him.

"Dad!"

The way Aiden says Dad is the most soul-crushing thing he's ever heard. He doesn't deserve for a kid to say Dad like that to him. Not after the mess he and Piper have made of their household.

"Are you crying?" says Aiden. "Don't worry. We made it! The championship! And if we win: DISTRICTS!"

"I know--I'm just. I'm really proud. You're awesome."

"Yo!" Butch motions for Aiden to join the team outside for warm ups.

"Gotta go," says Aiden. "Hashtag HOCKEYSTRONG!"

Justin doesn't know whether to laugh or cry. He does both.

Chapter Forty-One

 Kate Miller's Status Update: ⚙

Forgive my brag post, but Brett's team made it to the championship, and if they win, they go to Florida for the Southeast District Finals!! Send good vibes!!!!

#GoPolarBears #HockeyStrong

Charlie eyes the penalty box like the Promised Land. All morning he has been looking forward to standing in silence in the small space, eavesdropping on Butch, watching the hockey game without the commentary of the septuagenarian squad. Kate had thought it would be a nice gesture to invite the grandparents for the championship game, AND ask them to stay with them. Charlie begged her not to: districts would be in Florida, after all, just a few hours from his parents' home. But Kate reminded him there was no guarantee they'd make it to districts, and she felt as if they needed to reach out after leaving so abruptly from the retirement weekend.

Last night was horrible. Charlie and Brett had picked up his parents from the airport so Kate could continue cooking —as she had been all day long. As expected, his dad complained the whole way to the house about how turbulent the flight was, how windy the landing, how some kid wailed during the whole descent, and how confusing the airport was. Charlie had expected this, and just winked at Brett. Upon their arrival, dinner was laid out: capers and halibut, mushroom risotto, and steamed asparagus. Once everyone sat down, Charlie noticed that his mother only helped herself to rice and asparagus.

"No fish, Mom?" asked Charlie. "It's delicious."

"I'm allergic."

Kate blanched. "I'm so sorry. I had no idea."

"How could you, dear?"

"When did this happen?" said Charlie. "You live in Florida, for crying out loud."

"It happened three years ago," said Charlie's father. "If you had been speaking to us then, it might have come up. One day your mother woke up, and—Boom! Even one tiny bite of fish makes her blow up like a balloon and fall over dead."

Kate's face went from white to red. She ran to the kitchen, in search of something she could make quickly.

"We have chicken breasts," she called. "I could thaw one and cook it in the skillet. Or steak? We have a half a piece of strip steak leftover from the Outback."

"No, dear, I'm quite fine with the rice; thank you."

Charlie had to excuse himself to count to ten in the bathroom after he heard his father whisper to his mother, "You're not missing much, anyway."

This morning, his father bitched the entire way to the rink because Charlie made them hurry through breakfast and wouldn't allow his dad to go back for seconds. Then he thought Charlie was driving too slowly in the snow, then too

270

fast. Kate's parents were already at the rink when they'd arrived, and had started in about how ridiculous it was that the game wasn't cancelled for bad weather, and how crazy sports parents are.

Charlie practically runs to the penalty box, but when he arrives, Hank is there.

"I'm on the schedule," says Hank.

"This is my game, and you know it!" says Charlie.

"Guys," says Tina, sitting nearby with the scoresheet. "I literally can't take this any more. What's the confusion?"

"My schedule clearly said 'Hank' for penalty box for today's game."

"And mine said 'Charlie'!"

Tina pulls up the schedule on her phone. She reads it, and then makes a few clicks and swipes before looking up at them.

"Charlie, you must have had the old schedule," she says. "I had to revise it because of all the extra games Butch added this season. On the updated version, Hank is scheduled for today."

Hank grins.

"That's bullshit!" says Charlie.

"I even marked the new schedule email with a red exclamation point."

"It must have gotten buried or missed," says Charlie. "You send ten messages a day."

"Watch it," says Hank.

"Screw you."

"You'll get to work the box at districts," says Tina.

"IF we make it."

"If! Listen to this guy," says Hank.

"Yeah, where's your team spirit?" says Tina.

"We don't need those bad vibes anywhere near the ice," says Hank.

Hank glares at Charlie while he closes the door to the penalty box.

Charlie's heart races. He takes long deep breaths, and begins to walk slowly up the bleachers, his shoulders tingling and stiff, full of knots, his hands clammy. By the time he reaches his family, he can hear his father still complaining.

"This place is a dump. I thought you said Brett played for an elite team."

"The rink manager is terrible," says Kate. "And also happens to be the coach."

How Kate has managed to stay chipper throughout this ordeal is beyond Charlie. He's equal parts grateful for it and annoyed. If she can stay calm, why can't he?

"I'd file a complaint if I were you."

"Oh, after this season, believe me; we will," says Kate.

"Can you get them to turn on the overhead warmers?" says Charlie's mom. "What good is it to have cold warmers?"

"Tell me about it," says Charlie's dad.

The boys take the ice, and the stands erupt in noisy cheers. Charlie is fairly certain some of the Ice Dog parents are drunk, and knows his parents will somehow judge him for it. He can almost hear his father's voice: "How can you let your kid play for a sport that encourages this?"

A good question, really.

Brett, Aiden, and Bobby are back together, and their line is sent out first. Charlie feels a measure of pride that his son is starting the game, and points to Brett's jersey so the grandparents can see him.

The whistle blows.

Using his body to block the other center, Brett wins the face-off and chips the puck to Bobby. The boys spread out and Bobby hits the puck deep into the offensive zone where Aiden chases it, passes it to Brett in the slot, and BOOM! Brett scores.

Charlie and Kate scream. The Polar Bear parents cheer. Even the grandparents seem excited. Butch sends Mike's line out. Charlie feels slightly crestfallen that the shift was so short, but it did the job, so he'll force himself to focus on the positive.

"That's all he gets to play?" asks Charlie's father.

"They rotate them every thirty to forty-five seconds in hockey."

A minute ticks by. Mike's line remains on the ice, loses the puck, and now they are skating to the defensive zone. Butch has started screaming. Another minute goes by.

"Those boys get to stay out a long time," says Charlie's mother.

"It's because the coach's son is out there," says Kate.

"He's pretty good," says Kate's mom.

"No, he's not," snaps Charlie.

Everyone stares at him with the 'mind the lunatic' look, so he shuts up, until Mike gets a stupid penalty for knocking a kid on the ice after the whistle has blown. The parents boo. Tina plays *Bad Boys* from *Cops*. Gordie and Franklin's crazy brother runs down and bangs on the penalty box glass when Mike gets in, and gives him a thumbs up.

"Fuck, yeah!" says the crazy brother. "That kid deserved it!"

"Sit down, asshole," someone yells from the Ice Dogs' side.

"Oh my Lord," says Charlie's mother. "The language!"

"That's hockey," says Kate, sheepish.

The other team scores on the penalty kill, and the rest of the first period is a frustrating cycle of short shifts for Brett's line, endless shifts for Mike's line, and Mike doing double duty, moving from defense to offense. Though Mike spends most of the game on the ice, Butch is not pleased with him, and berates him every time he exits.

At the end of the second period, Kate runs to go to the bathroom, leaving Charlie with the complainers. Mee Maw and Poo Poo have made their way over and make introductions.

"It's so nice to meet you," says Mee Maw. "We're #44's grandparents."

"We're Brett's grandparents," says Charlie's mom. "I don't know his number."

Mee Maw laughs, nudging Poo Poo. "Can you imagine? We practically live here."

"Where are #44's parents?" says Charlie's dad.

"They're here today," says Poo Poo, pointing out the two people staring at their phones, ignoring each other. "Mostly we take Henry."

"Yes, his parents are so busy with their jobs, they can't possibly be as involved as you have to be with this team."

"What a load," says Charlie's dad.

Charlie grabs his dad's arm to censor him. His father scowls.

"Everything has changed so much," says Charlie's mom. "When Charlie was little, most of the time we just dropped him off at the soccer field."

"It's very different now," says Mee Maw. "Practices, nutrition, social media, tournaments--it's a full time job."

"Thank God we're retired," says Poo Poo.

Charlie's parents stare at Mee Maw and Poo Poo like they're covered in infectious sores. If Charlie weren't so stressed by the game and having them there, he'd feel a certain camaraderie with his mom and dad. As it is, the third period has started, the grandparents continue to talk—which aggravates the hell out of him—and Kate is not back from the bathroom. The score is tied 3-3, with goals from Mike on a power play, and #MariotheBeast. After two minutes, Kate comes running up the bleachers, her face red.

"What's wrong?" says Charlie.

"I feel like the biggest jerk on the planet."

"Why?"

"I drank like a gallon of coffee this morning, and since I didn't want to miss any of the game and all the stalls were taken, I used the handicapped stall. When I was about to flush, I dropped my glove in the toilet, and hoped to fish it out with a plunger, but there wasn't one in the stall. I knew the third period had started, so I just flushed the toilet and hoped for the best, but it overflowed. I went to sneak out, and there was an Ice Dog parent and her daughter—who was in a wheelchair—waiting, glaring at me."

"Oh no," says Charlie's mom.

"Yeah, I had to tell them the toilet was backed up, and then I just left them there."

"Jeez, that was rude."

"It's the championship," says Kate.

The grandparents stare at her.

Charlie turns his attention back to the game, but his parents won't stop talking about the bathroom incident, and Mee Maw keeps bragging, and now Dawn's son's running commentary of criticism is starting. Charlie can't take it. He sneaks down the bleacher steps to find a solitary place along the boards.

"Where are you going?" says Kate, with eyes like *don't you leave me with these people.*

He feels bad, but not bad enough to stay.

"I'm going to get some video of Brett's last period," he says, waving his phone. "This could be it for the season."

"Shhh!" says Linda.

Dawn swats the air around him, as if shooing away the negativity. "Do you wanna jinx them?"

He rolls his eyes and continues down to the boards. Hank gives him the stare down, and Charlie breaks the gaze first when he catches Amy in his peripheral vision. He narrowly misses a lunge from her, and feels like an ass ducking and running from an intellectually disabled child. When he looks up, Ice Dog parents are tittering.

Charlie has a sudden and savage wish that the Polar Bears will lose so he does not have to spend one more minute with these people. They have hurt his mental health, his physical health, and his family. He wonders what Kate would think if he confessed this to her. He thinks she'd understand—especially after what she just did—but it's hard to tell. They have never been under so much strain, and it's absurd to think that eleven and twelve-year-old hockey has brought it on. If this is the case, what will it be like when Brett is fifteen? Seventeen? Are all sports like this? Or is it coaches like Butch Johnson—deranged, loser, kid-bullies with unfulfilled dreams, acting out their NHL fantasies on children—who bring out the worst in parents?

The silver lining of this entire season has been his son. Brett is always so happy to go to hockey, he works hard, he doesn't seem especially fazed by Butch's yelling; half the time he can't even remember what Butch says. And in this game —the championship—Brett hustles like never before. He's unselfish and aggressive. In response, an Ice Dog forward has marked Brett, and puts pressure just shy of the penalty spectrum on him. Brett works hard not to retaliate—even when the kid trips him. The ref blows the whistle and calls the penalty, and the kid mouths off about Brett, who turns his back on the player. The kid is so amped up that his voice carries. Charlie can see Brett laugh and shake his head. He wonders if he could keep his cool after being physically and verbally assaulted. Probably not.

The ref tries to push the kid toward the penalty box, but he can't get control of him. All of the momentum feels like it has swung to the Polar Bears, and it's breaking this Ice Dog player. Maybe the kid has a dad who puts pressure on him, or a coach who bullies him, or maybe he's just a spoiled little shit used to getting his way. Whatever the backstory, the kid yanks his arm out of the ref's hand, crosses the ice, and punches Brett in the helmet cage. Brett looks stunned for a moment, but his instinct to protect himself takes over, and he pushes the boy away from him. The kid lands on his ass, still screaming, and the fans join in the cursing. Kate puts her face in her hands. The grandparents shake their heads. Brett is sent to the penalty box.

Charlie leaps into the air and bangs at the glass.

"No way!" he screams at the ref. "If you had kept control, he wouldn't have had to defend himself!"

Charlie rushes toward the penalty box, still screaming, ignoring the boos and shouts of the Ice Dog parents.

"You know that's bullshit!" says Charlie. "What, the kid can't defend himself after you let that little asshole punch him?"

"Keep it up and you're out," the ref yells.

Tina turns on *Rude* by Magic. Butch stands still as stone —dangerously silent. He looks at no one—only glares at the ice. Hank jerks open the door and slams it behind Brett. He wipes his snot along the arm of his Polar Bears parka, shoots a look of disgust at Charlie, and then shoves Brett on the penalty bench.

"Stupid."

The word echoes in Charlie's brain.

He sees Hank's rubbery, snotty lips say it, the man push his son onto the bench, and all time seems to stop.

Later, Charlie will say it was like an out of body experience—the racing of his heart, the blankness in his head, the black in his soul. Charlie will barely remember opening the door, or grabbing Hank by his parka, or the blood squirting all over Charlie's MILLER #HockeyStrong sweatshirt from the sickening punch he landed squarely on Hank's nose. He'll faintly recall his father pulling him out to the parking lot. The police showing up.

"It has been building all season," Dawn said to the cops. "This lunatic has hated my husband from day one because he can't stand that Coach wanted Hank in the box over him."

"In the what?"

"The penalty box!"

"Excuse me, are you talking about hockey?"

"Yes!"

"Kiddie hockey?"

The officer and his partner actually laughed and joked about calling a padded wagon.

After Kate persuaded Hank not to press charges in exchange for full penalty box duties for the rest of the season, she left Charlie sitting in the car, staring at the flickering ice rink sign through the half-peeled flip flop family. Minutes later she sent a text that Brett scored the winning goal, and they were going to districts.

Charlie barely remembers any of it.

The thing seared in his brain from the championship game is the look of horror on his son's face when he attacked Hank.

Chapter Forty-Two

 Piper Caldwell's Status Update:

Photo Album: REGIONAL CHAMPIONS!!!
DISTRICTS BOUND!!
Amazing families, Amazing Coach, Amazing Year!

#GoPolarBears #HockeyStrong

Justin clinks his beer against Aiden's lemonade. The family is at a celebratory dinner at Aiden's favorite wings joint. Piper hates eating here because the kids get messy faces and hands, and there isn't anything healthy on the menu, but tonight is all about Aiden and the Polar Bears win.

"You did it!" says Justin, shocked at how elated he feels. Just hours earlier, he was teetering on the brink of madness, contemplating divorce, and ready to punch a guy at a youth hockey event. Seeing Charlie Miller actually do so put things in perspective for him. None of this can be taken seriously. It's child's play!

"I can't believe it!" says Aiden.

"I can," says Piper, crossing her arms over her chest. "I knew this team would do it. As stressful as this year has been, it has paid off. You're a champion."

"We'll know for sure once we get through districts," says Justin.

"We know now. Just getting there is a line on the hockey resume."

The waitress arrives and takes their dinner order. Justin gets another beer with his wings, and is shocked that Piper hasn't ordered wine.

"Do you want a glass of something?" he asks.

He's hoping to work at reconciliation and show Piper he can meet her half way, but she shakes her head and narrows her eyes at him. Suspicious.

That's fair. Rebuilding won't be easy.

Aiden excuses himself to go to the bathroom. The girls stare at their iPads, and Piper sips her water and feigns interest in one of the many large television monitors featuring sporting events. Justin reaches for Piper's knee. She shifts away from him.

"Come on," he says. "Let's forget the last few months, okay?"

"What if I don't want to?"

"That's your choice. But do you want to complicate our lives?"

"You already seemed like you were willing to."

"I was at a breaking point. This year, this hockey season. The bad energy from all those nut-jobs. The travel. The money. It just piled up."

She continues to stare ahead, not making eye contact.

"I can see the light at the end of the tunnel," he says. "And watching Miller lose his shit was a wake up call."

Piper looks at him as if trying to read whether or not he's genuine. There's a twitch on the corner of her mouth, a softening of posture, but it's there for only a moment before her phone rings. She jumps out of her seat to answer it, leaving him alone with the girls.

Aiden rushes toward the table with Bobby Church.

"Look who's here!"

Justin feels his nausea returning. He struggles to hear who Piper is talking to, but she has wandered over to the bar, out of earshot. She's clearly happy to be in conversation with whoever it is. It better not be that dick, Cortland. Justin had to watch his wife drive off with Cortland to the airport after the game, and it almost made him puke.

"Any room at the inn?" says Bob Church.

Oh God.

"I don't think…" says Justin.

Tina and Bob ignore him and motion a nearby server to pull up three more chairs to the already crowded table. Piper returns, but stops short when she sees the Churches. Tina wraps her arms around a very stiff Piper.

"Forgive me!" says Tina. "We are buying dinner. Everything's on us. Even the booze!"

Bob winks at Justin.

Oh God.

Tina helps Piper sit and squeezes close to her.

"This is just like the end of last season," says Tina. "Lineys at dinner with their parents. But this time, we're number one."

"Hear, hear!" says Bob.

"If we want to win the whole thing, we need to restore team spirit, mend fences, and move ahead as one."

"That's very inspiring, Tina," says Bob.

Piper looks at Justin with wide eyes. He's at least grateful they can share in their loathing of the Churches. Common ground is a starting point.

While Aiden and Bobby talk about the game, Bob leans in and lowers his voice.

"Now, about next year."

"No," says Justin. "We can't even think about that right now. One day at a time."

"But try-out prep for next season is starting up soon," says Tina.

"Nope." Justin holds up his hands.

"You need to decide which team Aiden will play on to know where to try out," says Tina.

"Yeah, like will Aiden stay with Butch?" says Bob.

"I can say certainly, no."

"Wait a minute," says Piper. "We'll decide after districts."

"No way," says Justin. "That I know for sure. No more Butch."

"But if they were to go all the way next year," says Piper. "They could even advance past districts to *nationals*. They don't have nationals at this level."

"We're not discussing this here."

The waitress brings Justin another beer, and he drinks it quickly.

Tina gives Bob a nervous glance and then shifts her gaze to Piper. Piper actually raises her eyebrows as if to say, "We'll see about that."

Seriously? Is Piper taking sides with the Churches over him? Is she really giving him the look like he's the crazy one?

He orders another beer.

Chapter Forty-Three
One Day to District Playoffs

 Kate Miller's Status Update: ⚙

Shared Post:
Butch Johnson: Word of the Day: Neurasthenia
Nervous Collapse; break down, crack up

#HockeyStrong
♥ 💬

It has been snowing for forty-eight hours. Tree limbs encased in ice drop into five-foot drifts. School is cancelled, power flickers, a state of emergency is declared. The world is eerily silent—like Kate.

Kate hasn't spoken much to Charlie since "the incident," as they refer to it. Sometimes, when he catches her eye, he can't tell if he's seeing anger or confusion or sympathy, or some strange cocktail of all three, but it's clear she isn't ready for conversation. After "the incident," he apologized to his parents and to Brett. Kate and Brett seem wary of him, stepping almost lightly around him, as if he's an unstable surface on an icy pond.

Isn't he?

Fuck that. Any sane person who has lived through conditions like this would have done the same thing. Like Butch says, it's war, and all's fair in war. And now, the big event is upon them: Districts. Everything they have endured —the family drama, the practices, the games, the fees, the extra games, the tournaments, the dinners, the fundraisers, the sports' trainers, Butch—has led to this moment. And in wretched, icy form, the universe continues to prove itself relentless.

It is noon. Their flight is scheduled to leave for Florida at five p.m., and the airline website still shows that it's on time, but the morning flights have been cancelled one by one. Charlie refreshes the Flight Status page for the hundredth time.

On Time.

"Lying bitch."

"Who are you talking to?" says Kate as she walks in the office.

"Southwest."

"On the phone?"

"No, the Flight Status page. It keeps saying 'On Time.' I don't believe it."

Kate stares at him for a moment. Then she starts opening and closing drawers in her desk and the file cabinets. Brett runs in the office.

"Can we leave?"

Brett has asked this no less than four thousand times this morning.

"Soon," says Charlie.

"Argh!"

Brett stomps away and down the basement stairs, where he begins playing the drums Charlie's parents bought him for Christmas. Just what Charlie needs—banging. Brett hasn't stopped since Charlie assembled the set, but Kate pointed out that at least Brett has a healthy interest outside of hockey, and something to do when the weather is nasty.

Charlie's phone rings; it's his father. No. He cannot talk to him now.

Kate rustles through papers.

"What are you looking for?" Charlie says.

"A copy of Brett's birth certificate."

"Didn't we turn that in at the beginning of the season?"

"Yes, but we need new copies for districts, and Tina can't get to the file because it's locked in the rink, so we all have to scrounge."

Kate runs upstairs, continuing her search in the master bedroom. Brett bangs. Charlie hits Refresh.

On Time.

His father has not left a voicemail. That's a relief.

Between bangs on the drums, there is a clicking sound on the foyer window. Charlie steps out of the office— rubbing the chill on his arms he hasn't been able to shake for months—and sees that the snow has turned to sleet. He doesn't know what will be worse: flying in these miserable weather conditions or not flying in these miserable weather conditions. Panic rises. He has to get to warmth. It feels like life or death. He hurries upstairs.

"We need to leave. Now," he says.

"Five hours before the flight?"

"It could take us a really long time to get there."

"Charlie, the airport is fifteen minutes away. We don't need to leave now. Besides, you know our flight will be cancelled."

"Why do you sound so relaxed about that?"

"Because if our flight is cancelled, that means half the team isn't getting there tonight. Come to think of it, the whole team won't. The rest of the crew is on the seven p.m. flight. If we get cancelled, they get cancelled."

"Some families drove. The Gardenia's can't fly because Sal has some inner ear thing. They're already in Georgia."

"That's one player."

"I'm just thinking maybe we should drive."

"You have officially lost your mind. There's a foot of snow covered with an inch of ice, all the way down the east coast, through Virginia."

"If we left now, we could get there in plenty of time by the first game at 11:00 tomorrow morning."

"No, Charlie. We are not driving to Florida."

"Once we got through Virginia, it would only be like fifteen hours."

"Stop."

"You don't understand. If I don't get to warm weather, I'm going to have a nervous breakdown."

"Don't add to the drama."

"I'm completely serious."

"We can't leave until I can find that damned birth certificate anyway. Not to mention the load of laundry soaked and in the drier."

Charlie groans and hurries back down to the office. He hits refresh.

Delayed. One Hour.

"A-ha! Here we go!" he yells.

"What?"

"Delayed. One hour."

"What?"

Charlie runs to the basement steps and screams down at Brett. "Stop! Stop banging!"

"Can we leave?!"

"Soon!"

"Argh!"

Charlie's phone buzzes in his pocket.

GROUP TEXT

BUTCH: We're driving. Leaving in ten minutes. You better find a way to get to districts.

TOM: We decided to drive, too. Leaving as soon as we have David's birth certificate copied.

KIP: We're driving to Richmond—it's turning to rain there—and flying out at 11:00 PM. Just changed our flight.

LOUISE: We're in sunny Georgia, pounding beers by my aunt's pool. Suckers! Told ya you should have left yesterday.

TINA: We're switching to the Richmond flight, too.

A cold sweat breaks out on Charlie's forehead. Half the team has made other plans and are already underway. He has to convince Kate to let them go. He runs back upstairs.

"Kate, did you see the group texts?"

"Yes."

Her face is bright red, and she sits on the carpet amid the emptied contents of her bedside table.

"Did you find the birth certificate?"

"Not yet."

"I'm going to try to get the Richmond flight."

She does not respond. He takes this as agreement, and runs downstairs.

SOLD OUT.

"Fuck!"

His phone buzzes.

HANK: Just got the last three seats on the Richmond flight. #GoPolarBears!

Charlie is going to be sick.

"Found it!" Kate runs down flushed, holding Brett's birth certificate.

"That shithead took our seats," says Charlie.

"Who?"

"Hank. Got the last three Richmond seats. Now it's sold out. Fuck!"

"Geez, Dad."

Brett stands in the foyer. Kate's face is murderous.

"You should be thanking Hank right now," she says. "If he hadn't agreed not to press charges, you might be sitting in jail."

Charlie takes slow deep breaths. He's been listening to a meditation tape to get his anxiety under control. He got a new bulb for his Happy Light. If he can't manage, the next step will be Xanax.

"We need. To leave. For the airport. Now," he says.

"But the laundry. It's all underwear. We need it."

"We can buy new underwear in Florida."

"Come on, Mom. I want to go," says Brett, jumping up and down.

Kate looks like she wants to argue, but Brett's desperation oozes out of him.

"Fine."

#####

Their neighborhood hasn't been plowed since the sleet began. The car lurches and groans over drifts, and ice-crusted snow scrapes along the underside of the vehicle. It is stunning, humbling, chilling—a white nightmare.

"The main roads will be better," says Charlie.

He is startled to see Kate look at him the way she looks at Butch, making no effort to conceal her disdain. Brett is silent in the backseat—subdued by winter's gratuitous display. He doesn't even turn on his iTouch.

The two-lane road leading to the highway is not better than their neighborhood; it's worse. One lane has been plowed down the middle, trees are down to the left and right, and a pick up truck with a flimsy plow on the front heads toward them, flashing its high beams. Charlie stops the car, immobilized by the enormity of all they must conquer to get to Florida. There are so many steps between this treacherous road and a place of sun, and palm trees, and district championships.

"Back up, Charlie," says Kate.

The truck is getting closer, and it doesn't appear to be slowing.

"Back up! Do you need me to drive?"

Charlie shakes his head, checks his rear view mirror, and starts the slow reverse back to their neighborhood. The truck gets closer at an alarming speed, and Charlie is forced to take the backward turn into his neighborhood so sharply, their little sedan spins and hits a massive drift. The trucker flips them the bird as he passes, and Charlie swears the camo-clad asshole is Butch. But that's ridiculous; Butch is driving to Florida. He's probably already in Virginia. Charlie puts the car in drive. The tires spin, but the car doesn't move. He continues to push the accelerator to no avail.

"Shit!"

"Did you bring the shovel?" says Kate.

"Why would I bring a shovel?"

"In case the car gets stuck."

He grits his teeth and tightens his grip on the steering wheel.

"Do you want me to run back for it?" asks Brett.

"No," Charlie says. "I'll push us out. Kate, get in the driver's seat."

The air outside hits Charlie with an icy slap, and sleet stings his skin. By the time he gets to the back of the car, his jeans are wet to the knee and his tennis shoes are soaked through to his socks. It seems the foundation of the ice and snow is two inches of filthy slush. Excellent.

Kate gives him the thumbs up (he find this hysterically funny) through the window, and he leans down to push the car. While he struggles to keep from slipping, he notices—because of the slope of the window, snow clings to the little flip flop family. He also finds this funny, even when the car lurches forward and he lands on his hands and knees in the snow. He hurries back to the driver's seat, still laughing, closes the door, and nods to his family as if to say, "See! No problem."

They give him troubled looks.

It takes two hours for the Millers to get halfway to the airport. Charlie makes Kate refresh the airline page on her cell every minute, and it now says the delay will be two hours. Cars are spun out and abandoned on the sides of the road, and only one lane on the major highway is plowed, and not very well. There are few vehicles out, but Charlie manages to end up behind an idiot in a yellow Camaro spinning out left and right.

"Why would he take that car out?" says Charlie.

"Maybe his kid plays ice hockey," says Kate.

Charlie's knuckles are white on the steering wheel. He lays on the horn.

"What are you doing?" she says.

"He needs to know what an asshole he is."

"I'm pretty sure he realizes without you adding to his stress."

Charlie contemplates going around the guy, but the drifts on either side are about six inches deep and coated in ice. With Charlie's luck, he'd get stuck, so he'll just have to drive one mile an hour at a safe distance behind the dumbo.

"Refresh," he says.

Kate sighs.

"Oh God," she says.

"What?"

"Cancelled."

Chapter Forty-Four

  #PolarBears Public Page

Photo: Louise, Sal, Mario, and Dante selfie
by a sunny pool
Caption: All you stuck in the north: Suckers!

#DanteTheBeast #MarioTheBeast
#HockeyStrong

Justin and Aiden stand with Jack and Dominik at the airline counter.

"I'm sorry," says the young man at the desk. "Everything is cancelled tonight."

"Put us on standby," says Justin.

"You're pretty far down the list."

"Fine. We have a championship to get to. We're willing to leave on any flight, even if it's the middle of the night."

"Same," says Jack.

"What sport?" says the guy.

"Ice Hockey!" Aiden and Dominik say together.

"Right on!" he says. "I used to play. I get it."

High fives.

"What do you think our odds of getting out are?" says Justin.

The guy looks around, then leans in. "Don't spread this around, but there's a flight to West Palm that isn't cancelled, leaving at eleven fifteen. A couple of spots left. They're going to de-ice the plane before takeoff. Do you wanna switch to that flight?"

"Yes!"

"Cool. You'll have to pay an extra thirty dollars a ticket."

"Fine. Do it."

Justin's relief is profound. He had to fight with Piper just to get her to release Aiden to him in these driving conditions. She already switched her and the girls' flight to the next morning. They'll miss the first game. Aiden didn't want to switch, so he begged and Piper relented, and it was a good thing. Justin couldn't have handled Piper waiting around at the airport, bitching about economy airlines and losing beauty sleep, the little ones having meltdowns. Not to mention that she has been on the phone with Cortland once an hour since the championship game. She says it's to do with the house he wants, but the calls take a lot longer than Justin thinks they should.

Jack is uncharacteristically chatty. He leads them to a sports bar, gets the waitress to put on a hockey game, and the guys settle in for a long evening. Aiden and Dominik sit on one side of the table, alternating between playing Minecraft and watching the hockey game. Justin and Jack order a pitcher of beer.

"Your wife's not coming," says Jack.

"She's supposed to come tomorrow. But who knows. Things haven't exactly been…"

"I know what you mean. I've been there. Hockey stress."

Justin laughs. "I don't think it's just hockey."

"The constant tension, the cost, the testosterone, men and women put together in intense situations, traveling, drinking. The youth sports culture fosters it."

Justin is quiet. He looks down the table at the boys. They cheer over a goal.

"What, you think we should all take our kids out of sports to save our souls?" says Justin.

"Mine's still in."

"So it's an addiction."

"Maybe."

"It didn't used to be this way."

"No. But it wasn't the moneymaker it is now. Whoever figured out how to start the tournament machine is an evil genius."

"The kids love it."

"The kids would love playing on the pond, unzambonied, with hand me down equipment."

"True."

After they drink, Justin puts down his beer and rubs his eyes.

"Can I give you some unsolicited advice?" says Jack.

"Shoot."

"Don't be too quick to give up."

"On what—Piper or hockey?"

"Both."

"You're an optimist?"

"No. But I've lived through divorce. I mostly attribute it to our first hockey culture experience. And if my situation is anything like yours, you won't be happier on the other side."

"I'll keep that in mind."

Chapter Forty-Five

 Charlie Miller's Status Update: ⚙

Photo: Haggard, unshaven, wild-eyed selfie next to screenshot of Jack Nicholson from The Shining

#HockeyStrong

♥ 💬

Charlie watches Kate hit 'Redial' again, but she keeps getting a busy signal.

"I cannot believe we sat home all day, and when we get halfway to the airport, the flight gets cancelled," says Charlie.

"Why can't you believe it? We knew this would happen."

"We should drive."

"We are not driving to Florida in a blizzard!"

"I can't miss districts, Mom!"

"We cannot put our lives in danger for hockey! FOR SOME ASSHOLE COACH!"

Someone must have answered, because Kate is flustered, apologizing into her phone, talking with Southwest.

"I see. Uh huh."

"What's she saying?" says Charlie.

Kate swats the air at him and mouths, "Shhh!"

"So what should we do?" says Kate.

Charlie can hear the voice, but not the words. The Camaro has finally reached its exit and slides out of their way. Charlie accelerates and the car slips, but he is able to right it.

"She says we should go home."

"No," says Charlie.

"She says nothing will get out tonight."

"It might! If we stay at the airport."

"She says no way. And so many flights have been cancelled, it's a nightmare."

The person begins speaking again.

After a moment, Kate says: "She says to come to the airport early tomorrow. Get on standby. There are tons of morning flights to Florida that are full, but she thinks many people won't show up or will rebook. Standby tomorrow is our best chance."

Kate looks at her phone.

"Great, I'm disconnected."

"But he'll miss the first game!" says Charlie.

Brett whimpers from the back seat.

"Stop yelling at me!" says Kate. "I didn't make the weather!"

"But you're willing to give up so easily."

"I'm not willing to drive in this because I don't want to DIE for hockey!"

Charlie swerves and takes an exit to turn around, swearing and cursing the whole way. He is willing to accept that driving to Florida is a bad idea, but he thinks they should go to the airport to at least give waiting a try. And now his temper has got him going toward home, when that's the last place he wants to go.

It takes another two miserable tense hours to get there. Brett is crying by the time they pull in the driveway. Charlie thinks he could. Kate looks like she will murder the first person who speaks to her. She slams the door of the car when they arrive and storms in the house. Charlie goes straight to the office and spends an hour looking at nearby airports and flights. All are cancelled due to weather. Ice continues to click against the windows. Brett is up in his room with the door closed. Kate folds laundry, slams doors, and mutters to herself.

At seven o'clock, Kate makes Brett dinner. Brett's eyes are red from crying. Because they've been snowed in with plans to travel, all they have left in the house besides junk food is one egg, stale bread, and a bruised apple. Charlie doesn't want to eat anyway. He's sick over this.

"We should have gone to the airport," he says.

"To sleep on the floor with thousands of other people with no hope of getting out?"

"There's always hope."

"I don't want to fight with you any more. We are on the same team."

Charlie's phone buzzes. He reads it, and needs to sit.

"What?" says Kate.

He doesn't want to read the text aloud. It will crush Brett. Brett looks at his father and must sense he doesn't want to know. When he finishes eating, he says, "Can I go to bed?"

Kate nods, gives him a hug, and a kiss on the head.

"I'm sorry, buddy," she says. "We'll do everything we can tomorrow. I'll wake you up at three."

Once he's upstairs and Charlie hears Brett close his door, he reads his phone aloud.

"It's Justin on the group text: WE'RE GETTING OUT TONIGHT WITH JACK AND DOMINIK ON A FLIGHT TO WEST PALM. DE-ICING PLANE NOW. DISTRICTS, HERE WE COME!"

Charlie throws his phone on the counter. Kate leans over and buries her head in her arms.

"That leaves only Brett and Henry with no plan to get to Florida. Brett—arguably the best player on the team, the one who GOT them to districts, might not make it to districts."

"I'm so sorry."

"If we had continued to the airport like I wanted to, we might be on that flight."

"I don't know what to say. The lady told me there was no hope."

"She told you that because she didn't want another frazzled traveler in her face at the help desk."

Charlie walks upstairs and slams the door to their bedroom.

#####

Charlie doesn't sleep a wink, and knows from Kate's tossing and sighing that she doesn't either. He is relieved when her alarm goes off at three, and he smells the coffee brewing.

They are out the door by 3:15, travel mugs in hand, on the road, silent and strangely alert. The full moon glows bright and low—illuminating the glistening drifts and covered trees, revealing a cloudless sky. The roads have been plowed, and with no one out at this hour, they make it to the airport in thirty minutes. When they find a good parking space in the daily lot, Charlie begins to feel something like hope, but it evaporates the moment they step inside the airport. From the check-in counters, to security, to the coffee shops, mobs of weary travelers wait.

"Let's just go home," says Charlie. "I can't take it."

"No. I'll get in line," says Kate. "You two sit. Rest. I'll text you when I get to the front of the line to bring your ID. I'm going to get us on standby for the six a. m. flight. And if that doesn't work, we'll get on standby for the 6:30. And the 7:15 after that. There are flights to Florida all day long. I don't care if we have to drive an hour or two once we get there, but we are getting there, and Brett, you will make at least some of your games. That's better than none, right?"

Brett nods his head.

"Good. Let's do this."

Charlie cannot think. He can only obey. He takes Brett to the bench, and waits the forty minutes for Kate to switch their boarding passes from last night to standby. He is about to drift off to sleep when he hears his name being yelled across the airport. Kate is frantic. She waves from the front of the line. Why didn't she text him? He and Brett hurry over with their luggage.

"I need your photo IDs," she says. Charlie can see she is trying not to cry.

"Why didn't you just text us?"

"I left my phone at home. On the bedside table."

Of course she did. He swallows the bile. He will not be mean. This has been a nightmare for all of them. Deep breaths.

They check in and begin the hour wait at security. They eat a greasy breakfast at McDonalds that Charlie has no urge to Instagram. They report to the counter at their gate, and ask where they are on the standby list. The woman working has clearly been here all night—her hair is a mess, her eyes are half-mast; she's a soulless husk of a human.

"Numbers 34, 35, and 36," she says. There is an edge in her voice that somehow conveys, *If you complain to me about this, I will stick this pencil through your eyeball.*

"Can we put our names on multiple flight standby lists?" says Kate.

"Nope. One at a time."

Charlie sits and keeps his eyes closed. The twitching makes is almost impossible to see. Brett is silent—a zombie child. When the plane begins boarding, they call for standbys, one through three.

"Brett! Brett!"

They follow the voice and see Henry, waving frantically, with Mee Maw and Poo Poo. Brett runs over. The boys talk for a moment, but Mee Maw and Poo Poo hurry Henry toward the tunnel. Brett comes back with tears in his eyes.

"How did they get such great standby numbers?" says Kate.

"They came last night," says Brett. "The lady put them on the list so they'd be first this morning. I'm the only one who hasn't made it.

Charlie purses his lips and looks up at the ceiling. *Deep breaths.*

"Get your suitcases," says Kate. "We need to run."

A mass of humanity swells like a wave—it rushes toward the walkway, headed toward the gate around the airport that might be the answer to their prayers. The Millers are swept up in it, banging carry ons against other frantic travelers, desperate to get to warmer climates. They are in the middle of the herd, and when they arrive at the gate for the next flight, are given the unfortunate positions of 16, 17, and 18.

The flight lets on *one* standby passenger.

They run to the next gate—another wing away in the airport—for the 7:15, just beat by a huge guy pushing an old dude in a wheelchair that Charlie had to stop himself from throwing elbows to box out. They are numbers 8, 9, and 10. Only two standbys are let on. The herd sets off. Charlie collapses in the nearest seat.

"This is ridiculous."

"We're getting closer!" says Kate.

"I'm going to die of a heart attack if I have to run this airport one more time."

"We're almost at the finish line. I can feel it!"

"No. Stick a fork in me. I'm done."

The crowd disappears around the turn.

"Come on," says Kate, hopping up and down.

Brett sits next to Charlie.

"It's not going to work, Mom. Let's just go home. It's okay."

Charlie can see that it is not okay. Kate looks broken. It would be easier if Brett threw a tantrum. It's worse that he's willing to give it all away for his parents' sake.

Kate chews her lip for a moment, then leaves them to go back to the counter. He knows she is trying because she feels bad they didn't continue to the airport last night. He is not angry with her. It was an impossible situation. He just wants to go home and forget this whole miserable season. Maybe then they can start healing. After a few moments, she runs back to them, her face alight with joy.

"You've got seats!"

"What?"

"On the nine a. m. to West Palm. Two seats opened up for purchase! A couple must have gotten on standby. Who knows! I bought them. You guys will have to drive an hour when you get there, and you'll miss the first game, but Brett, you're going!"

Kate and Brett are hugging and crying and jumping up and down.

"Wait. What do you mean *two* seats?"

Brett stops jumping.

"It's okay," says Kate. "I'll get there eventually."

"We're not leaving without you," says Charlie.

"Yes, you are. I can run around this airport on standby all day. Even if I don't make it until tomorrow. I'll get there."

"No, mom."

Kate crouches down. "It will be okay."

Charlie grabs Kate and hugs her. When they pull away, they laugh to see they are both crying. He kisses her.

The nine o'clock flight is on the opposite side of the airport, of course, and when they arrive at the gate they are breathless and sweating and elated. Kate puts herself on standby for the flight, but the clerk tells her—though she is number one—it is unlikely she will get on because the flight is overbooked.

"It's okay," says Kate.

"Wow," says the woman. "You are the first person who has said that in twenty-four hours."

Kate tells the woman the entire story, and when she finishes, the woman stands with her mouth hanging open, unable to believe what they've gone through.

"If it were up to me, I'd let you sit on your husband's lap to get you there," she says.

"I'd be happy to accommodate," says Charlie.

"There are three people who haven't checked in yet, and one of them not showing is your only hope."

"So the odds are not in my favor," says Kate.

The woman shakes her head.

"What time do they have until to check in?"

"Ten minutes before we depart."

"It's really all right," says Kate. "At least our hockey player will make it."

"How are you going to get in touch with me to let me know which flight you'll be on without your phone?" says Charlie.

"I'll use a pay phone to call my mom. She'll text you the info. It'll be like the nineties."

"Throwback," says Brett.

With the time they have, they get snacks, coffee and juice, and Charlie texts the team that Brett will be there for the second game. A flurry of emoticons appear from various people conveying smiles to prayers to sad faces. Butch doesn't reply. When the boarding begins, Charlie is overcome with sadness. He and Kate hug for a long time.

"Still sucks," says Charlie. "The way this season continues to traumatize us."

"It's almost over," says Kate.

Their boarding numbers are called. Charlie and Brett start toward the tunnel, and while he knows everything will work out, Charlie still feels terrible about being separated from Kate. Brett feels it, too. He really would have gone home. They are some of the last people to board the plane, but—after some reshuffling—they are able to get seats together near the back.

"Please settle quickly," says the flight attendant over the loud speaker. "We are hoping to push off and get the heck out of this circle of hell on time."

Several people on the plane clap and yell, "Amen." Charlie is certain that none of them have gone through as much as they have to get here. He sees a guy hurry onto the airplane, breathless. He's probably one of the late three. Kate only has two more chances.

"We are about to close the doors. Please take your seats."

As the passengers settle and click into place, Charlie stares ahead. He's a sheet of ice on which the Zamboni forgot a swipe. A stick half-taped. A skate blade with a knick. Not broken, but not whole. Nearly healed, but still cut.

Two more people step onboard.

He and Brett look at each other, shake their heads. They fasten their seatbelts.

The flight attendants close the overhead bins.

And suddenly, a noise, a motion—up front.

Kate!

Chapter Forty-Six

 Piper Caldwell's Status Update:

Confession: I wanted to publicly let you all know
I've started an alcohol rehabilitation program.
If I have ever hurt you in any way as a result of
my drinking, I'm heartily sorry. I'm also reactivating
my real estate license. I've recently been inspired
to re-invent myself, and I'm going to post about it
on my new blog: "Hashtag Blessed." I hope you'll
all follow me on my journey. The struggle is real,
and I won't hold anything back.

#Blessed

Justin stares at the ceiling fan while Aiden snores next to him. How his son is going to play a hockey game in two hours is beyond him, but these kids seem to have unlimited wells of energy. Thank God Aiden can sleep anywhere.

Justin never fell asleep. Not last night, not all morning. The flight was turbulent and miserable. The rental car smelled like smoke and cat piss. The hotel sucks. He questions why he's here, he wonders if Aiden should stay with a guy like Butch or try out for a new team, whether or not he wants to try to make up with Piper. Butch and Piper feel like similar choices to him: the devils he knows. Or maybe he should take the old 'the grass is always greener' line to heart. After all, the parents seem more bothered about Butch than the kids do. Aside from the goalie David and his crying fits, the kids mostly ignore Butch or mock him behind his back. Maybe it's good for them to have a guy like Butch in their lives. Toughens them up.

His phone buzzes.

BUTCH: GAME MOVED TO 5 PM. FOG IN EVERGLADES MADE TRAVEL DELAYS FOR THE FLORIDA TEAMS. REST.

Justin wishes he could be happy about this, but he has no confidence that he'll be able to sleep. At least Brett will be there on time so they'll have a better shot at winning. And Piper. Her flight gets in at three. Aiden was upset she had to miss the first game.

He sits up and walks out to the balcony, turning his face to the sun. He surveys the palm trees and blue skies, and wonders why they all don't live in a place with weather like this all year round. Charlie and Kate are always going on and on about how great it is in Florida, even the hockey. Apparently NHL-ers retire and run camps and leagues. Several of the teams at districts are from Florida. He'll have to see how they play. He and Piper could get into Florida real estate. Maybe they could flip houses.

He texts Piper.

--HAVE YOU LEFT YET?

--NO. I'M KEEPING THE GIRLS HOME.

--YOU'RE NOT GOING TO DISTRICTS?

--FLIGHT WAS DELAYED. WE CAN'T MAKE IT.

--THE GAME HAS BEEN MOVED TO 5 PM.

--I DON'T THINK IT'S A GOOD IDEA.

--PIPE?

-WHAT?

--I'M THINKING WE SHOULD TRY FLORIDA.

--HUH?

--TO LIVE.

…

--I THOUGHT YOU WANTED A DIVORCE,
she texts.

--MAYBE I DON'T.

--IT'S TOO LATE.

--IT'S NOT.

--IT IS.

--WHY?

…

--WHY, PIPER?

--CORT'S MOVING IN.

Chapter Forty-Seven

 Charlie Miller's Status Update: ⚙

Photo: Airplane peanuts and soda.
I never thought I'd be so happy to eat this
for lunch. We made it!

#GoPolarBears #HockeyStrong
💙 💬

The flight was a breeze—sunny skies, fair winds, gorgeous color. Kate was able to sit one row up and diagonal from Charlie and Brett, and they all couldn't stop smiling at one another, especially after they landed and saw Butch's text. Finally! Fortune smiles on them. To celebrate their good luck, they switch their rental car from the sensible mini-van they reserved to a Jeep Wrangler Sport.

"Hydro Blue," says Charlie.

"Go Polar Bears!" says Kate.

"Do you have a stick family we could slap on the back?" asks Charlie.

Brett and Kate laugh. The rental car agent looks perplexed.

They change into shorts in the airport bathroom, and since they have some time, they stop at a waterfront restaurant with great views, fish tacos, and lemonade:

"electric" for the adults and regular for Brett. When they finish, they walk along the dock, looking at the fishing boats and allowing the sunshine to thaw them to the soul.

"I still can't believe you got on that flight," says Charlie.

"The airline agent said they keep one seat free for emergencies, but she didn't want to tell me about it until she was absolutely sure no one needed it."

"Wow."

Charlie's phone rings. It's his father.

"Do you mind if I take this?" he says. "While I'm relaxed."

"Not at all," says Kate. "I forgot to email your parents the game schedule. They might want to try to come to one or two."

"I don't know," says Charlie.

The memory of his father escorting him to the ice rink parking lot after he punched Hank comes to mind. He takes a deep breath and answers.

"Hey, Dad."

"I'm glad I got you. I tried to call yesterday."

"I know; I'm sorry. It was a nightmare getting to Florida. I'll tell you all about it some time."

"That's just it. You never sent us the game schedule!"

"Do you still want to try to make a few? I mean, after the, uh, 'the incident.'"

"Listen. I've been thinking about that. And I'm proud of you."

"Huh?"

"Seriously. You stood up to that asshole who had no right to push your son. If you hadn't intervened, I would have thought less of you."

Charlie is speechless.

"You manned up, Charles. I'm proud of you."

Charlie mumbles a thank you to his father and promises to send the schedule. When he hangs up, he tells Kate and Brett what happened.

"That's sweet," says Kate, squeezing his hand. "In a really twisted way."

"I'm proud of you, too, Dad," says Brett. "Mr. Hank was a jerk."

"But Dad's never…" mumbles Charlie. "It's the first…"

"What?' says Brett.

"It's just the first time my dad has ever really praised me."

He smiles. Kate puts her arm around him.

Charlie wishes they could stay there all day, basking in the moment, but the clock is ticking, and Brett needs to rest before the game. The drive to Coral Springs in the open Jeep is a joy, and takes less than an hour. Once they arrive, Kate and Brett head to the room for a quick nap, and Charlie goes to the pool to soak up as much Vitamin D as possible.

The hotel pool is shaped like an ice rink—rectangular, but rounded at the edges—and situated in a stucco and paver courtyard smelling of citrus and crawling with bougainvillea and clematis. Palm trees and bright green hedges line the inside of the brick walls, and a fountain provides a pleasant gurgling. For a mid-priced chain hotel, they have made quite a stunning little oasis. He'll suggest to Kate that they order carry out later for dinner, and eat at one of the tables on the patio. Even if Brett isn't allowed to swim, he can enjoy the outdoors.

Charlie settles into a chair facing the sun. Just as he begins to drift off, a shadow falls over him.

Butch.

He would have thought seeing Butch would set off his anxiety triggers, but after their success in getting to Florida, the warmth of the sun, and the call with his father, Charlie is relaxed.

Butch drops into the lounger next to Charlie with a grunt. He pulls a beer out of a case, cracks it open, takes a long drink and burps. A Ducks Unlimited T-shirt screams across his swollen belly, not quite meeting the waist of his camo bathing suit. His legs are almost as hairy as his neck and head, and his toenails look like bear claws.

"Cheers," says Butch, raising his beer.

"Yeah," says Charlie, eyeing the case of beer, thinking that any other guy on this planet would have offered to share.

"It's a damned miracle everyone's here," says Butch. "That fog was a godsend."

"Yep."

"You know, I lost a bet because of you."

"How so?"

"I said no way would you make it. Now I owe Sal twenty."

Asshole, thinks Charlie.

"I'll be honest; I like the level of commitment you showed to get here, Miller," says Butch. "I thought you'd give up, but you didn't. And you're here. Which leads to what I want to talk to you about. Helen checked the stats, and she claims Brett's the leading scorer this year. That makes him an asset."

"Wow, thanks."

I guess, thinks Charlie.

"Don't tell him I said that. Brett hasn't made it through boot camp yet. I don't want him letting his guard down or relaxing in any way before districts are over."

Charlie salutes. *What a nut.*

"We need to talk about next season," says Butch.

Fluttering begins in Charlie's stomach. He'd love to say, "If you think we'd ever let our kid play for a psycho like you again, you must be crazier than we originally thought." But he remains silent. They still have a tournament to get through. He'll unload the speech he's been fantasizing about all season on Butch *after* districts.

"I've been doing a lot of thinking, strategizing, planning. Watching the lines, seeing who can handle pressure best. Rating the mental toughness of the boys—as well as their parents. Look, Miller, it's no secret you've been a head case this season. But as someone who hasn't played hockey, you can't really be expected to understand the culture."

Charlie feels cold.

"Most people intuit it," continues Butch. "You obviously are not one of those people, so next year, I'll do a better job of communicating the unspoken rules to you."

Next year, my ass.

"I haven't always felt so magnanimous when it comes to you, Miller."

Word of the day?

"But seeing you punch Hank showed me something."

Oh God.

"It showed you have a hockey player in you."

The warmth returns. Charlie sits up in his chair, recalling the good feelings from the 'pat the helmet' dream. He looks at Butch to see whether or not he's being mocked, but Butch appears serious.

"Hank played hockey, so he's got the bug," says Butch. "You're starting to get it. We can work with that."

Though the compliments are shadowed with insults, its undeniable how validating Butch's praise feels—if one could call this praise.

"I know I'm harsh," says Butch. "I have to be. This world is too soft. We live in air conditioning and central heat. We can go to the store for butchered meat and snacks anytime we want. We get trophies just for participating. These kids need balance. And as hard as it is for parents, I'm part of that balance—the antidote to this sissified existence our kids are coming up in. Frankly, it scares me."

Charlie doesn't know if it's the electric lemonade or his general exhaustion, but Butch is starting to make sense.

No! Charlie shakes his head. He can't allow himself to be lured. Not again. Not after the hell of this season.

"Next year will be different," says Butch. "I'm hand-selecting my troops. We'll discharge the benders. We'll add off-ice training to the program so parents won't have to spend extra money for little Napoleon."

Compelling.

"I'll make the ultimate line: Mike, Mario, and Brett. I've got my hands on Viktor again for goalie, now that he'll be the right age. And here, I might as well give you this now. As long as you promise not to show it to Brett before the tournament."

Butch tosses Charlie a blue letter A.

"Assistant captain, next year. With Mario. Mike keeps the C. They'll go into the coming season as leaders."

Charlie stares at the letter. It's like a tiny little victory in his hand. They weathered the storm and came through, and they are stronger for it—all of them. They've run the gauntlet. They are winners.

Charlie has watched coaches on other teams, and many of them scream as much as Butch. A new team would mean new kids, new families—families who could be even loopier than the ones he knows. Brett loves his teammates. And now, it seems that Brett has finally proven himself to Butch. Everything could be different next year. Charlie knows he cannot speak for their family without talking to Kate, but his heart is turning.

"Thanks," says Charlie. "This means a lot."

Charlie places the letter in his pocket.

Butch nods, kills his beer, burps, and pulls another from the case.

"Hey, guys!" says Sal.

Sal steps into the courtyard drinking from a two-liter bottle of soda, munching on a super sized candy bar. He plops in a nearby chair.

"You tell him, Buddy?" says Sal.

Butch grunts a yes.

Sal holds up his hand to high-five Charlie.

"Unstoppable, my man," says Sal. "They'll be the three-headed monster. That dog thing. What is it?"

"Cerberus," says Charlie.

"Yeah! And our dog will crush those Ice Mutts every time next year."

"Every time," says Butch.

Charlie's eye twitches.

"Hey, Butch, you hear anything more from that psycho coach?"

"What psycho?" says Charlie.

"Some dude has it out for Butch. Says he shouldn't be coaching because of getting thrown out of a certain amount of league games. Whatever. He's sour grapes. Trying to get us disqualified."

"Is that even a possibility?" says Charlie.

"No," says Butch. "This whacko has been following our ranking all year, sending me heckling emails, baiting me. I shut him down. I don't know how he found out about me getting thrown out of games, but he can't do anything with that. He's just pissed because his team didn't make it to districts. They were below us in rankings, and we edged them out."

"He's probably the dickhead who narked on Viktor."

"Definitely."

"I can't believe an adult spends so much time on witch hunts in the name of Pee Wee hockey," says Charlie. "Get a life."

Sal gives Charlie the lunatic look, and then continues. "Yeah, anyway, he sent a letter to the head of the tournament with lists of all of our team infractions this year, including suspensions, toss-outs, and parent…uh…issues, and why his team should be here instead of the Polar Bears."

"Too late, asshole," says Butch.

Charlie's mouth is dry. He's dying for a beer. *Are he and Butch on good enough terms for him to ask?* Probably not.

"You should see the email he sent yesterday," says Butch. "Said we're lucky the tournament isn't in his home state, or I'd have to keep looking over my shoulder. I forwarded it to the tournament director."

"I'd love for him to try to mess with me," says Sal.

For a moment, the world goes grey. Charlie forgets he is poolside in Florida in March. It's like he's back on his icy street, careening, desperate to get out. He stands.

"Well, I'm going to ready the troops," says Charlie.

"Yeah, man," says Sal.

"We'll see you at the rink at 1600."

Butch opens his eyes. "Make sure Brett doesn't know anything I said. We can't have him let down his guard."

Charlie salutes.

Chapter Forty-Eight

⚒ **Justin Caldwell's Status Update:** ⚙

First Facebook Photo: Selfie with Aiden
Caption: Father/Son Hockey Championship Weekend

#RockinTheBlue #GoPolarBears
#GuysWeekend #HockeyStrong
🤍 💬

TINA: We didn't think we'd do any more episodes of #SportsTaxi this season, but after what we've been through, we knew there needed to be one more.

BOB: This has been an especially tough year, fans.

TINA: It has.

BOB: We knew there would be challenges going in, but we couldn't have anticipated exactly what Pee Wee, triple A, travel hockey would demand of us. I don't know if we would have gone through it if we'd known, but you know what? We're stronger for it.

TINA: We are, Bob. In our marriage, our family, our loyalty, our commitment to excellence in every area of our lives.

BOB: I confess: we wanted to give up along the way.

TINA: Multiple times, if we're honest.

BOB: Many.

TINA: But now that we're almost at the mountaintop, we can see the view.

BOB: And it is spectacular.

TINA: In one last gasp, nature tried to thwart all we had worked and sweat and bled so hard for this year.

BOB: Inclement winter weather threatened to keep us from districts.

TINA: But we came together as a family. We drove in admittedly unsafe conditions to find an airport that would get us to Florida.

BOB: At a premium!

TINA: We couldn't have done it if we all weren't committed—each member of our team, and our family.

BOB: But we were determined, and now we sit in our rented SUV under a palm tree, outside the rink where our son will play later today, and we feel...blessed.

TINA: Blessed by every hardship this season.

BOB: What didn't kill us made us stronger.

TINA: And whether we win or not, we made it to the Promised Land.

BOB: I'll tell you what: this experience has separated the men from the boys.

TINA: And when we look down that player bench—when we see who remains—we'll know who the real winners are: those who are truly triple A material.

#####

The Millers pull up to the rink—the arena where it will all happen. The zenith of the season. Charlie hasn't said a word to Kate about his talk with Butch because of Brett's presence, but as soon as Brett gets out of the jeep, Charlie will discuss next year with her. He can't believe he's considering suggesting they stay with the Polar Bears. He can't imagine what will happen if they decide to go. His mind spins with ideas, and he can't grasp what will be best for his son. It's so magnificently hot, Charlie wonders if his body is in some kind of shock from the change from yesterday. Maybe that's why he can't properly process everything. Kate will help him figure it out.

"Hmmm," says Kate.

"What's up?"

"Justin Caldwell just got on Facebook. Asked for my friendship. And posted a selfie with his son, and numerous hashtags."

"What's that all about?"

"If I had to guess, he's headed for divorce. Trying to show what a great dad he is."

"For custody."

"Yep."

Charlie shudders.

"Actually you can ask him," says Kate.

A taxi pulls up to the parking lot. Aiden gets out—red-faced and clearly uncomfortable—and goes for the trunk to get his hockey bag. Justin stumbles out of the back seat, knocking several cans of beer on the ground, before fishing through his pockets for money for the cab driver.

"Is he...?"

"Drunk," says Kate.

Most of the team is already in the parking lot. Kip has Kyle doing squats in the grass; Mee Maw brushes Henry's hair; Louise tries to break up a fight between Dante and Mario. Tom wipes David's eyes with a hanky; the kid is in the middle of his usual pre-game anxiety attack. Amy has her arms wrapped around her brother. Bob talks on the phone, smiling and gesturing wildly, while Tina encourages Bobby to finish his Monster drink and protein bar. Jack and Dominik are just pulling in, as are Butch and his family.

"The whole circus made it," says Kate.

"A miracle," says Charlie.

As Charlie puts the Jeep in park, Hank takes the space next to them, so close that Charlie can't open his driver side door. Hank leans forward and glares at Charlie. Hank's nose is still snotty, even in Florida, and he has an angry red slice across the bridge of it. Charlie can't help but feel pleasure at seeing the injury. He really must be turning into a hockey player.

"Here we go," says Kate.

They climb out the other side of the Jeep and help Brett get his things, while the families begin to migrate toward the rink. As they start forward, Mee Maw's voice reaches them from the front doors of the arena.

"WHAT THE FUCK?!"

Henry and Poo Poo stare at Mee Maw in shock. The families crowd the doors, pulling on them and groaning. A din rises. Moms scream at other moms. Dads yell at dads. The kids just stare at each other and their parents.

"Now what?" says Charlie.

When they reach the doors, they see they are locked. There is a notice taped to one.

DUE TO A RECENT CREDIBLE THREAT TO THE SAFETY OF THE PLAYERS AND COACHES, ALL GAMES IN THE SOUTHEAST DISTRICTS
ARE CANCELLED.
WE DEEPLY REGRET THE NECISSITY OF THIS ACTION, AND WILL REFUND ALL TOURNAMENT FEES, EXCEPT TRAVEL RELATED COSTS.

Charlie feels lightheaded. He looks at Brett in horror. Brett's face becomes a dark scowl.

Butch walks up. The crowd parts around him and becomes silent. When he finishes reading he makes an unearthly growl and slams his body against the door, as if trying to break it down.

"Can we swim now?" asks Kyle.

Kip throws Kyle's binder on the ground. Parents begin screaming at each other again—insult hurling, blaming. The children congregate, glaring at the adults. Soon, parents from other teams begin arriving—each group falling apart the way the Polar Bears have. There's pushing and shoving. Accusations. A storm of cursing and shouting. But only for the adults. Some of the kids have started a pick up game of soccer in the grass beside the rink.

"Let's go," says Kate.

Charlie is immobilized. "But…"

Kate takes Charlie by one hand, Brett by the other. She pulls them toward the jeep. Kate climbs into the drivers' seat, while Brett gets in the back. Charlie stands in the parking lot, staring, mumbling.

"Now," says Kate.

"Hydro Blue," says Charlie. "Go Polar Bears. Districts."

Kate puts the jeep in reverse and begins to back out of the space.

"Dad!" yells Brett.

Brett's voice calls Charlie out of his shock. He climbs in the jeep, and Kate starts driving before he has his door closed. Charlie can't take his eyes from the rink. Butch paces like a bull in the middle of the screaming angry mass. When he sees the jeep leaving, Butch catches Charlie's eye and glares. Butch's eyes are bloodshot. His face is red. His hatred white-hot.

Charlie reaches in his pocket and pulls out the letter A. It feels like the only real victory of the season. The banner. The trophy. The pat on the helmet.

At the traffic light, Kate sees the letter A and a look of revulsion crosses her face. When the light turns green, she grabs the letter, throws it out of the top of the jeep, and peels wheels.

Epilogue

2016
Eight Months to District Playoffs

Cars line up at the rink like a series of oversized dogsleds: Tahoe, Suburban, Lexus, Escalade, Hummer, a scattering of minivans. All of them are white—white as snow, white as nine-tenths of the players, white as the muffs around the tops of the armies of Ugg boots slapping the pavement in the pre-dawn on a summer day.

Charlie Miller parks his gray sedan.